Thoughts out of School

Studies in the
Postmodern Theory of Education

Joe L. Kincheloe and Shirley R. Steinberg
General Editors

Vol. 133

PETER LANG
New York • Washington, D.C./Baltimore • Boston • Bern
Frankfurt am Main • Berlin • Brussels • Vienna • Oxford

William Ray Arney

Thoughts out of School

PETER LANG
New York ▪ Washington, D.C./Baltimore ▪ Boston ▪ Bern
Frankfurt am Main ▪ Berlin ▪ Brussels ▪ Vienna ▪ Oxford

Library of Congress Cataloging-in-Publication Data

Arney, William Ray.
Thoughts out of school / William Ray Arney.
p. cm. — (Counterpoints; vol. 133)
Includes bibliographical references and index.
1. Schools—United States. 2. Teachers—Training of—
United States. 3. Educational change—United States.
I. Title. II. Counterpoints (New York, N.Y.); vol. 133.
LA217.2.A74   370'.973—dc21   99-053754
ISBN 0-8204-4876-1
ISSN 1058-1634

Die Deutsche Bibliothek-CIP-Einheitsaufnahme

Arney, William Ray:
Thoughts out of school / William Ray Arney.
–New York; Washington, D.C./Baltimore; Boston; Bern;
Frankfurt am Main; Berlin; Brussels; Vienna; Oxford: Lang.
(Counterpoints; Vol. 133)
ISBN 0-8204-4876-1

Cover design by Lisa Dillon
Cover photos by Hugh Lentz

The paper in this book meets the guidelines for permanence and durability
of the Committee on Production Guidelines for Book Longevity
of the Council of Library Resources.

© 2000 Peter Lang Publishing, Inc., New York

Printed in the United States of America

We must decisively divorce the realm of education from the others, most of all from the realm of public, political life. . . . In practice the first consequence of this would be a clear understanding that the function of the school is to teach children what the world is like and not to instruct them in the art of living.

Hannah Arendt, "The Crisis in Education"

As a matter of fact, it was a bit ridiculous. But because it was ridiculous, we know it must be true.

Tom Robbins, *Even Cowgirls Get the Blues*

Doctor Plarr sometimes had a longing to exclaim to his melancholy patient, "Life isn't like that. Life isn't noble or dignified. . . . Nothing is ineluctable. Life has surprises. Life is absurd. Because it's absurd there is always hope."

Graham Greene, *The Honorary Consul*

Contents

Acknowledgments

Several people contributed in material ways to this volume: Pamela Stewart, Rita Pougiales, Don Finkel, Chip Conquest, Alison Roth, and Jutta Mason. Together with the other faculty members in the Teacher Education Program—Gail Tremblay, Stephanie Kozick, and Josie Reed—these people have been my teachers in educational matters these past several years. They and a small group of others—Barbara Duden, Ivan Illich, Sigmar and Geka Groeneveld, Wolfgang Sachs, Adele Fiske, and Beate Zimmermann (and around them, rings of others)—have taught me the connection between criticism and friendship.

To the others who contributed to this work—other students in the teacher education program, their supervising teachers in the schools of this region, my son's teachers and principals, the administrators responsible for the documents I discuss—I extend a special thanks. Some of them have felt, as the superintendent of our local district wrote, exploited by having their good work examined critically. Some of them have been angered or hurt by my comments. But some of them have come to realize that these essays are an acknowledgment that I have noticed and tried to reflect upon what is happening in schools, and some of them have understood that this sort of reflection lies, according to many theorists, at the heart of education. The best among them have taken up the implicit invitation set forth in these pieces—the invitation to conversation and further reflection. They are true educators, and thanking them is just the beginning of the possibilities of life that lie between us.

Thanking institutions will never seem right to me, regardless of how common it becomes. But the institution that employs me, The Evergreen State College, is young enough to allow me to realize that the urge to thank this institution is, in fact, an urge to thank the people out of whose wisdom this institution was born. Indeed, the college is so young that many of those people still walk in our midst. Few institutions would allow a person without a degree in teaching or education to teach would-be teachers. It takes courage to respond to the predictable jab, "Isn't this the epitome of the old saw, 'Those who can, do, and those who can't, teach'?" with a firm, "Those we have selected to teach the teachers know something important about children, education, and the schools." I know the people who first gave voice to this courage, and I know the history of their efforts to institutionalize, in this wonderful and fragile college, their faith in the members of this faculty (something radically different from the much more common reliance on certification systems). In thanking The Evergreen State

College for the opportunity to teach in a teacher education program, I bow to all of them.

Finally, John—a son is never his father's teacher, even though the son may be the agent of some harsh lessons. I could thank him for the wonder of these past years, but it's likely he would be puzzled by that. When he was a baby, people commented most often on his wide-open eyes. "He's watching everything you do," they would say. I offer these essays to him as a small effort to reciprocate the gesture.

Thoughts Out of School

Every time they check, schools learn they are doing poorly, by their own standards. The recent national effort, the Goals 2000 project, shows a modest increase in math skills, a decrease in reading, little change in international standing of U.S. students in math and science, decreased interest in "lifelong learning" among adults, teachers reporting more disruptions in classes, and so on.[1] Connecticut led the nation in reading scores, but fewer than one of every two students could read "proficiently." Officials in Connecticut attributed their success—their relative success—to greater emphasis on evening and weekend school programs.[2] In return for doing worse, the schools, naturally, propose reforms and, ironically, expand their scope. Ever higher levels of schooling are required for ever lower level jobs, a fact that was neatly parodied when a college class chose as its motto "You want fries with that?"[3] Nearly a million homeschooling and no-schooling families are already opting out of a system that Ivan Illich calls one manifestation of "the mystery of evil." In this context I offer these essays and occasional pieces as "thoughts out of school." I mean that phrase in several senses.

First, I have taken the material for these thoughts out of the public schools. I am a faculty member at The Evergreen State College, one of the last remaining "alternative colleges" founded in the late sixties. Because the college is not bound by strict departmental and disciplinary structures,[4] I was able to teach in the Teacher Education Program even though I had no training or certification in this field. In addition to teaching graduate classes, I observed student teaching in the schools for two quarters. These essays come out of those observations and out of other experiences I had in the public schools around that time.

These essays are thoughts out of school in the slightly less trivial sense that these thoughts occurred to me after leaving the public schools. I had left the common schools, in one sense, through graduation. When I went back as an instructor and supervisor of would-be teachers, I found those schools very familiar and, yet, strange. So many practices and structures had persisted over a quarter of a century, but the schools were discernibly different, too. I had been out of school for a long time.

Beyond that sense of "leaving school," these are thoughts I could have only if I conscientiously left the schools at the end of each day of working in them. I could not have had *these* thoughts if I had allowed my mind to linger in the schools for too long. I had to get out, and I had to reflect on what I had seen. By conscientiously leaving the schools at the end of the day, I thought I stood a better than average chance of remembering what I had seen in them so that I could tell my own stories, not the schools' stories, about what was going on.[5] This was a difficult discipline because schools want to make everyone, even the most casual observers in them, grow up, move on, get better. They want people to forget what happens in school. They offer the future if only you will forget your past. To act against this offer of being able to forget what I was seeing in favor of all the promises schools make about a future when all will be better, I had to force myself to remember, and to do that I had to have these thoughts *out* of school.

Finally, these are thoughts offered as a *way out* of schools. Schools are impressive. They impress their logic on you and shape your mind to their ways. By using words that are as convincing as they are meaningless, they trap you in a web of thought that holds even though it has little substance.* Within days of beginning their student teaching, most of our teacher education students were good teachers. It wasn't that they could do no wrong, but they came quickly close to getting it right. It was as if "the rules of good teaching" were in the air they breathed upon entering schools. I felt it myself. "Professor Arney, both of us have the same interest in mind—the growth and development of our students—don't we?" I nodded. Who could disagree? But in order to get out of the schools' grip on consciousness, we *must,* if not disagree, then at least agree to think carefully about the effects of everyone so easily agreeing to take such a profound and persistent interest in the "growth and development" of students. We ought to give ourselves a chance to examine the violences, petty and large, inflicted on people in the name of "helping students" or "teaching pupils." There is nothing wrong with education. But there may be something frighteningly wrong with the set of practices called schooling. Perhaps recognizing that difference—between education and schooling—will encourage people to think their ways out of schools and into new ways of learning, teaching, educating. Perhaps it is possible to avoid denouncing schools because they are "bad," a tactic that leads to a kind of knee-jerk reaction to try to make schools into better schools, and instead see schools for what they are. If schooling is another manifestation of "the mystery of evil," then we might be able to respond to schools conscientiously and thoughtfully rather than systematically or programmatically. Instead of turning and running from the

---

* See the essays "Do I Need My Identity?," "Why I Won't Believe in Developmentalism," and "No Futures, Please, These Are Our Children" in this volume.

schools in a frenzy (an act that often lands us in more dangerous institutional arms), perhaps it is possible simply to think ourselves out of schools. That, at least, is my hope.

CHAPTER 1

It Matters

After an especially convivial dinner I asked our host if he could help me with a problem in language. I had decided, I told him, to open a school for those many students I was seeing during my visits to the public schools, and my school needed to have its motto rendered into a suitably dead language. Since the school would be founded on an honest recognition of the lives the students were being encouraged to lead, the school's motto would be "It doesn't matter."

Ivan Illich, my host, took the task of the joke seriously. His distant look told me he was sorting through his many languages, alive and dead, for an apt translation. Finally he said, "It can't be done. You can make this construction only in English. In every other language, the moment you say 'It,' *it* materializes. In every other language, *it* matters, all the time." Then he smiled, "You will have to render your motto in American."

The students I was seeing were good students. They had learned their lessons well. The principal lesson the schools were teaching them was "It doesn't matter": It doesn't matter if you get poor grades; the diploma's more important. It doesn't matter if you can't do math; you need to get a job (and the cash register will do all the work). It doesn't matter if you can't read; as soon as the bond issue buys computers for everyone, you're going to become computer literate. It doesn't matter if you act crazy; we have staff psychologists. It doesn't matter if the toilets are backing up; the district's priority is the gun control program. It doesn't matter if people can't get along with one another; we have playground rules to enforce. It doesn't matter if children prefer to watch television instead of playing together; there's an after-school sports program run by the YMCA. It doesn't matter if the traditions of our holidays are hundreds of years old; someone might sue if we taught tradition. It doesn't matter if the inner cities explode; our curriculum is multicultural.

A nearly trivial example: My son's test scores—scores from yet another round of standardized testing—arrived with a cover letter from his principal.* The letter included an explanation of the "summary narrative

---

* See the essay on "Testing: Letters to Which No One Wrote Back."

statements" generated by the California Test of Basic Skills' computer. Whenever a child scored "below mastery level," the computer generated the phrase "Further help may be needed in ———" and then listed the "particular objectives" on which the student scored low. The principal commented, "However, the *reason* for below mastery performance is not given. The important point is that low performance may be due to many factors. *One* may be that the objective has not yet been emphasized in our curriculum."[1] He did not list any other of the "many factors." It doesn't seem to matter if a student scores low on the test. There's always a reason for a low score; just call the school and they will explain everything to you; they can explain anything away. Nothing matters.

This example would be absolutely trivial, and not just "nearly" trivial, if it wasn't precisely the sort of cynical dismissiveness of their own activities that the schools generate at all levels. One week after getting my son's scores, the newspapers reported district scores throughout the state. This appeared in a Seattle newspaper:

> Seattle School District officials are downplaying the importance of recent standardized test scores ranking Seattle students below the national average in language, math and science. . . . Critics dismiss the CTBS [California Test of Basic Skills] test because too many other variables can crop up that would detract from allowing a student's true knowledge to show. For instance, the test is scheduled in October when schools have received an influx of new students, including many non-English-speaking schoolchildren.[2]

Whole school districts dismiss whole testing programs by explaining away their scores. No one in the schools is willing to acknowledge responsibility, not for my son's scores, low or high, and not for the scores of all the students in a district.

Martin Buber reminds us that God's question to Adam is not, "Why, Adam?," which would be an invitation to explain his sin, but, "Adam, where are you?" And what is Adam's response to God?

> Adam hides himself to avoid rendering accounts, to escape responsibility for his way of living. Every man hides for this purpose, for every man is Adam and finds himself in Adam's situation. To escape responsibility for his life, he turns existence into a system of hideouts.[3]

The schools have explanations or excuses for everything. They can tell you why a student or a district is doing poorly, why it's important to teach computers to pupils who can't read, why children carry guns to school.* But explanations and excuses are nothing more than an elaborate system of

---

* See the essay "Gimme My Gun, I'm Working on My Self-Esteem."

hideouts. By having an explanation or an excuse for everything, schools are able to avoid that crucial question: "Where are you?" They never have to stop and take stock of what they have done and what is going on, right now, in classrooms, on playgrounds, in the offices of administrators. People in the schools are too busy developing schoolish understandings and justifications of their activities to notice, exactly, what they are doing. Buber says of our collective fate, "Everything now depends on when man faces the question" of where we are.[4] Our failure to take note of where we are—no matter how good the planners tell us the future will be if we will just _____ (fill in the blank with the latest reform rhetoric)—is the ground in which the attitude that "It doesn't matter" takes rapid root.

These essays and occasional pieces are my effort to notice what happens in schools. Nothing that I saw while observing student teaching and nothing that happened to me or my son during the time I was writing these pieces is out of the ordinary. The events recollected here happen every day in most schools. Nothing that happened was terribly dramatic or even distinctive. Everything reported here can be greeted with an, "Oh, yes, that happens all the time," or, "I can tell you why we (or they) do that," or, "I can't understand why you get so worked up." All of these responses are simple variations on the theme of the school's primary lesson, "It doesn't matter." They are excuses for behavior that ought to be noticed, not excused. They are hideouts that allow everyone to keep their heads down, out of the glare of responsibility.

In order to notice what is happening in schools, I had to fight against explanations and excuses and encouragements to "calm down," to "try and understand," to "appreciate our situation." I have written these pieces to try to figure out what is going on. Sherwood Anderson had one of his narrators declare the following,

> "If I can write everything out plainly, perhaps I will myself understand better what has happened," I say to myself and smile. During these days I spend a good deal of time smiling at nothing. It bothers people.[5]

As I was writing about the schools, I did spend a lot of time smiling. And it did bother people. Schooling, everyone seems to understand, is serious business and is not the subject of smiles. Schools have to be reformed, the sooner the better, and this is serious. So the schools tell us. But, again, that's a line we must not follow because it leads us to thinking that things must change, that we must think together toward a better future, etc., and that what is going on *right now* doesn't matter.

But it does matter. It matters so much that we should learn to smile at the silliness of schooling instead of following the schools' logic, explanations, and rationales to the point where we are submerged under their seriousness.

Schools figure large in our lives. Children spend about 12,000 hours in these governmental institutions. Schools matter enough to respond to them, to everything they propose or do.

One unfortunate response to schools is to take them seriously, to excuse them by mouthing the available, correct, often school-supplied complaints about them. This act can lead to accepting schools and their logic (because complaints rarely lead to action and, perversely, complaints sometimes make us feel relatively good about a rotten situation), or it can lead to a blind rejection of them. Neither response is good because both are usually solitary. Either is antipolitical and dangerous because it is more a reaction than a conscientious response to circumstances. May Sarton wrote,

> I am more and more convinced that in the life of civilizations and in the lives of individuals too much matter that cannot be digested, too much experience that has not been *imagined* and probed and understood, ends in the total rejection of everything—ends in anomie. The structures break down and there is nothing to "hold onto. . . ."

> How does one handle it? The greatest danger, as I see it in myself, is the danger of withdrawal into private worlds.[6]

If we follow this route, we remain childlike and student-like throughout our lives. If we withdraw "into private worlds," some teacher will likely prepare a desk for us and get ready to grade us on our "complaining skills" or on our "making my school better term project." Schools are so large in our lives that some of us never escape their reasoning or their practices.

Instead of taking the schools seriously, we could think about them, smile, and try to "write everything out plainly." These pieces are works of criticism. I do not have in mind the common use of that term, which always involves faultfinding, which sometimes leads to explanations of trouble-some situations, and which often leaves one open to the seemingly ultimate and certainly conversation-ending jab, "So, what do *you* think we should do?" Instead, by criticism I mean, simply, saying what one sees, and doing so in a language that forms a judgmental matrix but that strives only for a precision of description that can move one to respond well. These pieces are highly personal. But because none of the circumstances that motivated these reflections is, in any way, exceptional, my comments are about issues that are or should be public. I have written with C. Wright Mills's final admonition in mind:

> Do not allow public issues as they are officially formulated, or troubles as they are privately felt, to determine the problems that you take up for study.

Above all, do not give up your moral and political autonomy by accepting in somebody else's terms the illiberal practicality of the bureaucratic ethos or the liberal practicality of the moral scatter. Know that many personal troubles cannot be solved merely as troubles, but must be understood in terms of public issues—and in terms of the problems of history-making. Know that the human meaning of public issues must be revealed by relating them to personal troubles—and to the problems of the individual life. Know that the problems of social science, when adequately formulated, must include both troubles and issues, both biography and history, and the range of their intricate relations. Within that range the life of the individual and the making of societies occur; and within that range the sociological imagination has a chance to make a difference in the quality of human life in our time.[7]

Schools may teach history and offer courses on "social problems," but only in ways that assure those inclined to worry that they need not be responsive to history and that it will never touch them. The schools make mighty efforts, including the hiring of armies of psychologists and testing specialists, to ensure that personal troubles remain personal, to ensure that difficulties in one's biography are dealt with at the individual's desk or in the privacy of the counselor's office. Mills encourages everyone to resist any institution that would wrench apart history and biography the way schools do. He tried to cultivate citizens who knew that quite a lot matters.

What matters? This is a question everyone should answer, every minute of every day. It is a variant of the very first question, "Where are you?" John Taylor Gatto, the New York State Teacher of the Year who resigned on the op-ed page of the *Wall Street Journal*, provides, in his partial answer, a distinction that can get us started:

All schoolteachers steal the time young people need to find out what really matters. Except in this negative sense, going to school doesn't really matter very much. . . . In what sense does school matter if it uses up all the time you need to learn to build a house? Or grow vegetables? Or make a dress? Or learn to love your family. Education matters, of course, but school and education are not remotely the same things.[8]

Education does matter—so do young people, and good friends, so does retaining one's "moral and political autonomy." But, then, so too do schools matter. We should attend to them closely. It is because education, young people, friends, and the possibility of understanding personal troubles in terms of public issues matter that I think about and write about schools as if they mattered, too.

CHAPTER 2

What Should Be Taught in Teacher Education Programs?

What should teacher education programs teach?

Perhaps it is best to begin negatively. Clearly, teacher education programs should not try to teach teachers all the tricks of teaching. They already know "how to" teach.

Consider this: My son comes home from his third grade class. It is the end of the school year.

"Do anything interesting in school today?"

"No."

Predictable so far.

"Nothing?"

"Well, the kids taught math."

"What?"

"The kids taught the math lessons."

"How'd they do?"

"Fine." He laughs. "They did just as good as the teacher."

After only three or four years in the public schools, the students teach "just as good as the teacher." And why not? Children are nothing if not observant. They see what's going on. They learn, very quickly, what counts as good work. And most children, even the poor students, are quick studies. Now, it is easy to figure that if children in the third grade can teach as well as their teacher, students entering teacher education programs, most of whom have been in schools for twenty years or more, know all the "methods" one needs to perform well in front of a class.

The students in our teacher education program were good teachers from the first day. That's not just my assessment. Most of the cooperating teachers in the schools where our students observed (during the first year of their teacher education program) and taught (in the second year) confirmed my view. Almost all of the seasoned teachers commented on the quality of work our students did in the classroom.

So, if you cannot teach would-be teachers to teach, what should you teach them? Here are three answers.

Don Finkel

In 1986, The Evergreen State College offered its first undergraduate teacher education program. Don Finkel was a member of the teaching team in the first iteration of that program. *At the end of the first year, Finkel wrote seven reflective essays on various components of the program. In this extract from the first essay, "The Prototype: 'Development: The Aim of Education,'" Finkel discusses the inspiration that the teacher education program took from his undergraduate program on "Development."*

The Undergraduate Program. In the spring of 1977, Dean Rob Knapp approached me and asked me if I would design an advanced group contract in education, so that students leaving an introductory education program offered that year would have some place to continue their studies. I agreed to plan and teach this group contract. It would be called "Development: The Aim of Education," after Kohlberg and Mayer's paper, "Development as the Aim of Education,"[1] and would consist of about 22 students and one faculty member.

I had never taught an education course, and, as a person trained in developmental psychology, and having formerly taught in a traditional psychology department, I had no acquaintance with the curricula in education departments.

I began planning the program by asking myself the following question: Besides the subject matter she will be teaching, what does a person need to understand or have experienced to be a good teacher? I answered with the following list: (a) an understanding of the nature of intelligence and its development; (b) a serious exposure to a set of alternative philosophical positions about the purposes of education and its relation to the surrounding social and political body; (c) a genuine understanding of the psychoanalytic concept of *transference*; (d) some understanding of the major issues of personality development; (e) a dose of direct experience working with children in the classroom. While the curriculum of the program included some things that went beyond what is implied by this list, these five items were the major factors determining what went into the program. This list may seem surprisingly short, but it was what I believed in 1977, and I acted

---

* Students at the college could take teacher education in previous years, but the program was sponsored by and under the control of another college. The program that began in 1986 was offered jointly with Western Washington University. The program was situated at Evergreen and generally followed Evergreen's "alternative" approach to undergraduate education. At Evergreen students usually take thematically organized, team-taught, interdisciplinary programs that last from one to three quarters instead of taking a collection of courses. Don Finkel was instrumental in applying this approach to undergraduate education to the preparation of teachers.

accordingly. I also believed firmly in the value of understanding deeply a small number of theories rather than spending time on "surveys," "coverage," or "reviews of the current research or literature." A strong understanding of theory would permanently alter the students' vision, and thus shape their decisions and their practice. That is what I was after.

To deal with the nature of intelligence and development, I intended to center on Piaget, the thinker who had shaped my own thinking about psychology and education. I would use Piaget for his notions of knowing and intelligence, and also for his concept of development. However, this latter idea I believed to be too complex to grasp simply from a study of Piaget. My idea was that the students would need to study several (at least three) developmental theories, all of which embodied the same structural notion of development. By this means, they would be able to generalize and extract the common notion, and thus make it their own. For this purpose, I included in the curriculum Kohlberg's theory of moral development, Perry's theory of intellectual and ethical development in the college years, and, to do double duty, Erikson's theory of personality development.

I was a novice in the area of philosophy of education, so to meet the aim of item (b) on my list, I arranged for the students to take a course co-taught by Ron Manheimer (a philosopher) and myself. I relied on Ron to take the lead in planning the curriculum for this course. The result was a progression of five philosophers: Socrates (via Plato's *Meno*), Plato (via the *Republic*), Aristotle, Rousseau, and Dewey. In later versions of this course, we added Locke.

To expose students to "transference," I designed the Self-Reflective Group. I have written about this teaching mode extensively in my essay "Democracy in Education: Education in Democracy."[2]

For personality development, I relied on Erikson. Here I was under the influence of Richard Jones's approach in his book *Fantasy and Feeling in Education*.[3] My notion was that Erikson's framework could give students a vocabulary and set of concepts for approaching emotional issues that arose in their classrooms, both issues dominant in an entire age group and those left-over, unresolved issues in individual "problematic" students. My goals were modest here, and item (d) had the lowest priority of my five.

Finally, to satisfy the experiential element, I incorporated an Evergreen internship into the program. This internship ran winter quarter and was to occupy only one-third of the students' time.

There were a number of structural features that seemed crucial to the design of "Development." (1) The program was organized around three "streams," the philosophy stream, the development stream, and the experiential stream. This meant that at first the program felt like three parallel courses to the students; as time progressed the students were able to inter-relate themes and ideas from the three streams, so that a convergence could take place. Eventually the three separate "courses" were experienced as one unified program.

(2) The program had a coherent *philosophy* which it embodied and a *theme* which was integrally related to the philosophy. The *theme* was implied by the title: What does it mean to take development to be the aim of education? One could think of the philosophy component of the program as helping the students to understand what is implied by the phrase "aim of education," while the study of psychological theories of development and the Self-Reflective Group helped them to grasp the complex meaning of the concept "development." (The internship would help them compare education as it is with education as it ought to be.)

The *philosophy* that informed the teaching of the program was that articulated by Kohlberg and Mayer; it may be called a cognitive-developmental or "progressive" educational philosophy, and it finds its fullest and most powerful justification in the writings of John Dewey. Thus, the subject matter and means of teaching in the program converged. The students were able to coordinate what they were coming to understand from their explicit studies with what they were beginning to see by reflecting on their own experiences as students and learners. This developing convergence made for a powerful intellectual experience, and, in my view, is one of the strongest and most noteworthy features of the program design.

(3) The program, while very well structured and planned, still allowed room for considerable student initiative.

(4) Large hunks and strands of work culminated in exams (usually, but not always, take-home exams) which were major intellectual and social events. Classes were called off, and the students were given time (usually close to a week) to work together in study groups on challenging, integrative questions, and to write their answers individually. These exams were important events in the life of the program because they provided opportunities for synthesis and crystallization and yielded great emotional payoffs.

(5) Finally, I should mention that the small size of the program led to a wonderful intimacy. There were only 23 of us. For a full year, we partied together, studied together, complained together, and we got to know each other very well indeed.

Transition from Undergraduate Program to Teacher Education. The "Development" model, while serving as the major inspiration for the first year of the Teacher Education Program (TEP), underwent major accommodations to meet new demands as it transmuted into TEP. TEP had a commitment to ongoing field experience from the start, so one of the three streams throughout the whole first year was field experience. We also had a major commitment to "social and cultural foundations" and to "curriculum design and teaching methods." The time necessary to do these three things changed the "Development" model. So in TEP, one stream that ran all the way through was a so-called "Theory" stream. In this stream, "developmental [i.e., psychological] theory" and philosophy of education alternated. Second, the sequence of philosophers had to be pruned. Aristotle and Locke were removed. It is not clear that the students saw the four remaining philosophers as representing a progression or a historical sequence; most probably just saw them as representing a variety of points of view. The component on history and the social-political context (including such writers as Michael Katz and Ivan Illich) was removed from the first year. The time spent in the field, and in the accompanying weekly "emerging seminars," meant less time in class for work on theory. Similarly, there was probably not quite as much time to work on Piaget as the students needed. At any rate, this corner was cut very sharply. Finally, even though the students had a big voice in the content of the Teaching Methods Workshops during spring quarter, they, in general, had less control over the curriculum than the "Development" students had. There was not nearly as much "free space" to play with.

A Good Model? The important question is whether the "Development" program is a good model for teacher education, one that deserves continued use. I think it is.

First of all, a coordinated studies model makes for good teacher education because it lets the students experience (often for the first time in their lives) what education ought to be about—intellectual inquiry by a community.

Second, the "Development" model has the advantage of cutting through the welter of things that students sense, fear, and are told that they need to be a teacher. This model says to them: "There are a few very important things you need; these are hard and require struggle, but the struggle is worth it. Understanding them will make all the difference; the rest you can easily pick up along the way." I believe these statements to be true, and I believe this approach has great virtue in teacher education.

Third, from start to finish, the model emphasizes the importance of reflection on experience as a means to learning. Nothing, I believe, will help future teachers more than the development of this habit. If they learn to reflect systematically on what they do as teachers, they will surely *become* good teachers, even if they start out as poor ones.

Fourth, the model emphasizes theory, and it emphasizes practice; it stresses Method at the expense of methods. All this is to say that we operate from the start on the assumption that the student will have to use her own mind to become a teacher; she will not be able to pick it up through imitation or memorization, or by gathering up a bag of tricks and strategies.

Fifth, the model has the potential to offer the powerful experience I spoke of earlier—the experience of discovering that what you are going through as a student makes sense in terms of the very concepts you are developing from the program materials. I think fewer students had this experience in TEP than the students in "Development" had, but the potential is there. This is the kind of experience that forges vision in people, and if it is vision that we want in teachers, then this is the kind of experience we want our prospective students to go through. As I write these words, I realize that I would want to work harder on just this dimension were I to work on revising the first year of the program. The changes necessary to push the program in this direction would be, of course, just those changes that would occasion the most resistance from fresh students and from outside reviewing agencies.

Bill Arney

I was a member of the teaching team during the first offering of Evergreen's new Master in Teaching Program. The master's program grew out of the Teacher Education Program that Finkel describes and was, in many ways, continuous with it. The first week, early in September 1990, we packed up the program—faculty and students—and went to the Makah Reservation at Neah Bay, Washington, to see a community that had taken its schools back from the federal government. The second and third weeks we brought in students, teachers, parents, administrators, school board members, the Director of the program, and others; we asked everyone to tell our students what he or she expected of these new teachers. We invited everyone to tell the prospective teachers what they should learn during the following two years to prepare themselves for work in the schools. We included ourselves, the faculty of the program, on equal terms with everyone else. This is what I said I expected of them.

You are already trying to teach me. Up at Neah Bay I said, somewhat casually, that in deciding to be a teacher, each of you has chosen to face a very big problem. "Challenge," you corrected. "We are facing many challenges, not problems. Problems are negative." It was nice to see, so early in people who want to be teachers, this impulse to teach.

I don't mind you teaching me, because I have so little to teach you. I am here, mostly, to teach *with* these three people [Gail Tremblay, Rita Pougiales, and Stephanie Kozick, the other members of the teaching team]. I didn't come to Evergreen to teach as much as I came to Evergreen to be a member of the faculty. I have little memory of the programs I have taught over these past nine years, but I have very vivid memories of the people with whom I have taught. What you learn over the next two years is much more dependent on what this team does—specifically on how we present and handle the many differences among us—in front of you than it is dependent on anything I could ever do with you or say to you. The book I am writing with Don Finkel, *Educating for Freedom: The Paradox of Pedagogy*, is about "collegial teaching." I suspect that by watching the four of us you may come to appreciate that term.

I am here because I think this team can help you think. By giving you my perspective on education and the schools, and by mixing that perspective with the three very different perspectives of my colleagues here, this team will give you the opportunity to think about what you are doing when you teach. One person who read a draft of Don's and my book wrote that we had discovered, in our discussion of collegial teaching, that the only thing worth teaching is confusion. He wrote, "By presenting always at least two truths, you teach not truth but confusion. And the students learn that if they are going to be able to think even one thought, they have to rethink everything. And they learn that they are going to have to do this on their own because their teachers, you two show them, are blinded. Each is blinded by his own truth." So my first expectation is that you will be confused by much of what goes on in here because there will always be multiple truths on the table.

My second expectation comes directly from the first. I expect you will rethink everything that you know (and your questions this week suggest that you know a lot about how schools run, about how they should be run, about what good teaching is, and so on) and you will do so for yourselves. I expect you to get into the habit of thinking. Thinking for yourselves (not thinking true and correct thoughts as they come from the textbooks and not re-thinking the thoughts of your favorite teacher) will provide you a firm ground as you begin to deal with the problems you have chosen to face as you become teachers.

I expect you to learn to deal with bureaucracies without becoming flexible. All of our speakers during these weeks have alerted you, in their own ways, to the fact that schooling involves bureaucracy and bureaucracies demand flexibility. Bureaucracies insist that you bend to their terms, and our speakers have helpfully advised you to become flexible so you will not break in officious winds. Many of your questions this week suggest that you are ready to comply. Underneath most of your questions, I have heard one question: "How can I adjust myself to fit into the system better?" The one thing bureaucracies detest and try to wipe out are people who are well grounded, who know with honesty who they are and who demand honesty in return, people who insist that they be treated as if they were persons. Bureaucracies do not function according to Emerson's urging, "Let us treat men and women well, treat them as if they were real; perhaps they are." I expect you to find—not now, but within the next two years—the ground under your feet. In two years, I expect you to know where you stand. I expect you not to be so ready to bend to fit.

Finally, I expect you to appreciate the indignity of speaking for others. I expect you, on one side, to experience many times the humiliation of having your own experiences reduced to a statistical accounting of the average behavior of a group. (This has already happened in these two weeks. Some of you have noticed.) I expect you to experience several times the disorientation and perhaps enlightenment that comes when, after you describe *their behavior* (whoever "they" are in the instance), a quiet voice not unlike Eunice Santiago's [one of the earlier speakers] says, "But it's not like that." I expect you to be surprised at least once by a child you thought you understood completely. I expect your teaching skills to improve, but I expect your humility to outgrow your skills as you think about what the problem you have embraced has to teach you.

Rita Pougiales

Rita Pougiales was a member of the teaching team during the first iteration of the Master in Teaching Program at The Evergreen State College. Occasionally, the four members of the teaching team would hold a faculty seminar in front of the students. We would discuss a question or a text among ourselves and discourage students from participating. One day, we must have been especially critical of schooling because one of the students shouted from the back row, "So what do you think we should do!?" Pougiales broke the resulting silence with this:

"You could open the door."

"What?" From the back row.

"You could open the door." No one interrupted her as she paused. "You know, the door to the school. The door is usually locked. They give keys to teachers. There are lots of neat things inside schools. Children enjoy a lot of things inside schools. In my opinion, it would be very good if you would let children get to those things. So, you could unlock the door. You could do this regularly and predictably, so your students could count on you doing it every day."

Then the children would have a chance to teach, "just as good as the teacher."

CHAPTER 3

Christy's Biker

"And you know what else? He smells. It was really hard to sit next to him."

Christy, a student teacher, finished telling me about Ray, an eighth-grade biker, with this reference to his smell. It was writing class. Earlier I had watched as Christy tried to get Ray to write:

"I can't write today."

"Why not?"

"Just can't."

"Is there something wrong?"

"Yeah."

"What?"

"My brain's blocked up."

"What does that mean?"

Christy's voice is somewhere between exasperation and panic: exasperation because she is ready to say something about having heard this all before (even though she's been teaching for only two weeks), panic because her supervising professor—me—is standing there listening.

"Do you really want to know?"

"Yes."

"Well, ever since the last day of school last year when my uncle was shot and killed in the Philippines, my brain feels like it's blank."

"You could write about that if you want. You should write about what's important to you." She means it. She's sympathetic, but she is, already, a teacher first.

"Can't. I want to write about my summer trip to Montana. The one where I went to the bikers' convention. This is what I've wrote so far."

Christy reads his work, talks to Ray, and asks what he's interested in.

"Knives," he says.

"Knives?" A little more panic, but not, this time, because her professor is there.

"Yeah, I make 'em after school. It's the only way I can get any money. My dad's been laid off for more than a year now. So I make knives. After school. Every day. For nine hours."

"You could write about that." Her sincerity is now, to Ray, as old as any twice-used line.

Christy asks him directly what he's interested in. "Passing. I wanna pass this course so I can get out of here." She tells Ray he can write about whatever he wants to write about, what's important to him. Christy moves on and I follow him back to his desk.

Ray tells me that he's a member of Hell's Angels, that he can't wear his jacket to school because even out there at the end of the valley behind the hills that back the industrial strip that runs south from Seattle they're also concerned about gangs, that he can "make a knife *that long* [he unexaggeratingly hold his hands about five inches apart] in three hours flat—start to finish," and that he really does want to write about his trip to the bikers' convention in Montana this past summer.

"My mother was born in Montana," I say. "Geyser, I think. A little town that just put in board sidewalks ten years ago. Or so she says. She's pretty old now."

"I was born in Montana, too. That's why I went there. To see the town where I grew up."

"Oh?"

"Yeah. I was born there and they put me on page one of the newspaper. On the last page of the same paper was a picture of my dad's truck. A brand new Ford truck. White. And I remember there were stories in the paper about the snow. Six feet deep the day I was born."

"You want to know how to write?"

"I guess."

I took his pen and wrote:

I rode back to Montana this summer. I wanted to see where I was born. When I was born, they put me on the front page of the newspaper. On the back page of the same paper was a picture of my dad's truck. A brand new Ford truck. White. The paper said there was snow, six feet of it.

When I got there this summer there was no snow, but _____.

I showed him the writing and said, "All you've got to do is fill in the blank. What happened then? I don't know. You do."

He read it and looked at me with a big smile. Junior high students—not even a member of Hell's Angels—have not yet learned to affect sullenness on demand. "This is good," he says.

"They're your words. I just got you from what you said about your trip to where you have to write some more. The trick of writing like that is to not let words like yours go through your brain. From what you said about your uncle, it sounds like there's a good reason why your brain might be blank. So, to write you just have to get the words on paper."

Later, Christy and I talked about Ray. That was the conversation that ended with her comment about his smell. She was right. He did smell—bad. It *was* hard to sit next to him.

Later still, sitting in my study in front of a computer that this kid would never to be able to buy no matter how many knives he made, still warm from a shower that this kid could not get at his house, I wrote to Christy:

So here's this kid, a big kid in a Harley shirt. He says he can't write because every time he does his mind goes blank, and that happens, he thinks, because on the last day of school last year his uncle was shot and killed in the Philippines. And he's pissed off because he can't wear his Hell's Angels duds to school. And he makes knives after school because he's damned good at that. His sole concern, which he voiced to you, is that he pass this year. And to top it all off, it's hard for you to sit next to him because he smells. Ray's what? 14, 15 years old?

So what do you say? "It's important to write what you want just for yourself." Now wait, Mrs. R. I don't think Ray would choose, given a choice, to write anything, not for himself, not even for you. He just wants to pass. It was a "good move"—a good teacherly move—to tell him to write for himself. But I think you are, as I put it to you yesterday, trying, with that kind of line, to "take him on." You are challenging his principal reason for being there, which probably goes by a name close to "doing time."

I strongly encourage you not to take this kid on, not with the most sound educationism, not with the best pedagogy in the world. I strongly encourage you to meet him right where he is. If he wants only to pass, tell him precisely what that is going to involve. Maybe when he sees that the schools have such low standards that even a poor student like him (I'm speaking, you know, about the kind of self-perception that the schools have encouraged him to adopt—it's so evident with Ray!) can pass, maybe then he can learn to write too. And maybe he will tell you (he will tell you) some pretty amazing and interesting things (which your comments, before class, about some of the other students' work, tell me you are interested in hearing).

I encourage you to listen to this guy, very closely. He said some beautiful things to me in just the two minutes I sat with him. Show him how to write them down before they get anywhere near going through his mind, which I think you should accept is, in fact, "blank."

And don't send this guy to the counselor. Lots of kids with blank minds have learned a lot in school.

I rarely give advice to student teachers, so it was a sign of Christy's character that she could accept *so much* advice as gracefully as she did. She acted on the last bit of advice immediately. She didn't send Ray to the counselor. She went herself. The counselor contacted Ray's father and learned that they didn't have hot running water or a shower or bath in their house—and no way to wash clothes. The counselor asked Ray's father if he would allow Ray to come to school early to shower there and whether it would be okay to wash his clothes with the laundry done for the athletic teams. "Sure," he said, "that would be great." The counselor also invited Ray's father to use the school's showers if he wished.

There's no end to this story except, very likely, the obvious and statistically predictable one. Ray will eventually cause enough problems in one school or another that he will be thrown out; and, eventually, he'll be old enough that no one in a position of authority will be able to come after him, even if they cared to.

But the interim ending is nicer. At the end of her student teaching assignment, Christy showed me the final pieces of writing done by some of the students. One piece was by Ray. It was about hunting bears, about skinning them in the woods and cutting them up and carrying the meat, 300 pounds of it (Christy wrote in the margin, "What does 300 pounds of bear meat feel like? Tell me. Write it."), and the skins miles back the truck and then to his father's "haus." Christy was especially proud of that paper. She didn't say how Ray felt about it. And she didn't say anything about how he smells.

CHAPTER 4

What Do You Teach after the War Begins?

January 17, 1991, five students show up for seminar today. Yesterday, in time for prime time on the East Coast, a war started. "The liberation of Kuwait has begun," Marlin Fitzwater said with as much of a snarl as a seasoned, cynical news guy could manage. I was in the car on the way to hear Christopher Lasch talk at Elliott Bay Books. Nancy had invited me. "Well, I wonder what he'll say now," she said as we listened to the bombs behind the voice-over on the radio.

Lasch didn't say anything. He didn't show. The folks at Elliott Bay weren't even apologetic. David, a friend who had come with Rudy in a separate car, knew Lasch and asked after him. "He's staying in his hotel room. Called in to say he was really upset and wouldn't be coming. I told him about the demonstration that's going to be at the federal building at 8:00. You might catch him there." David and Nancy and Rudy and I went out for dinner: fine pasta, good company, and serious talk (filled, as it had to be with this group, with many laughs).

Those five students in the seminar were very serious and without laughter the next day. Four sat on the far side of the table opposite me, the fifth to my right at the head of the table. "It's so depressing. What do you think?"—looking at me. More than any other day this year I was the center of the seminar even though I had avoided the head of the table.

"I really don't think much about it. I'm still bothered that Christopher Lasch didn't come to Elliott Bay last night and talk. I mean, really, here's this guy who writes a book on progress and here we are trying to progress through the Middle East and he's so depressed that he stays in his hotel and doesn't say anything. What's the world coming to when a smart guy like him doesn't have anything to say publicly at a time like this?"

Not the response they wanted.

"Now wait. We think it's important to talk about this war."

"Whatever you like. It's your seminar." A gambit I used often.

"No, it's important that you talk now. What do you think? I mean, when we're teachers and in situations like this, with a war starting and all, and the students come to class and they're upset, what do you think we should teach?"

"Math? History?"

Not the response they wanted.

"Math?! At a time like this. Look, Bill, there's a half a million troops over there. Men and, this time, women. Fathers and mothers. Just up the interstate there are huge military bases that only have the women and children and dogs and cats still there. Some of the students in the schools we're in have their fathers—some of them have their mothers—over there. And you think we should teach math?"

"Or history. Or anything else that you think is important to teach."

"It's important to teach about this war."

"Then teach history. George Bush started this war by drawing that damn 'line in the sand' months ago. Right then—right at that moment!— you should have started teaching about how all those lines in the sand that we call 'national borders,' those lines that a whole lot of people are going to start getting killed over, got drawn in the first place. Did you ever notice on a map just how straight *those* lines in the sand are? Do you think they follow the 'natural features' of that region? So George Bush talks about lines in the sand. Teach about the history of lines in the sand.

"Or teach about math. You say there are half a million American soldiers there today? How many calories does each one need each day? How much food is that going to be over the next four weeks? How about the next four years? I bet you anything that the supermarkets all over Kuwait are going to shut right down once they hear that there's a war going on. How are the generals going to get all that food to all those folks? Teach about math. In fact, I heard just the other day that the Defense Department is recommending that each soldier drink something like eight quarts of water every day. How many Boeing 747s full of water is that going to be each day? Teach math."

"You've got to be serious for once. The children are going to come to school upset. You've got to deal with that."

"Where did your students learn to be upset?"

"From TV. From hearing their parents talk. It's upsetting. Look at our seminar. Only a third of the students came today. We're upset too."

"What is there to be upset about?"

"Bill . . ."

"I mean it. This war, this *particular* war—let's leave aside all the Middle East problems—started last summer. Remember, there was this State Department announcement about Iraq massing 30,000 troops on the Kuwait border. What happened? The stock market went down fifty points. The next day the market comes back and no one thinks about it after that until Bush, 'after conferring with our allies,' starts sending *half a million* troops into that region. Then things go along pretty much as normal for the whole fall. People talk about how long this war is going to last once it starts, as if that is a normal thing to talk about. And all the news stations go over and tape these interviews with the troops saying how they're glad to be able to do their duty and how they wish they were home for the holidays, and everyone treats *that* like it's normal. But then the war starts and everyone sits in front of their television sets thinking that they are learning something about the war. Just doing what's normal. And now they get upset?! I can't believe that even a smart guy like Christopher Lasch is upset. When, in the normal course of events, you say that you're drawing a line in the sand and will go to war if someone crosses it, and then, normally and naturally, you send half a million troops 10,000 miles away and you give them guns and other stuff you normally give to people in the army, and then you conduct these normal training missions all over somebody else's sand, it seems only normal that you might expect a war to start. I don't see any reason to be upset about events just following their normal courses.

"But you have given me another idea for something to teach about. Why don't you teach children how easy it is to learn to be upset by watching worried adults or by listening to TV announcers who treat war as if it were a normal thing?"

"The children are worried in the schools. It seems to me that we have a responsibility to care for them."

"Perhaps. But you are paid to *teach* them. It's damned difficult to decide what to teach on any given day. Having a war start in prime time the night before when everyone's sitting around the dinner table makes that decision on this particular day a little more difficult, but it's the same decision I hope you'll face conscientiously every day."

"Some schools are hiring psychologists part-time, to be 'on call,' so that if a kid freaks out, there'll be some help."

"I know that most schools have too much money and that they make very bad decisions about how to spend it. I just hope that those of you in the poorer districts don't think *you* have to be psychologists just because your school isn't hiring them for you. You're hardly trained to be teachers yet; we haven't done anything to train you as psychologists."

"But you don't have to be a psychologist to care for people."

"I think teachers care for students best by teaching them well."

* * *

"Is it possible to be a teacher at all in the schools?"

I'm afraid I laughed.

I had just finished giving a typical critique of the schools in an undergraduate program with a typical title: "Meaning, Power, and Learning." Some of the students had been irritated, some charmed, some puzzled. One of the puzzled ones came to me afterwards to ask his question: "Is it possible to be a teacher at all in the schools?"

"It's possible to be a teacher every nanosecond of every day you are in the schools. From where would such a question ever come?"

"I read Illich and now I listen to you and the schools seem like such hopeless places. Who would ever want to teach there?"

My laughter, already on the wane, subsided entirely when I realized that once again I had failed as a teacher. This young man was, it seemed likely, headed for a career in teaching. He was sensitive and thoughtful, a little rebellious, probably concerned about improving society (and convinced it could be done). You could tell he was one of those students who had had one, maybe two, possibly (even though it was unlikely) three good teachers in his course through the public schools. He had tasted good education in the schools. He knew it was possible to be a good teacher in public schools, but all the critiques that he was reading and hearing concerning the schools had left him discouraged. He had listened closely to what I had to say, and, if my talk had not been the final straw to push him toward a job in ecology or some such new venture outside the schools, the next one would. He was serious, so I had to be, too.

"I hope that lots of people will want to teach—in the schools. The best teachers are often people who wonder why anyone would ever want to teach there. Don't forget: Illich is *not* opposed to education. That *would be* a little silly, wouldn't it, given how obviously educated he is?" We laughed together this time. "Somewhere in *Deschooling Society* he says that the problem is not the value that people attach to education; rather it's *the institutionalization of values* that concerns him. It's not education that worries him; it's schooling. There's a difference. I think it's possible for education to occur, even in the schools. It would take some courage, and a remarkable ability to keep your head clear in the face of the fog that schooling creates, to go into teaching nowadays, but I hope that nothing I said will discourage you from it, if you're inclined that way."

He thanked me in a formal sort of way and walked away without tipping his hand concerning his plans. That poker face, I thought, will serve him well in the schools.

* * *

The problem teachers face, in the schools, is not whether they can be teachers. There are good teachers—true educators—in the schools. Even if there were only one, it would be sufficient evidence that it is possible to be a teacher, even there. The problems arise only when teachers forget they are teachers. When they become psychologists, surrogate parents, deputies of the local police force, mouthpieces of the government, safety experts, or adjudicators of the rules of extracurricular life, they run into problems. They aren't trained to those tasks, and doing any one of them, even for one moment, takes time away from what a teacher actually can do in the schools—teach.

One student teacher I know had an especially difficult class to which he was charged to teach Washington State history. His first quizzes and tests came back blank from some of the students. There seemed to be a hard core of eight students who could not or would not—in any event, did not—do any of the work he assigned. Then, not because of his tests but because a bureaucratic clock had gone off in the administrative offices, the requests for documentation started arriving from the counselors and the specialists and the remedialists closeted around the school. Everyone, it seemed, wanted some information, if you please, on just those eight students. Instead of completing the forms as requested, he went looking for the form senders.

"Why these eight?" he inquired.

"They're all special ed or on watch for it," said the remedialists. "She gets beat up by her father if she gets lower than a B," said the psychologist. "He's next on the list for reading enhancement," said the specialist.

"Why didn't you tell me?"

"Didn't want to stigmatize them in your mind. Wanted to give them a chance in your class first."

"Great. So I've been trying to teach these kids for five weeks and you knew that they were going to have problems learning anything from me and you didn't tell me, much less help me. Is that right?"

"Uhhh . . ."

It's easy to complain about all the programs for special education and special help and psychological assistance and this and that in the schools nowadays. This student teacher knew all those critiques, but he had a wonderfully naive and productively literal view of them: *If* there are these specialists and remedialists and psychologists salted around the school, *then* they should do their jobs, so he could do his job, which he knew to be teaching. He was willing to do his part, even to fill out all the forms; but he expected to be allowed, then, to teach. He is a man who will never forget that he is a teacher, no matter how much the schools try to get him to think or behave otherwise. The toughest problem in the schools is not being a teacher; the toughest problem is not forgetting that you are one.

* * *

I was very pleased that those five students came to seminar the day after this particular war started. They helped me remember what I am paid to do.

And I'm still bothered that Christopher Lasch forgot, at least for that evening, that he's a teacher, too. It's a bad sign for our times when learned people find reasons not to talk about what they know.

CHAPTER 5

D.A.R.E. to Ask Questions about Drugs

This is about the day the D.A.R.E. cop came to class. The class consisted of 65 would-be public school teachers in the Teacher Education Program. The D.A.R.E. cop tried hard to give his 17-hour drug-education curriculum on how to "say no" and how to find other things to do with your life in the one hour allotted to him. He did it, but not without a few questions.

School Reform, D.A.R.E. Style

Anyone interested in reforming the schools should pay attention to D.A.R.E. It's a model of curriculum reform. In my son's school district, the local police department is given all the children in two grades for 17 seat hours. The D.A.R.E. folks have imposed their curriculum on schools across the country. Here, from their example, is how school reform should be accomplished:

First, pick a topic a lot of people are concerned about. It should be a topic that worries people but that not a lot of them are doing anything about. "The war on drugs" generates a lot of worry in parents who, before the start of the "war," were confident about their abilities to teach their children to stay away from dangerous things. The war on drugs is an exemplary starting point for creating a reformed curriculum.

Second, assemble a lot of "research." It turns out that one or two Ph.D.s in southern California assembled most of the research that is used by all D.A.R.E. programs. They researched everything, including, the D.A.R.E. cop will tell you, the black and neon pink colors of the D.A.R.E. logo: "Research has shown that hot pink on black attracts kids' attention better than any other combination." Not incidentally, this research keeps the people in California well-heeled because they get to hold seminars and institutes, and cops from all over the country come to southern California to learn about the research so that they can go home and answer all the questions of the local folks with sentences that begin, "Research has shown . . ." You don't have to have a Ph.D. to sound smart; you just have to have been in the presence of one or two of them.

Third, get the local business community on your side before you approach the schools. Ask the car dealers to donate a van. For the war on drugs and a tax write-off, one of them will do so. Make sure part of the deal is that local businesses paint your van with the logo—in the "research has shown" colors—so that you can drive to the school board meetings as if you are ready to go. And get them to donate bumper stickers, so the catchy title of the catchy curriculum reform gets around.

Fourth, design a curriculum. Make it thick. If people are really worried and have no idea what to do, it helps to seem like you have something— better if it's a lot—to say.

Finally, when you go to the school board meeting and ask to be allowed to teach the community's children for such a long time, wear a uniform with a badge, but leave the gun in the van. Research has shown they'll think you're thoughtful.

(Incidentally, don't worry about whether the curriculum has any effect on students. If someone asks if D.A.R.E. reduces the likelihood that kids will use drugs, don't say, "Research has shown . . . ," because it hasn't. Concentrate research on things you can actually do something about, like the colors of your logo.)

Once you get into the schools, the nearby university or college will invite you to give the people in the Teacher Education Program a little presentation on the kinds of things you do in the schools. They will send a letter that says something like, "We hope you will take part of the hour to tell our students something about the D.A.R.E. program and a little about what you do when you are in elementary schools. We'd like you to leave half the time for questions." No matter what the invitation says, it's best to plan to fill the whole time with your material. Hand out an outline of seventeen hours of curriculum and plow through summaries of the whole thing. If you don't fill time, they will ask questions.

A Few Questions

The D.A.R.E. cop came to our class late one afternoon. He handed out his outline of the seventeen hours. He told everyone to ask anything they wished; he'd like to keep this as informal as possible, he said.

"Do you wear a gun—like that one on your belt!—when you go into elementary schools?" "Oh my gosh! No, not at all. I always leave that in the van. I'm sorry. My mistake. Let me just put in here on the table while we talk."

But nothing flustered the guy, not making the mistake of bringing his gun to class, not having a loaded gun on the table while he talked. Research probably had shown that if you ever get flustered when talking about drugs, if you ever show any kind of strong sentiment one way or the other, if you show any sign of weakness in your rap—they'll smell you out and ask questions. So, gun on the table, he started.

"Anyone in here want to say whether or not they've used drugs and maybe tell us something about the circumstances?" Nervous stirring. After all, the D.A.R.E. cop did have a badge and there was a gun on the table. Finally, though, a few people volunteered responses. A guy in the back row said, "I used drugs in Vietnam. It was the only way I could get to sleep sometimes." "Thank you. . . . And thank you. . . . And thank you. . . . So not all of you are strangers to drugs. So let me tell you about the D.A.R.E. program. Back in . . . , two psychologists in Los Angeles started looking at the research . . ."

And so it went. For fifty minutes we heard about the research and the colors and the new van every year and the seventeen lessons and about the way that, yes, the curriculum is controversial, but participation is voluntary ("But the kids really like learning these skills."), and the parents can come to the sessions, and so on.

Finally, I had to ask, "I've been reading this theological scientist who has called, throughout his life, for the decriminalization of all means of self-destruction. He says that, in these times, the use of drugs may be a reasonable response to a bad situation. So I was wondering, in your view, what is so bad about drugs?"

"That's an interesting comment. What exactly do you have in mind?" Research *had* shown you should never get flustered.

"Well, I have in mind something like Mr. ———— in the back row said at the beginning of the session. Sometimes you have to take drugs just to get to sleep. Sometimes you find yourself in a very bad situation that is nothing of your doing, but it's very bad. Some people drink to kill their pain; others take drugs. So what is so bad about drugs?"

"But the kids I'm talking to are not in Vietnam."

I was beginning to suspect that research had shown it is better not to answer questions, but I tried again.

"I don't know about that. I read a lot about child abuse these days. I read about more and more kids growing up in poverty or going to bed hungry. Recently I read a story about violence in Washington, D.C. It said one-fourth—25 percent—of the children in the public schools of our nation's capital *have witnessed a murder*. Now, of course, the kids you talk to are not in Vietnam. But I am not convinced they are not in situations to which the use of drugs might not be a reasonable response. So I was wondering, what is so bad about drugs?"

"You raised a very interesting point." (Research had probably shown that one way to get people to desist from asking questions is to tell them that they had asked interesting questions.) "I guess my only response would be to ask you a question: Who's in control of your life if you use drugs?"

"I'm afraid I would turn it back to you and ask you a question: In a city where one in four schoolchildren has witnessed a murder, *who* is in control of their lives?"

"Well, that's interesting . . ."

At precisely this interesting moment, the students in the program got involved: "This kind of exchange could go on forever," one woman said. "The man only has ten minutes left and he's only up to lesson eleven. I hope you'll let him go on with this now."

He did. He finished without getting flustered.

I don't know what the would-be teachers learned that day. I learned that if you dare to ask questions about drugs, the D.A.R.E. cop will probably find your questions interesting.

CHAPTER 6

Should We Value the Teaching of Values?

Perhaps some will say, "Why cannot you withdraw from Athens, Socrates, and hold your peace?" It is the most difficult thing in the world to make you understand why I cannot do that. If I say that I cannot hold my peace because that would be to disobey the god, you will think that I am not in earnest and will not believe me. And if I tell you that no greater good can happen to a man than to discuss human excellence every day and the other matters about which you have heard me arguing and examining myself and others, and that the unexamined life is not worth living, then you will believe me still less. . . . If I had been rich, I would have proposed as large a fine as I could pay: that would have done me no harm. But I am not rich enough to pay a fine unless you are willing to fix it at a sum within my means. Perhaps I could pay you a mina, so I propose that. Plato here, Athenians, and Crito, and Critobulus, and Apollodorus bid me to propose thirty minae, and they guarantee its payment. So I propose thirty minae. Their security will be sufficient to you for the money.

Plato, "Apology"

We know Socrates as a man who would do anything to keep a conversation going. Here in the "Apology" we find one of Socrates' most stunning maneuvers. He turns away from discussing "human excellence . . . and the other matters" that have occupied him, his friends, and his interlocutors every day, and he initiates a discussion of values. He is willing to make, to the good men of Athens assembled in judgment, *proposals concerning the value of his own life.* If one mina is insufficient in exchange for his life, perhaps 30 will do.

Immediately following his proposal, Socrates is condemned to death. Critical thinkers raised on "values clarification" curricula will have already spotted the problem: Plato and his friends don't value their teacher's life highly enough. They should have taken up a bigger collection; perhaps they should have entered into negotiations. We know from our experts in communication and mediation that reasonable men can usually reach what they call "consensus" on values. Socrates simply stopped. These things happen to the unschooled.

But Socrates' turn toward a discussion of values was a device, a tactic to keep things going as his case neared its end. We ought to recognize that while values might have been the terms on which the men of Athens might have found their way into the conversation with Socrates, Socrates' main interests lay elsewhere: in the discussion of human excellence. Socrates' turn away from excellence and toward values poses questions for us: Should we value the teaching of values? Why aim so low?

Two Nexuses

Most of what now passes for education in our schools is organized around a nexus of three terms: information, fitness, values. Good teaching and learning is organized around another nexus: knowledge, character, virtue. We live in a period of functional confusion between these two nexuses.

We pursue information, fitness, and the study of values and think—we are led to think by those who school us—that we are gaining knowledge, developing character, and learning something about virtue. In fact, we have left behind the world of knowledge, character, and virtue entirely, even though we are still in a position to know, appreciate, and comprehend its difference from the world of information, fitness, and values. Peter Drucker uses a topographic image to suggest how some historical changes occur. Some changes in landscape don't mark real changes at all, he says. "But some passes are different. They are true divides. They are often neither high nor spectacular." But once traversed, there is no going back. One may still carry memories of the other side, but, as Drucker puts it, *"There are new realities."*[1] Our current reality is grounded in the information/fitness/values nexus.

Sometimes, something suggests that a course toward the realm of information, fitness, and values is not a good way to live with one another and with ourselves. However, we proceed without protest because of our functional confusion. We find ways to reassure ourselves that in our rush to embrace the new nexus and find a life in the world of information/fitness/values we are not necessarily leaving behind virtue, character, and knowledge, in general, excellence.

Information/Knowledge

We know what information is. It is that which may be reduced to bits (0 and 1, the on/off of the millions of switches in, first, transistors and, later, chips), bytes, and the luminescent displays on video screens. Information is inert. It can be useful or useless, but there is nothing about information per se that makes the distinction. By itself information cannot be right or wrong, correct or incorrect. It takes something more to impose such assessments. It takes knowledge, a term we should use in the strong sense to include what some people have called "judgment."

Michael Oakeshott makes a distinction between information and knowledge:

> When I consider . . . how I first became dimly aware that there was something else in learning than the acquisition of information, that the way a man thought was more important than what he said, it was, I think, on the occasions when we had before us concrete situations. It was when we had, not an array of historical "facts," but (for a moment) the facts suspended in an historian's argument. It was on those occasions when we were made to learn by heart, not the declension of *bonus* (which, of course, had to be learned), but a passage of literature, the reflection of a mind at work in language. It was on those occasions when one was not being talked to but had the opportunity of overhearing an intelligent conversation.[2]

Oakeshott is not a mere rationalist for whom an "argument" is the application of a logical, deductive apparatus of rationality to a body of facts. He recognizes that knowledge requires embodiment and human intercourse. We are in the presence of knowledge when we hear "an intelligent conversation" or see "a mind at work in language." Rousseau tries to grasp the difference between reasoning from facts and participating in knowledge in *Emile*:

> One of the errors of our age is to use reason in too unadorned a form, as if men were all mind. In neglecting the language of signs that speak to the imagination, the most energetic of languages has been lost. The impression of the word is always weak, and one speaks to the heart far better through the eyes than through the ears. . . . Reason alone is not active. It sometimes restrains, it arouses rarely, and it has never done anything great. Always to reason is the mania of small minds. Strong souls have quite another language. It is with this language that one persuades and makes others act.[3]

It is this other language that is the language of knowledge.

Information can be transmitted anywhere; knowledge must have a place in which it resides. One becomes aware of the operations of knowledge "dimly" at first and gradually becomes enlightened; the reasoning with which information is manipulated can be learnt by anyone, even by the very young now being raised on courses in "critical thinking skills." Knowledge must be embodied and have people whom it moves and through whom it circulates; information is necessarily disembodied (the body can only mimic, more or less successfully, the operations of machines that function according to the position of on-off switches). Knowledge is always local and particular; information and reason have the peculiarly modern property of being international, of being able to cross boundaries marked by mere differences, as we are now able to say, in culture and language.

We can turn to a contemporary report to see just how recently we, in modern circumstances, have crossed the pass from the regime of knowledge to a world governed by the flow of information. Shoshana Zuboff's *In the Age of the Smart Machine* chronicles changes in a paper-processing plant as the plant was automated.[4] She shows that in older paper-processing plants the workers possess, in their bodies, knowledge of how the plant operates and of how to make paper. (Of course, this manufactured paper is not the paper of the 16th-century craftsperson, but the fact that workers in modern factories still have the opportunity to possess knowledge regarding their work highlights the fact that our transition to a world of information is even more recent than our passage into the industrial era.) They know the meaning of a vibration here or a change in ambient temperature there. With their fingers they can test the consistency of the slurry and know what it will mean for the paper that will result.

Zuboff reports that an engineer in the plant said of the people who ran the older, unautomated plant, "The operators run the mill, but they don't understand how. There are operators who know exactly what to do, but they cannot tell you how they do it." In fact, however, these operators of the old mills have a good *working knowledge* of the plant, knowledge which they could not turn into *information* that engineers could put into algorithms that could be fed to computers that would run the plant in a newfangled way. Workers cannot turn their understanding, their knowledge, into information because knowledge of how to run the plant is in them, in their bodies; it is inscribed in their habits and everyday activities. It is not that the workers do not understand how they run the plant, as the engineer claims; they understand very well and they can convey this understanding to another *person* through education. The problem, in this instance, was the engineer's implicit demand that they disembody their understanding and try to convert their knowledge into information for the benefit of the soon-to-come smart machine. In comparison to the sacrifice of knowledge on the altar of information that will occur as the plant is automated, the fact that a few workers will lose their jobs seems trivial.

Fitness/Character

Character results from the world shaping a person as he or she interacts with the world in some essential activity. Having character means a person has the capacity to carry out the activities proper to himself or herself. If one is a hunter, the activity of hunting gradually causes one's body to take the shape of a hunter. The Seattle Art Museum's Katherine White Collection of African Art contains several hunters' shirts. These shirts are covered with leather thongs, tufts of hair, and teeth. The shirts bristle through the village as they are worn by men returning from the hunts. The shirts help define the characters of the hunters whose shapes they contain and whose activities they announce. One who would wear such a shirt can be nothing other than a hunter whose body *and* mind have come to be what they are through pursuing what a hunter does. If one is a berry picker, the same thing happens. One develops the character of a berry picker by being a berry picker.

Character depends upon the pursuit of activities that give definition to characters. Harold Baillie distinguishes between "activity" and "motion":

> An activity is a life function that contains its own end or purpose, and thus it may be both complete and continuous.

> On the other hand, a motion has its purpose or end outside itself, and thus is never complete while it exists. For it to be complete, that is, for it to attain its end, a motion must cease to exist.[5]

The hunter hunting is involved in an activity. The hunt is a completely self-contained activity and thus can build the character of hunters. But, one might ask, doesn't the hunt have an end external to itself, namely, the feeding of the tribe? No, others engage in the activities called "preparing food," "cooking," and "feeding." The hunt remains continuous only with itself and completes itself, at which point other characters in the tribal play, engaged in other essential activities, come to do the work of which they are knowledgeable.

Are you a person of character? used to be a question that could be asked. It meant, simply, are you capable of engaging in those activities specific to who you are in yourself and in your relationships to everyone else? We have lost the capacity to ask this question.

Now we ask, Are you fit? The depressing thing is that people answer this question without ever asking, Fit for what? Robert Crawford conducted a study of health and wellness by asking people, simply, Are you healthy? How do you know? Crawford showed that concepts of health and fitness, along with the socio-medical discourse that surrounds them, have become the modern terms in which people think about and judge their moral worth.[6] People are fit, they say, because they are flexible in body and spirit, because they use machines that let them bicycle to nowhere, because the numbers announced by blood analyzers are within limits they are told are normal. All references are to externalized, abstract, depersonalized standards. People no longer think about character, their capacities to pursue the activities proper to who they are. They think about their fitness to do what they are called upon to do, their ability to meet whatever challenges their lives put before them. Educationists, guidance counselors, therapists will tell you that one of the biggest mistakes you can make today is to outfit yourself for something in particular. Being able to engage in an activity is not the way to be fit, even if it was once one step on the way to character.

The workers in plants and offices about to undergo automation have to make themselves fit for anything, ready to fit anywhere. Today it is smarter to be generally flexible than particularly capable. One is better off if one is ready to move and able to seize opportunities whenever they present themselves.

One must be fit for the mundane reason that our times—the times organized around information, fitness, and values—are discomforting. Zuboff writes about women working in an office that converted from a "paper and pencil" approach to processing documents to a fully computerized system. She says,

> Jobs [in the stock and bond transfer agency] that had been able to utilize at least some small measure of [workers'] personhood now emphasized their least individually differentiated and most starkly animal capacities. They had been disinherited from the management process and driven into the confine of their individual body space. As a result, the employees in each office became increasingly engulfed in the immediate sensations of physical discomfort.[7]

We can imagine that hunters, especially young hunters-in-training, experienced physical pain, but they lived enmeshed in a group of people who could explain to them why they should expect to feel this discomfort. They might say, "You just don't *know* yet," or, "You are not yet of sufficient *character* for this activity," and they might offer the novice certain instructions that had a clear purpose—the perfection of an activity—and that had a secondary effect—the relief of discomfort. Now people experience discomfort and the best explanation someone can give is, "You're probably out of shape." No wonder there are wellness programs and hundreds of people leaving their offices at lunchtime to march through the streets with no purpose other than trying to get away and to get fit, fit for nothing but fit nonetheless. These new marchers to nowhere are, like Zuboff's workers, "lost in space," just going through the motions. They have no place in which to engage in activities that will help them develop their character, that which is proper to who they are.

Value/Virtue

Martin Ostwald says this about Aristotle's use of *areta,*

> *Areta* was eventually generalized to denote the functional excellence of any person, animal, or thing. . . . In other words, *areta* is that quality which enables its possessor to perform his own particular function well. . . . [A person's] *aretai* or "virtues" are those qualities which make him function well in relation to his fellow men, that is, the qualities which make him play his

part in human society well. . . . The value of *areta* is that it is an end in itself, realized in living human society.[8]

Baillie, following Aristotle, says this of virtue,

> An action in accordance with virtue is an activity, not a motion. It is a perfection of human life that completes and retains both the life and the activity. In virtue, one can attain one's end and live a full life within it.[9]

Baillie adds to the essential idea of virtue being the perfection of a human life the notion that virtue needs a *place* proper to the action, a place that supports and encourages virtuous practices. Aristotle's virtue of "political wisdom" is realizable only *in* the state; it is not a theoretical ideal realizable in the mind. Courage requires a battlefield just as temperance requires a household. Recently, the so-called "Hebenshausen Declaration on Soil" linked a definition of virtue to the "soil beneath our feet":

> As philosophers, we search below our feet because our generation has lost its grounding in both soil and virtue. By virtue we mean that shape, order and direction of action informed by tradition, bounded by place, and qualified by choices made within the habitual reach of the actor; we mean practice mutually recognized as being good within a shared local culture which enhances the memories of a place.

> We note that such virtue is traditionally found in labor, craft, dwelling and suffering supported, not by an abstract earth, environment or energy system, but by the particular soil these very actions have enriched with their traces.[10]

It is worth considering these several ways of thinking about "virtue" because virtue holds together an orientation to the world, an orientation organized around the knowledge/character/virtue nexus. Virtue is place bound, character bound, based on the judicious use of embodied knowledge, and it is inherently social. You cannot be a "virtuous person." You can only act virtuously in relation to other persons in some specific social context. Indeed, the theologian F. Forrester Church has argued, in *The Seven Deadly Virtues,* that virtue becomes destructive, deadly, when it takes on an individualistic cast.[11] Virtue, he suggests, must be conceived always as "corporate virtue," which is characterized by righteous actions that do not violate the order of things, all things.

In stark contrast to virtue stands value. Value is more an attribute of any thing than it is a perfection of some particular thing. Value enables comparisons. Socrates' life can, imaginably, be valued. Students in schools are taught "values clarification." Once they cover such a curriculum they will be in a better position, so they are told, to make personal decisions between the value of spending a little quality time with a child and the value of going to a meeting that might boost one's career. The ambitious can imagine graduating from such a course prepared to face the "difficult decisions" and to make the "tough choices" that today's politicians tell us are their everyday fare: Are prisons or schools more valuable? Food for people or arms to protect them?

Value is, the dictionary says, a "suitable equivalent for something else." One could never compare "friendship" to "community" to "courage" to "blessedness." There are no terms in which any of these virtues could be conceived as the "suitable equivalent" of another. These virtues are different activities that take place in incommensurable realms of life. But once one grasps the value of a thing, it can be compared to or exchanged for anything else, anything of comparable value, of course.

In a world organized by value, one might be able to live, as they say, a "balanced" life: career, home, solitude, community. Clarify values, prioritize, and go through the motions. "You can have it all," as long as you take everything in the right amounts (which, if you get your values ordered right and are rich, can be glutinously huge). Virtue, in opposition, admits no balancing. Virtue drives one to perfection, and, if we follow Martha Nussbaum's thinking, admits the possibility of total, utter moral collapse.[12]

Value begets arguments over, of course, the value of a thing, and it is on the basis of arguments over values that schools build many of their curricula designed to teach "ethics," "responsibility," and, especially, "personal choice." But under a regime of value, the only thing that people can ever do together is argue. "Value" is etymologically related to "valency," the positive or negative, the inevitable 0 and 1 bit of the information age; and the *Oxford English Dictionary* tells us that "value" came into common use only in the late seventeenth century as objects became linked through their valuations in money. Within the information/fitness/value nexus, we can argue only the relative value and valency (positive or negative) of a thing; and then, once the price is settled, we can go about substituting in the "suitable equivalents." We can make tally sheets for a life, Socrates', grandmother's in the ICU, ours, or anyone else's life. And we can talk about living life in terms of risk/benefit ratios and in terms of net worths and in terms of networks and relationships and all of the other benefits that are valuable in the information age. We live in a time when a governor of a state can actually talk about the responsibility that old people have to die and make room for others because the old people have lost their value to society.

Virtue is pursued by people of character through knowledge, not argument. According to some traditions, it is intelligence, a capacity

different from reason, that permits human beings to discern the good.*
Discernment (*discretio*) of the good from evil was, for Hildegard of Bingen,
a "joyful knowledge" (*laeta scientia*), the "light of the second day of
creation which allows the accomplishment of good works," that which
"permits the individual to choose consciously his role in the universe and to
live it."[13] The knowledge/character/virtue nexus effects an impulse toward
good living within diversity that is directly opposed to the conflictual
existence that necessarily arises from the information/fitness/value nexus,
which encourages differences of opinion.

What Should We Teach?

It should go without saying that we live in the world of value, the world
where we must choose the "relatively better" or "the lesser of two evils,"
not the world of virtue and of the good. We think it is our job—each
individual's job (for which he or she always has an "individual responsibility")—to produce goods whose values can be established in a market, to
develop the skills necessary to value correctly (or, as Carl Rogers puts it, to
become reliant on a "valuing process" that is inherent in the organism[14]), to
make decisions according to correct valuations. We do not think that it is
our job to try to engage in virtuous actions with an eye always to the
implications of every action on the perfectibility of life in community. We
live according to the videotext and the information-processing screen and
have opened for ourselves the possibility of creating "virtual realities,"
realities like those on *Star Trek* where the crew is provided a room that can
be programmed to produce any reality a person wishes. We can live
between the earphones of our individual Walkmen, with our personal
computers and in our cars with sound systems so sophisticated that we will
never again have to risk paying fifty dollars for a symphony ticket with the
possibility of hearing a poor performance; we can claim that we are an
interconnected species since we have our phones, faxes, and e-mail with
which we can, we are assured, "reach out and touch someone." We can do

---

* INTELLECT is "the highest faculty in man, through which—provided it is purified—
he knows God or the inner essences or principles of created things by means of direct
apprehension or spiritual perception. Unlike the *dianoia* or reason, from which it must be
carefully distinguished, the intellect does not function by formulating abstract concepts
and then arguing on this basis to a conclusion reached through deductive reasoning, but it
understands divine truth by means of immediate experience, intuition, or 'simple
cognition' (the term used by St. Isaac the Syrian). The intellect dwells in the 'depths of
the soul'; it constitutes the innermost aspect of the heart. The intellect is the organ of
contemplation, the 'eye of the heart'" (from the glossary of the two-volume *Philokalia* "a
collection of texts written between the fourth and fifteenth centuries by spiritual masters
of the Orthodox Christian tradition").

this and claim these things because we live in a world of information, because most of us are more or less fit for that world, and because we value it.

But we should pause to raise a question about our "new reality." The question is whether "living" is a term that is appropriately applied in this world defined by the information/fitness/value nexus. The essayist Benjamin DeMott, wrote in 1960 about "a deeply lodged suspicion of the time . . . that events and individuals are unreal, and that the power to alter the course of the age, of my life and your life, is actually vested nowhere." He wrote of generals and other modern "warriors," the men who command the modern war-making system, and he showed how, in them, we cannot see even the shadows of warriors of old, people whose courage on the battlefield showed others the meaning of nobility. DeMott wrote that the modern general, "unable to recall the style of the lost, spikily independent military self," asks, "Who am I?" and is answered,

> I am not a maker of events but a remover of obstructions. For progress's sake, and in acknowledgment of the insuperable uncontrollability of "forces," I march with affairs—and am in truth hardly a man of war at all. Patron of industry? Supporter of research? Even these titles imply an improper separation from the huge machine that encompasses all. I am simply "of the community," and in the service of things as they are.[15]

DeMott said that the reasonable thing to do in these times is to cultivate a little maturity, develop a little disinterestedness, affect a little sophistication. We could add to this: gain access to all the information, make yourself fit and ready for anything, learn the values of all things, and be ready to negotiate. For all of this we get to "half-live" (DeMott's term).[16] We don't even live in the world of the truly alive anymore.

We have passed into a new time. In the previous century, Chief Seattle recognized his people's passing into their new time as "the end of living and the beginning of survival." It's a distinction we can use to answer the question, What should we teach? We can teach people to work within the information/fitness/values nexus. That is, we can teach survival, which, of course, the schools would insist on calling "survival skills." Or we can teach living. But if this is the choice we have to make, we should do so not on the basis of the relative values of the two options.

CHAPTER 7

May Mania Month

June 1. During the next to the last class meeting, our student teachers were grousing about all the things that the schools were doing—in their views, *not* doing—as the end of the school year approached. The discussion was prompted by the widely publicized visit to Washington of some guy trying to convince teachers that schools should operate year-round. These student teachers were already convinced, by what they saw around them, that schools could not sustain themselves even through June, much less July or August, and should probably close at the beginning of May.

"They've just given up trying to teach anything. The teachers just do things—lots of *things*—with the students."

"Yeah, at my school they call it 'May Mania Month.' The graduating seniors are already gone, but the teachers still have to find something to do with the students' shells that show up for class everyday."

"You ought to see what's happening in *my* classroom. Everyone is in love."

"Aren't you teaching kindergarten?"

"Yeah. I tell you what: When the girls fall in love, it sure slows the boys down."

That evening, after class, I was left to imagine what a school might be like if every month, not just during May Mania Month, the teachers did things—lots of things—with their students instead of trying to teach, if everyone was in love, and the boys slowed down. That could be a school even teachers might want to go to year round.

CHAPTER 8

Learning through Fighting
Rita Pougiales

"There is nothing wrong with kids fighting back." I was surprised to hear myself say that to the teacher education class. I believe it—I have since my own children came along—but I was surprised by it, and surprised that I had to defend it. This sentiment is opposed to common assumptions: fighting leads to asocial behavior; fighting springs from aggressive impulses that children must learn to control. I don't accept either assumption. What I believe is that children live and learn through their bodies and that they can achieve great clarity about themselves and others if they are allowed to do just that. In fact, I believe that children will be less violent as they grow older if they are allowed to express their rage (and their joy) and if they are allowed to see and appreciate the consequences of their actions.

Once I was speaking with Jin Darney and Sarah Williams. We spoke about the conditions that we think would characterize women's education, i.e., education influenced by and conducted in the interests of women. I recalled some of my memories from when I first attended Outward Bound. I remembered how that experience immersed me in bodily situations. I couldn't miss the point of anything. I was frightened, tired, elated, euphoric. The meaning of each situation came to me through my body. And I was in the company of others having comparable experiences. The clarity of our experiences, although often painful, allowed me to learn and to understand some things that are muddled in the rest of my life. Just one simple example: To stop and help someone else in pain often caused me more pain. Outward Bound allowed me to learn that.

What does that have to do with fighting? Fighting is just one of the ways children live their views through their bodies. It is a particularly clear way to express themselves and to understand how their actions can hurt others. Can we allow such learning? What responsibility does a teacher have to children who are fighting? What do you deny children when you restrict their fighting?

Many well-meaning adults see a direct connection between children's fights and adults' violence. The connection may be the opposite. Fights, and the urge to fight, surface for children as matters of great importance to them. Teachers could do something other than snuff out those urges. They could grant children the right to understand themselves better.

CHAPTER 9

The Scandal of Commercial Television in School

Criticism is almost too easy nowadays. Channel One TV offers to put televisions in any school that will show its ten-minute program every day. School districts all over the country have public discussions. Finally comes what seems to be the key question, and the oh-so-predictable answer is yes, the ten-minute program will have commercials, about two minutes each day. Everyone goes critical. Just imagine: Commercial television showing programs with commercials in the schools! It's a scandal. The commercials, that is. "Our kids shouldn't have to watch two minutes more of commercials every day, at least not in the schools." But that's what everyone in all the districts says. Especially the newspapers, those commercially supported organs of commercial criticism of our time. They say so and say so: No one should accept commercial television trying to show commercials, especially to children, and not in the schools.

I watched Channel One for several hours as I supervised student teachers. The scandal is *not* that commercial television shows commercials. In fact, the commercials are the best part of Channel One. The scandal is the way the schools respond to this newest aspect of modern schooling. *The scandal is that almost no one in the schools responds at all to this "new," old idea.*

I didn't see anything like a sample of Channel One TV. I only saw four programs, one each day I visited a Washington State history class. The programs were aired at a time that allowed the class to assemble, roll to be taken, and the television sets to be turned on. Ten minutes later at the moment the program ended, the television sets were turned off and the history lesson of the day began.

I happened to see one of the first programs of the academic year. It had a standard television news format but the reporter was a teenage woman. She introduced herself and the concept of Channel One to newcomers and then read some sort of lead into three minutes of world news and sports. The only difference between the evening news and these three minutes was that the Channel One news was intercut with educational "hits." On this day Soviet tanks were rolling into one of the Baltic states. Instead of letting this headline news item develop from beginning to end, it was interrupted with a little history lesson on how the Baltic states became part of the Soviet Union. You could tell that this was the "educational" part of the program because the voice speaking over the graphics was a monotonous drone. It was exactly the voice that high school students might associate with A History Lesson. After this educational hit, it was back to the tanks and on to a tennis match and over to something about a television star suffering some sort of something.

Then there were the commercials, one for M&Ms, one for Nike. More on that, as they say, in a moment.

Following the commercials, there was a special segment for the beginning of the school year: "New Faces on Channel One." For almost a minute—for this was new news, too—they showed, for a few seconds each, faces of the people who would be reporting for Channel One for the year, just faces, no names, no indication of what each face might be reporting on—just faces—head shots, with one exception: One of the reporters was in a wheelchair. If they had shown just his face, no one would have known he was in a wheelchair. So, still without commentary of any sort, the camera began with a long shot of this guy rolling down a ramp in his chair. Very quickly the camera zoomed in and you got the head shot, his face, yet another "new face on Channel One." It was so obvious that Channel One was trying, by showing all these new faces, to show that they had all the categories covered to be "politically correct." There were male faces and female faces and African American faces and Asian faces and Native American faces and. . . . And you could just imagine Channel One's problem: how to show that they've got a "differently abled" face, too. They had worked it out.

Then it was over. Headline news, commercials, new faces, all with quick but smooth cuts from one to the other, and that was it.

"All right, turn off the TVs, turn on the lights, and turn to page 41 in your books." The teacher, the student I was observing, said nothing about what had just happened during the first fourth of his class. In fact, he hadn't really been watching Channel One. Like the students, he had other things to do, a lesson to think about, notes to make, forms to fill out. One can do lots of things while the TV is on. But then it was over and class could begin. "Take out your books. . . ." Another quick cut, perhaps less smooth—but this is a teacher still learning his craft.

Now, about those commercials: I liked them. So did almost all the students. I surmise they liked the commercials because they watched them. (They tended not to watch the news stories, and the "new faces" segment didn't have anything to watch, except a few faces.) But the commercials were good to watch: fascinating shapes and figures and movement and colors in the M&Ms commercial, Michael Jordon making good moves to good music ("I like Mike") that the five women in the front row sang to and moved with in the Nike commercial. The commercials were perfectly constructed for this narrow audience. The students paid attention, which showed that Channel One was doing very well what it was designed to do.

The teacher had other things to do, and he continued to do them, even through the commercials.

Two other episodes of Channel One followed world news and sports with segments on teenagers. One was about the changing nature of family configurations. One of the new faces on Channel One was out in some large city interviewing some actual teenagers about their actual living arrangements. Cut into these interviews with the teens were interviews with experts. A sociologist talked about the "changing shape of the American family." A psychologist talked about "stress" caused by changes in families. Then it went back to the actual teenagers talking about their actual families and how their families changed from time to time and how much stress it caused them. Then there were statistics. So many percentage points live in families in which parents are married and so many percentage points live in families with divorced parents. Of that latter percentage, so many percentage points live with two parents, so many percentage points with one parent, and 13% live with no parents. Cut to a young man who says something like, "That's right, I'm not living with either of them," then to a voice-over saying, "So, more of us are spending more time alone," and then more about stress and the difficulties of being a teenager nowadays. This brief minute or two of Channel One television was enough to keep any teacher interested in critical-reasoning skills or in the use of statistics or in the relationship between experts' pronouncements and real-life experiences in business for weeks. But this was a class in Washington State history, and while Channel One was on, the teacher had other things to do.

But so did the students. They showed very little interest in any of the "substance" on Channel One. With the bit on living arrangements of American teens, their behavior said, "We know how we are living. We have other things to do." And they talked to their friends and looked through their books and made notes and did all the other things that students do during the lulls in school. Besides, after a particularly engaging rendition of "I like Mike," everything else has to be a comedown.

The absurdity of Channel One was put into high relief the following week. After the taking of roll and the adjusting of the TV sets, there was the headline news and sports, then the commercials (including yet another reprise of "I like Mike"). And then there was a long segment on the representation of teenage boys on—what else?—television (with a politically correct promise of a segment in the spring on the representation of teenage *girls* on television). So here it was—so blatant that one would have to be well into the latter stages of "dust to dust" not to notice—the true scandal of Channel One television: Teenagers go to school to watch television that tells them about the representation of teenagers on television. The television and the class were like elements in an Escher drawing. Everything folded itself around and transmuted itself into something else, and as long as you remained inside the frame, it all remained stable and made sense and you didn't go crazy. But step just one millimeter outside the frame of the experience—you'd have to spend a long time thinking about just what was going on and how anyone could ever think to do *that*.

But no one was paying attention. Well, almost no one. There was one fellow sitting in the front row. He seemed interested. I say that only because he spent a lot of time asking his classmates to be quiet so he could watch television. Then he appealed to the student teacher. "Mr. S., will you make them be quiet so we can watch television?" Mr. S. had other things to do.

I talked to Mr. S. later. "Why don't you say something? Why do you just turn on Channel One and let it run for ten minutes and shut it off and tell them to open their books and not say anything?" "Because that's what the contract says." "Huh?" "The contract says we have to leave it one for the whole ten minutes. In fact, they have timers on the TVs to make sure that they are on for the whole ten minutes." "But I was asking why you don't say anything about the content, about the way things are presented, about—" "It's because I've got other things to do. Besides, they don't watch it anyway." "Oh."

As I think about it, it may be more right than I thought to say criticism is almost too easy nowadays. To say that almost no one in the school where I did my observations responds to the material on Channel One TV is perhaps the easiest criticism of all. After all, who responds to anything on television anyway?

CHAPTER 10

The Hard Work of Teaching vs. Teaching with Grace

"I have to prepare a math lesson for today." "I have to read them a poem and get them to think about images of fall in poetry." "I have to teach them about money." "I have to conduct an enrichment session in writing." "I have to get them interested in the separation of the Baltics from the Soviet Union." And my favorite, "I have to provide them the structure so that they can have their freedom."

Teaching is very hard work.

Teaching that begins and ends in the assumption that everything that happens in the classroom is the effect of the teacher's teaching efforts would, indeed, be very hard work. But that kind of teaching is bad teaching. Good teaching rests in the discipline to remain on the right side of a fine line: the line between, on one side, thinking that every educational effect is the result of some teacherly cause and, on the other, noticing every effect that happens in the classroom and resisting the urge to attribute it to *any* cause. Those who are willing just to notice effects permit themselves to move on and do the very next thing; those who think that they are the cause of every effect will always be hopelessly mired in figuring out what they ought to do next. Those who spend time figuring out what they should do next will be the ones who get awards for being good teachers, but they will work terribly hard. They will burn out in five years (with a standard deviation of 1.3 years). Those who are willing just to notice effects and do only the next thing stand a chance of being able to teach for a lifetime because they are teaching with grace.

It is very easy in teaching to think, as the Zen master put it to Eugen Herrigel, "that what you do not do yourself does not happen."[1] There is, to begin with, the compelling purposefulness of teaching. "I have to teach *so that* _____," and you get to fill in the blank: so that the children will learn their math; so that they will grow up well accommodated to the demands of that real world just beyond the edge of the schoolyard; so that they will be good citizens in a democracy; so that they might reach the pinnacle of the Perry scale, that lofty status of being able to make "judgments in context." Beyond the general goal-directedness of teaching in the schools, there are those curricular materials, the textbooks and the workbooks and, most important, the teachers' manuals, that say, in every way, that if you do thus-and-so, then such-and-such will happen. Just be careful in what you do, because there are so many ways to make mistakes in teaching. (But that is why you went to teacher education school in the first place, to avoid making mistakes in teaching.) Beyond purpose and beyond the theory and practice of teaching, there is the evidence of the senses. Jennifer does learn to add, right there in your classroom, in math class. She couldn't add at the beginning of the year and now she can. Before you started teaching them about that troubled region, they only wanted to know if the West Bank was better for surfing or for finding shellfish. After drawing fifteen maps, one for each country in the region, and coloring the flags and writing reports, almost all of the students in social studies actually seem interested in the Middle East. The classroom is a convincing place. You teach, they learn. It's enough to convince anyone to try to do it better. No wonder teachers work hard.

But what does that kind of cause-and-effect teaching do to one's soul? To enter a classroom every day and see not young people but objects of one's teacherly ministrations, not children excited by the newness of things bigger than they but small things progressing through some or another developmental scheme, not people able to test the limits of life unto death but beings who deserve only slightly more protective attention than the grade book during fire drills*—this must impoverish the soul of a person committed to teaching.

It is no wonder that some teachers bore easily. Every year you can expect only more of the same: another batch of second graders that you have to move on to the third grade, another textbook carefully designed (and field tested) to help you do so, more of the same sort of policies and procedures and special new programs that will make sure that those not moving along at the prescribed rate are enabled (or worse, empowered) to do their very own, individual best even though they are bound for failure. And all a teacher can do is try to do better, to work harder: better lesson plans, better curricula, better delivery techniques, better assessment schemes, better interpersonal communication skills, better record keeping that will lead to a better titration of teacherly effort so that better individualized learning might occur out there in that mass of humanity called your students, whose number will surely be bigger next year—the one fact of schools that will require you to be better still. It is no wonder that those who don't burn out aspire, after ten years of getting better and better, only to become a principal or, worse, a designer of better curricula—because teaching is very hard work.

---

* Everyone knows that the schools know that they can go a long educational way on the basis of a little humiliation. One story from student teaching was about a fire drill. All the students were outside in their lines and properly accounted for. Then the principal made his rounds. A student teacher had not been told that the grade book had to be rescued, too. In front of the assembly, she was ordered to reenter the building and retrieve it. When she returned, the drill could end, successfully.

We must step decidedly outside contemporary educationism, but not far back in time, to get a taste for the alternative to working hard as a teacher. Martin Buber, a man of our time, described the approach to existence that is enacted in most teaching as an I-It relationship. The hardworking teacher must turn her students into lots of little Its, an effort that also turns herself into a slightly larger It. Everyone and everything in the classroom becomes an instrumentality, an object of a specific, usually technical sort of attention. The alternative, of course, is Buber's dialogical mode of existence, the I-Thou relationship. Maurice Friedman comments,

> The difference between these two relationships is not the nature of the object to which one relates, as is often thought. . . . The difference, rather, is in the relationship itself. I-Thou is a relationship of openness, directness, mutuality, and presence. It may be between man and man, but it may also take place with a tree, a cat, a fragment of mica, a work of art. . . . I-It, in contrast, is the typical subject-object relationship in which one knows and uses other persons or things without allowing them to exist for oneself in their uniqueness: The tree that I meet is not a Thou before I meet it. It harbors no hidden personality that winks at me as I pass by. Yet if I meet it in its uniqueness, letting it have its impact on me without comparing it with other trees or analyzing the type of leaf or wood or calculating the amount of firewood I may get out of it, then I may speak of an I-Thou relationship with it.[2]

To enter into an I-Thou relationship requires a different kind of attention than that extended by the person concerned with causing an effect. It means listening. "The mark of contemporary man is that he does not really listen," says Buber. "Only when one really listens—when one becomes personally aware of the 'signs of address' that address one not only in the words of but in the very meeting with the other—does one attain to that sphere of the 'between' that Buber holds to be the 'really real,'" Friedman says.[3] Ivan Illich, writing out of a slightly different tradition, approaches the necessity of listening this way:

> Obedience in the biblical sense means unobstructed listening, unconditional readiness to hear, untrammeled disposition to be surprised. It has nothing to do with what we call obedience today, something which always implies submission, and ever so faintly connotes the relationship between ourselves and our dogs. . . . When I listen unconditionally, respectfully, courageously with the readiness to take in the other as a radical surprise, . . . I bow, bend over toward the total otherness of someone. But I renounce searching for bridges between the other and me, recognizing that a gulf separates us. Leaning into that chasm makes me aware of the depth of loneliness, and able to bear it in the light of the substantial likeness between the other and myself. All that reaches me is the other in his word, which I accept on faith.[4]

Imagine a teacher ready to be surprised by a student instead of being poised to record progress on a grid of observations against a developmental trajectory. Imagine a teacher able to let a student be a child, herself with the discipline to remain an adult, refusing to search for a pedagogical bridge between the two. Imagine a teacher who does not use her students in any way, not even to establish herself as "the teacher," but who meets each student in his or her uniqueness. Imagine a teacher willing to listen to children, unwilling to penetrate them for the purpose of figuring out what's going on "in there" for the good end of helping them out. Imagine a teacher ready to accept her students' words for what they are: merely their words and not some sign ready to be read for what it might indicate about the educational readiness of a child to learn what the books say it is time to learn. Imagine such a teacher and you see someone able to teach with grace. She will never work too hard.

It is important, I think, to notice the effects that manifest themselves in one's classroom. A good teacher notices what is happening to students. Equally crucial, however, is refusing any invitation to determine the cause of those effects, even the effects that everyone agrees are the "educational effects." A teacher should, simply (so to speak), notice effects so that she can decide what to do next, *not* so that she can determine the next step in some program of teaching, not so that she can figure out what needs to be done, not in order to do something *so that* ———— To try to determine the order of the classroom and act in accord with it, to try to assess cause-and-effect relationships so that they can be used to make one's teaching better—these are paths into the abyss. A teacher should notice what is happening to her students so that she can take the next step—a step away from the abyss—gracefully.

One student teacher told me of a little incident in her second-grade class. Matthew was one of those kids who, for some good educational or administrative reason, had a specialist following him around for most of the day. In a math game that had the students going one-on-one with flashcards, Matthew had tried so hard to please. He excitedly told everyone that he remembered from yesterday that the competition had finished just before his turn so it was certainly his turn today to go first. He lost the first round, swiftly. But he remained excited. In fact, "excited" was, from the school's point of view, part of Matthew's problem. On another day that had had its share of difficulties the student teacher had ordered Matthew to a corner of the room to work on math by himself. Soon the student teacher noticed him "messing around" with some books and sort of talking to himself. She headed for him, ready to set him straight with a sharp I-thought-I-told-you-to-work-on-your-math. "Then," she said, "I noticed that he was counting the books. He was using the books as counters to work out his math problems." She had set her mind to teach him how to behave in class, how to follow instructions, and how to get his math done. Something, some fit of grace, interrupted her course and allowed her to notice that Matthew was already doing his math, and learning.

It is possible, if difficult, to notice the effects of teaching and not follow common logic further than that, but only after one stops making teaching such hard work.

CHAPTER 11

Report Cards: An Exchange of "Letters"

In the March issue of the newsletter from my son's school appeared the following "letter" about the forthcoming report cards:

Dear Mom and Dad,

In a few days I'm going to bring home a "snapshot" of myself. This picture will be a time exposure of me that's been developing during the past weeks. Considering my many likes and dislikes, my mood changes from day to day, I think it's a pretty good likeness of me.

When you see my snapshot, remember this is a report of someone near and dear to you. So, please don't get too uptight if you see a blemish. I hope you will accept me as I am.

Please do not picture me as being better than all the other children. Remember that all children do not learn to talk or walk at the same time, nor do they learn math and reading at the same rate. I ask you not to compare me with my brother, my sister, or the kid next door. You can set realistic goals for me, but please be careful not to push me to succeed at something that is beyond my ability.

I want you to understand that my report card is a picture of my school progress. From my teacher, you will learn many things about my life at school, even some things that might surprise you.

My teacher knows me as I am at school. You know how I am at home. The "real" me is somewhere in between. When these two pictures become blended with acceptance and understanding, I hope my "snapshot" will be a shining portrait.
Your Child

I decided to write back. I sent the following to the school. A letter (to no one, from no one) deserves a letter in return. I asked the principal to publish it in the next issue of the newsletter.

March 22
Dear Child:

I read "your" letter to "Mom and Dad" in the *Flyer* for March. I put "your" in quotation marks because I know it was written by someone else who has not yet learned the indignity of speaking for others. You would never talk to me as that letter talks to Mom and Dad. You never speak of "the 'real' me," with or without quotation marks. You are always real—very, very real—to me. You are a part of my life and I love you. But that you know, so let's get on with this.

"You" tell me that you'll be bringing home a "snapshot" of you. I learned later in the letter the reason for *those* latter quotation marks. What the letter from "you" is about is the fact that you will be bringing home a *report card*, the third this year. (I evaluate my students twice a year and *that* takes a lot of time. I sometimes dream of the education that could occur if report card preparation time were spent in loving engagement around your education. But you know that I dream often.) I think "you" have a very great misunderstanding of this thing called, properly, a report card, and as a parent is sometimes wont to do, I want to try to set "you" straight.

Your report card is something required by law. People who are paid to be teachers have to send these things home several times a year, again, at times specified by law and rule. Lots of people spend lots of time trying to convince parents that these report cards mean something. Lots of smart people spend lots of time trying to find ways to make these virtually meaningless things mean more. (I recently read a doctoral dissertation—all 66 pages of it—from the University of Washington School of Education comparing the perceived meanings of literal and numerical scales. That's how some very well-schooled people spend their time.) The marks on these report cards have as much meaning to me as did CNN's "coverage" of this recent, nasty, vicious war that our country so proudly waged. Just as happens when I watch a war on television (and try to remember that something real is really happening a third of the way around this globe), I see some things in your report card that I can recognize as having something to do with the you I know. But very little. Yes, your handwriting has gotten sloppier, but you tell me that you have been working on writing fast. That's probably because you see me writing quickly (and you know how my writing looks, don't you?). (I must tell you: There are many other ways—all of them much more humbling—that you are like me.) Yes, you are doing less well in math than you did at Olympia Community School, but at OCS math was connected to real things in your life (map making, vacation budgeting, real money used to buy real things in a store some of the students opened in your school); math was not something confined to endless worksheets. And, yes, I know you are good at sports and I know you are a little bossy sometimes. I know. I know. But that I know these things has nothing to do with your report card. It has to do with the fact that I pay attention to you. I know you pretty well.

Your teacher did us a fine, friendly favor during the first parent-teacher conference. After telling us her impressions of you, and despite the fact that we ran well past our allotted twenty minutes together because she, in fact, listened to some of our thoughts about you, she kept her report card on you to herself. I wrote to a friend, "This was an act of considerable friendship in one sense that you have used that term: friends are people who can protect you from information. Now my task is to remain uninformed about my child's progress through school for the next 10 years. It will be difficult." And it was. The next card came without consultation, so I had to read it. And I'll probably read the others you bring home.

Not that I will ever understand them. Have "you" looked at the scale "they" use? In my day, everyone knew that grades were either used to sort you out against your peers (something "your" letter explicitly urges me not to do) or to compare you to some standard (something that "your" letter seems to suggest is irrelevant in this age of developmentalism and statistics). Now "they" use a scale that is relative only to someone's assessment of "your" own individual abilities. I had a hard enough time understanding your teacher's narrative evaluation of you. If I had to understand, first, her assessment of what she thinks are your abilities before I could even look at her grades, I'm afraid we would have to have spent much more than 20 minutes together.

So, my child, please expect no understanding from me when you bring home this next report card.

But you have never been one to look to me for understanding. You look to me for love. With respect to that, no report from any person authorized to make a report on you will ever matter. You know that in my office I have a snapshot—a real one; no quotation marks—of you. I took it when you were halfway out of your mother some eight and one-half years ago. It was then I started to know you. Not know you "as I am in school" or "as I am at home." Just know *you*. Not "my child," but *my son, John*. God granting, I'll have many more years to continue to know you. And all these other people who must report to us on their "knowledge" of "you," well, we can smile and thank them for their efforts. Right?
Your father,
Bill

The principal of the school wrote back to me. She did not write about the substance of my letter; she wrote to tell me that she would not be publishing it in the newsletter. She said that much of the material in my letter was personal and therefore inappropriate for publication; she urged me to "share" my letter with John.

The sociologist C. Wright Mills wrote that democratic politics begins by seeing "personal troubles" as "public issues."[1] One way organs of the state ensure that politics remains undemocratic, besides denying people access to public forums which those organs control, is to assure people who try to turn a "personal" matter into a "public issue" that the matter is, in point of true fact, really personal. They make sure that everyone thinks he or she is very special and they encourage everyone to share that personal specialness with his or her intimates. And they go to great lengths not to notice the substance of any matter brought before them, because then they would have to respond substantively.

CHAPTER 12

The Evaluation Conference: Letter

My son, John, had attended Olympia Community School (OCS) for the equivalent of kindergarten and first grade. OCS was a private school that used a college-owned house on a beach as its schoolhouse. John started in the public schools in the second grade. The first parent-teacher evaluation conference was in November. I wrote this letter to a friend following that conference.

November 9
Dear ———,
    Rain all night. A nice patter to fill moments of wakefulness. Then hard rain this morning. Two more inches by the end of the day, so they say. But the day is warm. And *this* rain is worth walking in, slowly. I think I will never grow used to the rain, but it is hard not to welcome it back at this time of the year.
    But that is not the topic. This letter is about our first Parent-Teacher Conference. The subtitle is "Or Why I Don't Know How My Child Is Doing in School."
    Debbie and I arrived at the conference table at 3:05 P.M. (I really wonder where schools get their idea about time, viz., that nothing can be scheduled for a proper time, like 3:00 P.M. straight up. John has asked several times why they get out at 3:23 P.M.)
    The conference was supposed to be a well-orchestrated 20-minute ditty. It turned into a 45-minute Stravinskyesque extravaganza. After it was over neither the teacher nor Debbie nor I quite understood what had happened, but we all left, I think, with our eyes a little more open.
    You might, if you used such words, call this a "multi-vocal" evaluation conference. First, there was the presentation of John's responses to a set of questions that the teacher had asked each child. "What do you want your parents to know?" "That I like coming here to school. It's better than the school last year." "What are your favorite subjects?" "Reading and math." "Least favorite?" "Art." "Friends?" Three, with names. She: "But John likes a lot of other kids and they like him."
    Then, enough of the small talk, "How do you think you are doing in school, John?" "Good." "How about your behavior?" "I don't know." (Is he

my son, or what?) L. L. [the teacher]: "This really surprised me. I thought he'd say, 'Good,' or 'I have some things to work on,' but he said, 'I don't know.' Unusual." Me: "Why?" She: "Most kids have an opinion about this." Me: "Well, it may be the case that he understands this situation." She: "What do you mean?" Me: "What John tells me about is how he must behave and how that behavior must be structured according to some rules that sound, frankly, odd to me. He may understand that the judgment about his behavior rests with someone else and that he is not a legitimate judge of his behavior. He may have been suggesting that this question should not be directed to him. Just a guess." She: "Hmm. I see."

The first atonal chord sounds, but softly, because we went on and harmony was maintained.

"I want you to see these [she pulls out plot summaries of *Charlotte's Web*] and John wants you to see his whale book." The first was a series of single sheets with a picture at the top of each (the disliked "art") and several sentences at the bottom. Plot summaries of each chapter of E. B. White. "John is doing very well with these. [I would have said "brilliant," but I'm flexible.] The problem I'm having with some of the kids is that they want to tell the story back word for word. They like it so much that they want to remember it all. We're working on shortening, getting the ideas down in a few sentences." I giggled a little, but held it. I mean: this *is* the E. B. White of Strunk and White, isn't it? Rule 17: Omit Needless Words! I know White heeded Professor Strunk's dictum and, somewhat perversely, I suspect these kids know that he did Omit Needless Words! and that fact might naturally lead some (the obsessive, but not necessarily the "brilliant") to want to remember *all* the words. But never mind: I held the giggle. Harmony in the hall.

Then whales. "John really likes studying whales and he's doing very well." (I was coming to like this "very well.") Debbie: "He's seen whales." She: "Oh really?" Now wait, I thought. You spend weeks talking about whales and you don't know that one or more of the children in class have seen whales? Debbie: "Yes, we were on a cliff on San Juan Island with a group of friends and John was the first to spot this mother and baby Orca swimming together very close to shore. We watched them for a long while." *That* sounded more like something worth writing about than, "Humpback whales live in the sea but they are not fish," which I read at the bottom of one of the sheets. But I held it.

Then, the narrative evaluation. I understood this part of the conference since this is what we do at Evergreen. What I did not understand was the way she used our rather short time together to read to me what she had already written. But, you know, I'm flexible. Writing: doing fine. Reading: You could work on oral reading at home. Math: OK when he attends to his work. Sports: Super. He is really coordinated and plays wall ball every day and likes soccer. In class: He has a relationship with Perrin, the girl who was born on the same day as he. "But you know," she says, "some of the time [this is written on the sheet and I've read it already] some of his behavior is really not appropriate. He and some other boys feed on one another and get into some really inappropriate and harsh language. And sometimes I've seen him mocking me."

I couldn't hold it: "On what basis do you distinguish between the hypothesis that his behavior is, simply, 'inappropriate behavior' and the hypothesis that he is trying to make the classroom an interesting place to be?"

Silence—the greatest music!

"What are you getting at?" (With an invitation like that, who could hold it?) "Well, what I hear about, often, is how John has to do these work sheets and has to sit for long stretches at his desk, and how he has to put his head down and be quiet before the row he's in is allowed to go to recess, and so on. I should think that in that situation, your average [a word that would very soon come back to haunt me] eight-year-old would try to find some ways to make the class interesting. What some teachers think is 'inappropriate behavior' is often 'trying to make things interesting' to an eight-year-old." She: "I think my class is very interesting. We do lots of different things." Me: "But I think John is often bored." She: "I think there's something you should know. John is not a brilliant student. He's good in some things and not so good in others. He's really quite average."

This jab evoked a complicated response. First, of course, I worried about what I could possibly write to my friends who teach in Ivy League colleges. Could I write in our Christmas letter that "Our child is average. We know this now because we've been told"? Perish the thought. The second reaction was to realize that this woman felt under attack and she had decided to attack back. But I couldn't resort to a salvage operation yet. Me: "I'm not sure you have to be brilliant to be bored by school. I was just telling you what John tells me—that he is bored. I worry about that more than I worry about his academic competence. Six hours a day is a long time to spend being bored, no matter how smart you are or aren't." She: More on the many different activities that she spends so much time inventing, the hard work of teaching, etc. I.e., more defensiveness.

Time to tack. Me: "Let me put this positively. John, I think, likes to do things. That's how he learns. Last year John really liked math because he didn't have 'math class.' Math was just built into everything else the kids did, mapping, collecting and measuring things, planning a vacation within a budget, etc. This year he has work sheets. He's not doing anything, so it's not surprising to me that he doesn't like 'math' as much, despite his report that it is a 'favorite subject.' Now, this *Charlotte's Web* stuff: he obviously likes that. He's *doing* a lot with this, even though it's art." She: "We do a lot in my class. I remember having to sit in my seat for years in the public schools. I never got to sing a song in elementary school. I made a vow never to have that happen to my students. So we do a lot, pattern blocks, ordering exercises, lots." Me: "I hope you can appreciate that I know nothing about what you do in class and I'm not trying to make a comment on the way you run your class. I'm talking about what I know—my son—and how he seems to learn. I think it's interesting that in your class he learns writing when he learned very little of that at OCS. At OCS writing was a drag; it didn't involve him in doing anything. You've involved him here, so he likes writing and reading. I just wonder if it's possible to pay attention to how this particular child learns and not be defensive about how you run your classes? John obviously likes being here. But he's also bored. I wonder if we could talk about John?"

She followed me on this tack. She: "Why did you put John in public school?" Debbie: "It was a tough call. OCS was very good for him. But we thought it might be time for him to start seeing places like this. So, it's mostly about the social part of adjusting to schools." Me: "I tried to tell him that you can't go to school on a beach forever. Sometime he needed, I thought, to get used to real schools, with a teacher, lots of students, desks, big but well-regulated playgrounds, rules, etc. Frankly, what academic subjects he learns here is almost irrelevant to me. He's learning a lot, a lot of what he needs to know."

At this point, we experienced a breakthrough. L. L. made a brilliant—I know, it's an overused word—maneuver that demonstrated a rather complete understanding of the situation. She said, "Well, why don't we just forget about the report card. I have a hard time categorizing kids anyway." Debbie and me: "Fine." End of conference.

I remember you saying, in the context of my father's and Paula's illnesses and in light of the Ted Rosenthal story, that one function of friends is to protect you from information that demands that you adjust to it. In this instance, L. L. showed a little friendliness. She saw it as one possible part of her job to protect people—John's mother and me in this case—from information. She realized that it was not important for us to know, in truth, how John is doing in school. Actually, it may have been better than that: She may have realized that knowing how he is doing could be dangerous to us and to him. What a wonderful thing she did by filing that state-required report back in her file! . . .

Now, of course, this little moment of friendliness raises an interesting question: Is it going to be possible for John to progress through all of the public schools without us ever knowing how he is, in fact, doing in the schools? It's an issue to work on, as *they* say, no?

The Christopher Parkening concert last night was wonderful. In the first two numbers he had a little trouble getting his hands to work together, a *problemacita* for a guitarist. But then it came together and the music washed over me.

* * *

My friend responded with a letter saying that I should be quite happy with an assessment of "average." She reminded me that children who do not show up in the tails of anyone's distributions tend not to get noticed and they avoid getting shunted into this program or that one. Her letter reminded me of a paragraph from Marilynne Robinson's *Housekeeping*. The tale is of two young sisters who are eventually raised by an eccentric aunt. At one point, the narrator, one of the sisters, says,

> Because we were quiet we were considered docile, and because our work was not exceptionally good or bad we were left alone. Hours of tedium were relieved by occasional minor humiliations, as, for example, when our fingernails were checked for cleanliness. Once I was required to stand by my desk and recite "I Heard a Fly Buzz When I Died." My cold, visceral dread of school I had learned to ignore. It was a discomfort that was not to be relieved, like an itch in an amputated limb.[1]

Not all average children experience a "cold, visceral dread of school." John, in response to the questionnaire administered before our arrival, wanted to make sure his teacher reported that he likes going to this school, that it's better than the one last year. If he can only manage to be left alone anyway, then I can work on the problem of not knowing how he is doing.

CHAPTER 13

Do I Need My Identity?

Do I need my identity? Teachers, and therapists of other sorts, are sure that I have an identity, and their activities make it clear that they are, in various ways and to different degrees, concerned about it. Teachers are schooled to understand identity's importance both to me (for the ways in which it conditions my behaviors and responses to the world about me) and to them (for the ways in which it either empowers them to educational effectiveness or undermines their efforts to be sensitive to my personal idiosyncrasies and needs).

But to say that the experts know I have an identity does not answer the question, Do I need one? To answer this question, it is perhaps better to inquire into a prior question: Where did my identity come from? And to avoid having this discussion fall back into the hands of the therapists, we must answer this question not individualistically, but historically. It may turn out that I need my identity only because there is something historically peculiar about our times that requires me to have one.

I know that teachers are schooled to appreciate the importance of identity and self-image because even our somewhat unorthodox teacher education program put considerable effort into increasing the sensitivities of our charges by having them read stories and reports from people of widely varying identities and with various challenges, as they say, to self-image and esteem. Our readings included Audre Lorde's *Sister Outsider*, Saxton and Howe's *With Wings*, Uchida's *Jar of Dreams*, and a raft of shorter pieces. Indeed, the theme for the quarter in which we read this material was "Yourself as a Learner." We were trying to get prospective teachers to think about themselves—their backgrounds, their self-images, their own identities—before they assumed the duties of a profession that concerns itself so insistently and rigorously with others' identities.

While planning our teaching on identity and self-image, Gail, a woman from the Onondaga tribe (one of the many features of her identity), suggested that we all try to talk quite personally before the students about our identities and our self-images. My response to the teaching team, all women, was, "I have an idea for this section on identity: I'll be the man." Gail said, with one of her easy smiles, "We've noticed." Perhaps it was in response to having my little joke turned back on itself that I began to wonder, in the spirit that Michel Foucault wondered, "Do we need a true sex?"[1] whether I need a true identity.

"Identity" Has a History

At one time a person might be named, recalled, remembered, or recognized. One might have a history, a family, an association, and a reputation, but one did not need an "identity." Literature is filled with scenes of recognition and naming that do not involve a person's identity. One of the earliest in our tradition has Telémakhos arriving as a stranger at the palace of Meneláos. The stranger, of course, is welcomed by the king and seated at the table. The king says to Telémakhos,

> You must have heard your fathers tell my story,
> whoever your fathers are; you must know of my life,
> the anguish I once had, and the great house
> full of treasure, left in desolation.

Meneláos is jogging his guests' memories so they might realize who their host is. Then Meneláos mentions his special memory of Odysseus. As Telémakhos weeps in response to this recollection of his father, the king realizes with whom he has dined. Moments later, Helen enters and instantly recognizes and names the young man:

> Never, anywhere, have I seen so great a likeness
> in a man or woman—but it is truly strange!
> This boy must be the son of Odysseus,
> Telémakhos, the child he left at home. . . .[2]

One might know another's history, all the stories told by and about another person; one might rely on family resemblance in order to recognize someone. But none of these operations involves the identity of the person. Identity is a modern concept that sweeps over naming, recognizing, etc., and turns this multiplicity of human activities into a psychosocial and technical, even a bureaucratic, phenomenon.

The second edition of *The Oxford English Dictionary (OED)* reminds us that "identity" is a latecomer to our lexicon. The definitions are prefaced by a note:

> Various suggestions have been offered as to the formation [of identity]. Need was evidently felt of a noun of condition or quality from *idem* to express the notion of "sameness," side by side with those of "likeness" and "oneness" expressed by *similitas* and *unitas*.[3]

And then it shows that the first uses of the word are coincident with the beginnings of modern times in the early seventeenth century.

From the course that "identity" followed in the early part of the modern period, the "need [that] was evidently felt" appears to derive from a concern about the persistence of a thing in light of changes in appearance. Thus, for example, the ancient Phoenicians are judged to be originally the Canaanites "from the Identitie of their Languages."[4] The early philosophers of government were concerned especially about the persistence of the "person" throughout changes in his or her life. So John Locke (1690) would write, "The Identity of the same Man consists . . . in nothing but a participation in the same continued Life, by constantly fleeting Particles of Matter, in succession vitally united to the same organized Body." If the change, decay, and death of autonomous persons were natural, there still had to be an enduring subject that remained constant through all apparent changes if natural law or the various theories of human nature were to have something to which they might apply. We still struggle with the problem that Locke thought he solved. We agonize over the criminal who says in his legal defense, "I wasn't myself," and whether he was or not then becomes a matter for the court to decide.

Around the middle of the nineteenth century, identity shifted from being something that connoted the persistence of a whole from one time to another to being an attribute that was judged not so much by resemblance but by relationships to external things. An entry in the *OED* from Washington Irving in the early part of that century shows that identity still applies to the whole person even though the person, not a philosophical onlooker, has become the judge of the persistence of the self: "He doubted his own identity, and whether he was himself or another man" (from the *Sketch Book*, 1820). Forty-five years later, a most modern sense of identity has taken shape so that a character in *At Any Cost*, by "E. Garrett" (1865), would establish his identity through his orientation to his possessions: "Tom . . . had such a curious feeling of having lost his identity, that he wanted to reassure himself by the sight of his little belongings."

It seems only a short step from an identity derived from its relationship to things to an identity ascribed by a thing, an identity bracelet, card, certificate, disc, paper, patch, etc. The entries in the *OED* suggest that this use of "identity," as an attribute of any device that accords its bearer an identity, is peculiar to the 20th century.

At the same time that identity was being externalized by the bureaucrats who would prefer to recognize persistence through papers rather than through philosophical judgment, identity was also being internalized by the psychologists. In their hands, identity became multidimensional, malleable, and, in some respects, fragile.

Roger Brown's *Social Psychology: The Second Edition* says,

> The self-image has two components: a personal identity and many social identities, as many as the groups with which the individual is identified.

> Identity is a concept no one has defined with precision, but it seems we can move ahead anyway, because everyone roughly understands what is meant.[5]

So, identity, as we have it from the psychologists, has two dimensions, the personal and the social. Personal identity retains the old idea of persistence. This is from the *Dictionary of Behavioral Science*:

> IDENTITY 1. The condition of sameness in essential character. 2. The temporally persisting sense of being the same person, whereby the individual orients himself or herself to the external world. It is based primarily on cenesthesia and the continuity of goals and memories. Psychologically it is called personal identity.[6]

But then there are Brown's "many social identities," identities based on one's identification with social groups. That phrase, "I as a . . .," where I get to fill in the blank with any number of categorizations and cross-classifications, becomes not just possible but an essential part of establishing who I am. It is no longer the case that I have an identity simply because my Particles participate in the same Life; now, my identity becomes me.

Even though part of my identity is based in my personal persistence, the social sciences have made it clear that identity can be changed and shaped through personal effort. Again, Roger Brown writes,

> The theory of social identity . . . assumes that an individual can make an effort to improve his or her self-image either by trying to enhance personal identity or by trying to enhance social identity, and the theory undertakes to explain when the one sort of effort will be made and when the other.

> If in-group preference or ethnocentrism raises the value of a social identity and ultimately of the self-image, then we have a partial answer to the question: What is cultural affirmation good for? It is good for the individual pride of all the persons whose culture is being affirmed. Fanon and many others who have exhorted their groups to be themselves, to be different, and to be proud of what they are have understood the benefit on the level of individual psychology that would result.[7]

Self-image can be enhanced by good work on all the social fronts demarcated by the "I as a . . ." statements. Just as identity can be enhanced, there lurks on the other side of this possibility the destruction of self-image, the denigration of the identities of people because of their identification with a group that is not culturally affirmed.

It is on the basis of the possibility of a diminished self-image that schools have based their elaborate curricula to build "self-esteem." Without entering into the debate over the importance of image building or identity enhancement, we can at least note that it is only in our times that it is possible to have such a debate. It is only in our times that identity has become something more than a fact of personal life. It is only in our times that identity has taken on the possibility of being a project.

The importance of thinking of one's identity as a project was highlighted by the appearance of a concept new in the latter half of the century, "identity crisis."

> Erik Erikson describes the eight-stage process of ego-development characterized by a series of psychosocial crises. In adolescence, the main task is that of solving the identity versus role diffusion conflict. During this process, an identity crisis (IC) may occur.

> Because identity is considered by psychoanalytically oriented theorists one of the most important aspects of ego strength and ego development, the identity crisis is emphasized. Erikson . . . himself has wondered, "would some of our youth act so openly confused and confusing if they did not know they were supposed to have an identity crisis?"[8]

The first *OED* entry for this mutation of the concept of identity is from 1954. Rather quickly it became possible for anyone to have an identity crisis. So, for example, a 1974 number of the *Times Literary Supplement* contains reference to "a middle-aged cuckold with piles and an identity crisis."

Identity is a most modern idea. It is instructive that Roger Brown's first edition of his popular text in social psychology, published in 1965, contains no discussion of the term. Where we find the discussion of identity in the 1986 edition, we find in the 1965 edition only an overview of how one forms an impression of another's personality and how to identify, accurately, one's own emotions. Whereas the 1965 text is written in a dispassionate, impersonal, scientificized prose, the 1986 edition contains a remarkable, long discussion of the ways in which the author's (Brown's) self-esteem once got linked in his own mind to the opera career of Renata Scotto. Identity has become such a necessary thing in these times that even the author of a college textbook goes to considerable lengths to show that he has one.

Uwe Pörksen lists "identity" among his *amoeboid words*. These are words that, lacking definition (recall Brown: "Identity is a concept no one has defined with precision, but . . ."), capture many activities in their scope. Pörksen says of amoeboid words (a small set that includes, inter alia, "communication," "relation(ship)," "process(es)," "partner," "strategy," "solution," "resource," and "modernization"):

> They resemble the building blocks of science. They may not have precise meaning of scientific terminology, but their meaning is still assumed

to be constant and independent of context. They are stereotypes. The speaker is powerless to define them.

> They transport the authority of science into colloquial language and impose silence. Not their factual content but their aura predominates, the social function and effect that they exercise. Their usage establishes the social elite.

> They can be transformed into hard cash.

> They are part of an international code. . . . [In them] we have . . . the fundamental code of the industrialized nations, which is step by step encompassing the globe.[9]

There is something about our time that encourages me to think in terms of "having an identity" instead of being who I am, of "enhancing my self-image" instead of reflecting on my history and pursuing my ambitions, of "responding to threats to my self-esteem" instead of apologizing for the mistakes I make or developing a critical appreciation of the social apparatuses that constrain my fantasies and my actions. Human activities are invalidated by the rise of the technical project centered on the amoeboid word "identity."

Pörksen makes it clear that the colonization and mathematization of language, in which "identity" participates, serves new structures of power. No longer can people simply say who they are or wait for recognition by others who may have heard of them, for amoeboid words undermine speech. Now one must declare oneself accurately and sincerely, according to accepted categories, in terms that can be digitized and that self-effaced experts can understand:

> As soon as a child is born [in Germany], a certificate of health is issued, along with a booklet documenting medical inspection. The child is checked against a computerized catalogue of 66 criteria . . . and, all being well, receives a cross in the box "no distinguishing characteristics." A computerized customer and citizen has been born, ahead of him a life of being checked, stamped and registered, of being defined and numbered by increasingly flawless sets of words. The yard-sticks of the experts, catalogues of criteria, examination papers, marks and points, tests, test results and percentages will accompany him. The relentless diffusion of geometry and numbers is reaching the furthest recesses.[10]

The access to those furthest recesses is through my identity, which I must have.

Alternatives to Having an Identity

In response to the pleas of his critics, sympathetic and otherwise, that he be clear about his way of working, that he tell them more about himself and his approach to the world, Michel Foucault wrote, "Do not ask me who I am and do not ask me to remain the same. Leave it to our police and our bureaucrats to make sure our papers are in order."[11] In these times there are oh-so-many people who have invented oh-so-many businesses based on the possibility of assessing, judging, adjusting, manipulating self-image—that is, there are oh-so-many police and bureaucrats of self-image manage-ment—that I think I must have a self-image on their behalf. It is certainly in their interests that I have one.

Maybe not first among the self-image police and bureaucrats but somewhere in the first rank are educators. Somewhat like dentists who put themselves out of the tooth-care business when they virtually solved the problem of cavities and then went on to develop new lines of the dentistry business based on a clinical interest in our jaws, gums, and tongues, educators have put themselves out of the knowledge, information, and skills business (not because, like the dentists, they were successful at what they professed to be interested in, but because they were, according to their own criteria, hopelessly unsuccessful). In its place, they have developed a passionate interest in self-image, self-esteem, identity, empowering the self, and so on. On their behalf, and with the effect of protecting their jobs, I find myself caught in the rush depicted by Octavio Paz, "I'm in a hurry to be. . . . Who and what is that which moves me and what awaits my arrival to complete itself and to complete me? I don't know. I'm in a hurry."

Under the sway of those who have a compelling professional interest in our having an identity, we are often in a rush to become who we have identified ourselves as being. That rush is signalled by the use of that phrase, "I as a . . ." Audre Lorde fills in her blank with "black lesbian feminist comfortable with the many ingredients of my identity, and a woman committed to racial and sexual freedom from oppression." Some might say, "I as a man, father, son . . ." But any particular filler is not so much true as it is a device to make one's response to the world easier. "I as a . . ." will always be a quicker response than "I . . ." ever will. "I as a . . ." can hurry to be. Many people who interviewed Foucault were interested in the influence on his work of what we—we who have had the word for some 100 years—would call his "homosexuality." They wanted him to say, "I as a gay man . . ." In response to what he regarded, I think, as immoderate or indiscreet (as the police are sometimes indiscreet) questions, he sometimes gave an answer like, "I think the problem we face is not to *become* a homosexual (or any other categorical identity, or any combination of categorical identities); I think the problem is to *be* gay."[12] Being who one is, instead of striving to become what one is identified as being, seems a way to avoid hurrying.

But what is the alternative to identifying oneself through a series of carefully chosen, scientifically certified identifiers? What is the alternative to that easy construction, "I as a . . ."?

As for the self, that can be left to others. The philosopher Stanley Hauerwas recalls a chance meeting between a member of "a team of evangelical Christians [that] invaded Shipshewana, Indiana, to bring the lost of Shipshewana to Christ" and a Mennonite farmer from the area. "Brother, are you saved?" the saver asked the possibly lost.

> Wanting not to offend, as well as believing that the person posing the question was of good will, [the Mennonite farmer] seriously considered how he might answer. After a long pause, the farmer asked his questioner for a pencil and paper and proceeded to list the names of ten people he believed knew him well. Most, he explained, were his friends but some were less than that and might even be enemies. He suggested that the evangelist should ask these people whether they thought him saved since he certainly would not presume to answer such a question on his own behalf.[13]

As an alternative to laying claims to an identity through "I as a . . .," we can leave the matter of public declarations of the nature of our selves to the judgments of others who know us, remember us, recall and name us.

That would leave room for a certain selflessness, the sort of selflessness that is captured in Foucault's notion of "being gay." I read his admonition to mean, at least in part, lighthearted (in opposition to the heavyheartedness of the very serious, very modern person bent on formulating and enhancing a self-image), open to others, willing to turn the self to others in unconventional ways. Leaving matters of the self to others leaves room for compassion, something I understand to be a capacity to see one's own suffering in the eyes of another.

It is useful to hear both parts: compassion involves the capacity to see oneself as a suffering being, where suffering has that old-fashioned meaning of simply "allowing," *and* compassion involves the capacity to see one's own suffering in the eyes of the other who is also a suffering being. Compassion does not allow you to see yourself as equivalent to the other. Quite the opposite: it focuses you back on your own suffering, in part, because you can never know the suffering of the other. Hence, the compassionate person cannot see himself or herself as even "statistically different from but comparable to," much less "equivalent to," the other. Compassion does not instruct you to get connected with the other or to network or interface with him or her. Quite the opposite: it forces your attention to the unbridgeable gap between yourself and the other. Compassion does not tell you what to do. Quite the opposite: it leaves the field of possible things you might responsibly do radically open. Compassion does not focus you on solving your own problems to the neglect of others. Quite the opposite: it illuminates your own helplessness with regard to your own suffering and enables you to do what you can for all others. Compassion does not have a purpose, a goal, an end that points toward the overcoming of limitations. Quite the opposite: it shows one, first, that everyone is a limited being, and it turns one toward the other with a kind of purposeless, unlimited intensity that one can never know if one begins all speech by saying, "I as a . . ."

Teacher education programs, and other therapy-training curricula, have to make a choice. They can train their charges to be responsive to others' identities, to enhance others' self-images, and to do nothing that would degrade others' self-esteem. They can have their faculty members talk before their students quite personally about identity and self-image. They can make sure that, in the name of not treading on someone's sensitivities, every statement that even verges on the personal begins with "I as a . . ." They can train people to police themselves and others so that everyone remains within the bounds of his or her identity. Or teacher education programs can focus on the way that sometimes people are recognized for who they are, on the fact that sometimes a facet of person's existence is noticed by those around him, on how this noticing is sometimes accompanied by a smile of recognition. They can attend to the fact that sometimes people encounter one another with a mutuality that has nothing to do with their identities.

CHAPTER 14

How Quickly We Learn
Anne Liu Kellor

The director of the preschool called me in to work on my day off. "We have a new little girl from China," she said. "She's having a real hard time. We thought you might be able to talk to her." I went in and found her with my eyes right away. I squatted down low beside her and spoke quietly, unsure of my Chinese, self-conscious of speaking too loudly this private tongue that others hear only as a Charlie Chan singsong, *It's all Chinese to me.* I'm not sure what she understood, but it was clear that she knew I was different from the other teachers.

The children in class were "writing" letters and "addressing" envelopes to their parents. On her envelope I wrote the Chinese character for mother, *ma ma.* I tried to get her involved with the rest of the children but wondered if this was what she needed. She clung to me for the rest of the afternoon.

I like to watch the Chinese children in our preschool. I try not to give them more attention than the others, but I do. My senses zone in on them like an internal radar, and I watch them—intently.

Caroline was fascinating. She was a blaze of directed energy spun out of control, bouncing gleefully off all surfaces, quick to laugh ecstatically or to throw a temper of childish fury. She was not yet two years old, but vocabulary spilled from her lips: farm animals, body parts, names of things. She had learned she was Caroline, but she called herself *mei mei*, little sister, a familial name that she obviously went by at home.

"Isn't it funny," one of the teachers commented, "she thinks she's *mei mei?*" Isn't it funny, I thought, that we think she's Caroline. Later I heard that teacher say to Caroline, "Anne's a *mei mei* too, you know." Caroline stared at her blankly.

Five o'clock diaper change, my turn—a dirty job, yes, but secretly I loved it. It was time to be one on one with a child, together, private, away from the rest of the room. I could dazzle, entertain, win the affection of the children during these times alone, with their focus directed, staring into my face from below. It was my chance to vibrate lips on their tummies like my mom used to do. They loved it. And when I would stop they would always purse their lips and lift their shirts to say, "More, more." This was my chance to give all the private affection I felt discouraged from giving in my role as "teacher" or "childcare provider," one who must not show favoritism, especially to little Chinese girls.

"Ni de bizi zai nali? Ni de yenjing zai nali? Ni de erduo zai nali?" (Where is your nose? Where are your eyes? Where are your ears?) I spoke softly to Caroline as I wrestled her into a fresh diaper. She pointed delightedly to the different parts of her face, in full understanding.

"Ke-ai de mei mei, sweet Caroline. *Xiao zu shuo shenme?"* "Oink, oink!" she exclaimed. *"Xiao mao shuo shenme?"* "Meow, meow." Yes, she knew her animals, too. But I think they spoke only in English.

The first time I had spoken to her in Chinese, Caroline had looked at me with the confusion of a little dog, head cocked, ears pricked up with curiosity. Around the other children and teachers I usually only spoke to her in English. But tucked away on the corner of the playground or on the changing table, we carried on our own private dialogue—a blend of Chinese and English. She floated easily between languages in mid-sentence. She was still young. And although she was aware of the distinction between the languages, the boundaries were not yet set solidly.

When I work with the older children, the three- and four-year-olds down the hall, the boundaries have already become more rigid. Each language has its place: English for school, a public place; Chinese in private, if at all. I watch these children with fascination and remember myself in their place amidst plastic shapes and colors. I squat beside them and introduce myself, gauging their reactions. "I'm Chinese, too, you know." They look up at me from their play like they aren't quite sure what I'm talking about. *"Ni keyi zhang Zhongwen, ma?"* (Can you speak Chinese?) I ask. Their eyes question me. "Hey, how come you said that?" "Why are you talking like that?" They hear me. They understand. But only in English will they reply. How quickly we learn what is private and what is public. How quickly we learn.

At the end of the day the parents come to pick up their children, hurrying them with hidden impatience. "Caroline, where are your shoes?" Her mother calls after her, trying to gather her things. I don't tell Caroline's mother that I can speak Chinese and sometimes do with Caroline. I am not sure how her mother would feel—innocent as it seems. I wonder if she wants Caroline to speak only English at school, so she will grow up to be more "American," without a telltale accent.

"Caroline . . . ," her mother calls after her again in English. This dialogue between them sounds unnatural to me, and I wonder if it feels this way to them, because I've heard Caroline's mother's voice relax back into Chinese the moment they've stepped outside the classroom door. I hear the sounds of this language, so familiar to me, drifting down the hall as they leave the school to go home.

CHAPTER 15

Why Won't the Schools Teach about Anything Real?

Just after completing her first quarter of student teaching, a woman wrote, "School doesn't seem real most of the time." In her experience, the school rarely taught about anything real. But more important to her, the school led this young teacher to treat almost everything that happened as if it was artificial. Even her reactions to human events impressed her as unreal. Her reflections on her first quarter began:

> I was walking down the hallway of ——— Middle School one day last week and came upon a small boy lying on the floor, his leg crumpled under him, obviously in pain. I think at any other time in my life I would have stopped immediately and asked him what was wrong. But I had a very long day of teaching every period, and taking care of over a hundred students, and for some reason I passed him by. I hadn't gotten but a few feet away from him before I stopped myself and went back. I asked him what was wrong. He said he had fallen and hurt his leg. Some other students went for the nurse, who wasn't in school that day, and the principal. As the other teachers gathered around I stood there feeling helpless. They kept asking him questions about his injury. It was almost as if they didn't believe he was hurt. . . .

> Thinking about the situation later I couldn't believe I had actually hesitated before going back to the boy. There was a child, obviously in pain, and I had passed him by with hardly a look. I had almost not wanted to acknowledge the pain. There is so much pain that goes on in school. I had to take a long look at myself to try to figure out why I almost didn't go back.

If she can take a long look at herself, at least we can take a brief look at these things, called schools, that would induce their agents, our children's teachers, to question, however briefly, a child's pain; and perhaps we can try to understand why they won't deal with anything real.

At least the outline of an answer is apparent in the reactions of one other student teacher. At a seminar, she wanted to tell others of a particularly difficult decision she had had to make the previous week. It was just after the concluding sessions of the Senate Judiciary Committee's confirmation hearings on Judge Clarence Thomas. Her high school, like many others, encouraged teachers to discuss sexual harassment after Anita Hill's testimony at the hearings. She, along with her cooperating teacher, planned a short series of lessons. "But," she said to her colleagues in the seminar, "I won't be teaching this lesson in one of my classes. One of the students in there was sexually molested last week. Her parents and the school principal, after talking with her therapist, told me that I should not mention anything having to do with touching or sexuality. If anyone does so in this girl's presence, they tell me, she breaks down and cries."

Some members of the seminar questioned the wisdom of this decision. Isn't it possible that this young woman might appreciate the fact that the class was talking about something that happened to her without directing their discussion at her? some wondered. Why, others asked, would she not teach this lesson because she *knew* that one student in her class had been molested? Shouldn't she take seriously the statistics that say that half, or more, of all females have experienced incidents of sexual assault? Why not just assume, they pressed, that in a class of 30 there are perhaps several young women who have been molested and teach about what is real in these students' lives? One person even recalled C. Wright Mills's admonition to see personal troubles as if they were public issues. As long as this woman is encouraged to see her molestation as simply a personal matter, as her parents and her principal and her therapist and, now, her teacher were doing, she will never develop any sense that this personal fact has any public or political dimension to it, this student teacher was told.

But no, her decision was clear and firm. If a principal tells you not to discuss something, and if a student's parents say that they will surely remove her from the classroom if a lesson on sexual harassment proceeds, and if she does, in fact, break down when sexual matters are mentioned in her presence, then there was no argument that could sway her.

Why? Because her first responsibility was to protect this child, this student teacher said. It sounds ironic but logical: In the name of protecting a student, don't discuss the harm that has just befallen her. Don't treat the child's pain as if it is real.

As I listened to her speak, I recalled a day two years earlier when my son had come home from school. He was obviously frustrated. "What is it?" "Drugs," he said. That got my attention; he was in the equivalent of first grade in a small private school run by teachers who had never completely left the sixties behind. "We talked about drugs today in school. I don't know what the big deal is about drugs. In fact, *I don't even know what drugs look like.*" I called the teachers and told them what he had said. "Why not show the kids what they look like?" "Can't; the police won't let us." "Well, have the police come in and bring some samples from the evidence lockers. Make this topic real. How are they going to be able to say no to 'drugs' if they don't even know what drugs look like?" "Why don't you call the police?" I did. "Sorry, it's against department policy to take real drugs into the schools, and it's against the law to remove drugs from the evidence locker except for use in cases." To this day, my son has not been shown what drugs look like—not by any of the people so bent on protecting him from the danger they tell him that drugs are. Drugs will remain for him an abstraction, at least until the day that someone on the playground shows him drugs. But that person won't be so obsessed with my son's safety.

Press them and many teachers will say that their first responsibility is for the *safety* of their students. Safety is above all else. One student teacher—an especially able student—wrote some reflections about a time when she saw two students leave the school yard. She followed them off the school grounds, but they ran. They stopped and looked back. She approached them and they turned. She said, "I finally yelled, 'Freeze! Get back into the school yard this instant!'" They obeyed. "This incident is important to me," she wrote,

> because it was the first time I had to draw the line of what was important to me as a teacher. I had a lot of time to think as I was going after the children. My first reaction was anger, because they did not obey me. Then I thought of the game that they were playing. . . . But the catalyst for my action was concern for their safety. That will always be my primary concern as a teacher and, luckily in this instance, that was the point at which I was able to assert my authority and provide guidelines for my students' future actions.

Accepting her authority forced this student teacher to face a dilemma; as she put it, "I realized that my actions stemmed from a conflict between . . . giving students their freedom and keeping them safe. *I will always conclude that the foremost of these should always be the safety of the student. Only within the parameters of personal safety is the freedom to allow students to grow and experience what their world contains.*"

This student teacher has already developed a view of the world and her place in it that is as peculiar as it is common in the schools. The world, according to a well-schooled, teacherly view, is a threatening and dangerous place. Students learn only from their experiences (she *had* read Dewey and Piaget), but those experiences must always be mediated by a teacher who, because of her overarching concern for students' safety, will grant students a certain freedom to learn "only within the parameters of personal safety." If a student wanders too far outside those school-established parameters some safety-conscious teacher will always be there to yell, "Freeze! Get back into the school yard this instant!" because unless you are safe you will never learn just how dangerous the world is. It's an ironic logic, but it's the schools' logic.

One student recalled a speaker hired by a school district to address all the teachers in the district on the day before school began for the year. The speaker was a man who studied satellite photographs of the earth. "He gave us honest information about the things he loved—his wife, his children, photography, and this planet," she wrote. This "honest information" was, she said, "grim." In his own lifetime this man had seen changes in the photographs, changes that threatened the planet he loved. "He commented bitterly on the bureaucracy and stupidity of people and governments." Some of the teachers in the audience got up to leave.

> Cami commented that he seemed pessimistic. . . . I later found a line of teachers [who had left the talk] in a nearby office waiting to laminate their foo-foo name tags, posters, etc. I mentioned to my cooperating teacher that it would be great to have this speaker talk to our students. She mentioned the students' comfort levels. "I don't know if students would feel comfortable hearing about this." Of course not! I'm not comfortable hearing about this either. . . . I think that learning concrete facts about what is happening to our planet is one honest and clear way of understanding the severity of what is happening. All the rhetoric about "save the earth" is just that without real information about the massive destruction of it. But that's just not nice and we all want to have a nice day now.

It used to be that sometimes the truth hurt. Now the truth cannot make you more than just a little uncomfortable. The schools can't deal with real things because they are not comfortable with making people uncomfortable. But as the schools are the first to assure everyone, there's always something else to do—laminate name tags, complete math work sheets, think up 50 more simple ways to save the earth—and many of those things that you can do will allow you to stay well within your comfort level. As least this student was able to say, "I cannot think of a time I learned anything and felt comfortable."

I remember the sign on the door of a colleague at Dartmouth College. He was an assistant professor of education, later fired. The sign said, "Danger to Souls—A Specialty." This man knew what all good educators from Socrates on know: to take an interest in the educations of others is to put their souls in danger. To talk about the harsh realities of today's world openly and honestly in the schools may very well put the rather comfortable souls of our students (and their parents and their teachers) in no small danger.

It is so easy to do great harm—educational harm—to young people in the name of safety, in the name of protecting them from what is real about their world, but if teachers will not teach students about things that are real out of an interest in the safety of their charges, let them think about themselves. The young woman who passed the boy in the middle school hallway—a child in pain—turned and went back. She had the courage to recognize that her actions were wrong, that questioning the reality of the boy's injury was wrong, that inflicting further pain by not recognizing the reality of pain is wrong. She had the strength to see these signs of a soul—her own—already too comfortable with the callings of her profession and already eager to pass by the real because of a commitment to the necessities of teaching and immersion in her work. But she had only been a teacher for eight weeks. She hadn't even been issued a nicely laminated, foo-foo name tag.

CHAPTER 16

The Great Debate, or The Day That One School Taught One Thing That Turned Out to Be Real

"Hey! We can't have a debate in here about abortion. That would be too personal. Some people in here have had an abortion." More softly and with a smile to her friend: "Not me, but some, right?"

The student teacher ignores it. The debate is joined: "Resolved: that the government should make all abortions illegal."

So which students would take which position? A table with three young women says, loudly and unanimously, "We want the pro!" Then one says, "Of course, they should be illegal. Can you imagine doing that? I mean . . . how disgusting." (One of these women, Susan, just before this project started, had arranged with a few of the other young women in the class to have them come over after school for her daughter's first birthday party. "Yeah. There'll be guys there, so come," she had said to convince another woman to make the effort of dressing *her* child and making the outing.) "But," says the student teacher, "Scott's table wants the pro position too. We've got to have a con. Who'll be against making abortions illegal?" "Flip a coin," they say. "Okay, Scott, you call it, and Susan, you flip it." Susan and her table win the pro position and get to argue against abortion; Scott and his group agree to argue in favor of legalized abortion.

The school is one of those run on a small budget in a makeshift building on the social margins of a rural school district (even though the building is in the middle of town). The teachers don't seem like they would be happy in the regular school system and the students are, as the student teacher explains it to me, those who don't want to go to the regular schools. They are the young mothers and the academically suspect and a few young men who would never let their sexual orientation out of the closet in this small town. They are kids who "don't want to go to the regular schools" because most would not be welcome there.

"This will just be a practice debate today. Do as much research as you can in the next fifteen minutes or so, then get an opening statement together, then we'll have the debate." I'm surprised that there's only a little grumbling before everyone in the room sets to work. The student teacher explains to me, "There's a waiting list to get into this school. They like it. Maybe it's easier than the high school, but they feel better here. So those who stay work hard."

The pro team spends a little time discussing their case. They don't do any "research" in the few almanacs and textbooks and encyclopedias lying around the building. They are pretty much of one mind and act as if they've heard all the contrary arguments before. They spend their time making what they call "visual aids," signs that say "Abortion is murder," "Killing is wrong," and the other slogans that appear in news clips of the latest targeted clinic.

The con team heads out of the room and comes back a few minutes later with literature from the women's clinic in the area. Scott seems especially diligent about reading the material and taking notes.

"Okay. Get all the tables out of the way. Put some chairs up front there. Make room for an audience. Just a few rules and then we start. . . ." No grumbling now. Everyone helps get the room in order and the abortion pros and cons move to the front.

"Killing is wrong. . . . I don't know how anyone can carry a baby in her body and have an abortion. . . . And there are always people wanting babies. You can always find a place for a baby to get adopted. So there's never any need for anyone to kill their baby. . . ."

"Okay. Thanks. Now the con."

"It's a fundamental right that women have got to have control of their bodies, so you can't stop a woman from having an abortion if she wants one. Besides, if there weren't abortions, there would be 2 million more births a year in this country. And you know the conditions under which a lot of those kids are going to grow up—"

Becky breaks in from the other side, "Yeah, I know the conditions. Once I had my daughter, you grow up real fast and you take care—"

"I'm not talking about you. I admire you for having ———. But I'm talking about 2 million babies that women didn't want to have. Do you want to have 2 million—"

"They could be adopted—"

The teacher breaks in from the audience, "Okay. Now, are you following the rules? Right. You're not. You get the chance to make a statement. You give them the chance. Then you get a rebuttal time. And it goes back and forth. Okay, let's wrap this up. One more round of statements from everyone."

Everyone makes his and her statement without too many more interruptions. Then the student teacher asks if anyone in the audience has anything to say. Some do. They mostly reiterate the points they have heard, but each adds a bit from his or her personal background. Some speak to the panelists about experiences with sex and childbirth and children.

I sit in amazement that I am hearing a thoughtful, courteous, sustained discussion about a serious topic grounded in the lives of these teenagers. And it is happening in a school.

Time to vote: 7 for the con, 6 for the pro. Just as the teacher is asking whether the debate changed anyone's mind, Susan's eyes well up with tears. She heads for the door at the back of the room saying, "I've got to get out of here." The student teacher watches her go. He seems to look at her closely as she leaves the room and then continues: "No. I didn't expect this would change your minds. But this was just a practice debate. In a couple of weeks, we're going to do a full-fledged debate. They'll have done a lot more research and they'll have their arguments honed a little better. You might find yourself thinking more about abortion. Okay. Any questions?"

He fields a few, none of which concerns Susan or the couple of her pro-teammates who have joined her outside the room. Then, after glancing at the clock and gently issuing orders to get the room back in shape, he says, "I just want to go check on them out there."

I follow him.

"You okay?" he asks Susan.

"Yeah." She has a few tears.

"You did real well. You coming back to class?"

"Yeah. Later."

"Okay. See you then." And he leaves.

I stay.

I say, "Pretty interesting in there. Seemed like you all knew what you were talking about."

"Yeah. Well, it's just Scott."

"What about Scott?"

"He's just so good. You know he doesn't believe anything of that stuff he said, right?"

"He wanted to take the pro position at the start."

"Yeah. That's his position. That's what he thinks. It's just that he's a good debater and . . . well, he just got to me . . . made me upset. I usually don't get this upset. . . . Today's my daughter's birthday."

"I heard. Congratulations. . . . So you'll go back in there."

"Yeah. Soon."

Whenever one school teaches about one real thing, even one time, and when one teacher treats one student as if her real reactions matter, it gives you reason to think it is possible to teach about real things in the schools. It makes you realize that not everything is a lesson.

CHAPTER 17

What Do You Teach When the Students Know the Answer?

"Who knows what the biggest mammal is? . . . Yes?"

"The blue whale."

"Uhhh, that's right. How did you know?"

"We had a unit on whales last year, in the first grade."

"Oh." Then the question was how to fill the twenty minutes of the lesson that was supposed to be devoted to discovering that whales are really mammals and not fish and that the blue whale is a mammal and the biggest of them all. It wasn't a time to panic, but it was a time to wonder, What do you teach when the students know the answer?

Same school, different day, different classroom: before the lesson the student teacher comes to tell me, her supervising faculty member, that she is going to teach a lesson on place value. "This is difficult," she says. "I remember I didn't really understand the importance of 'place value' until high school, maybe even college. I remember sitting in some math class and thinking, 'Oh, so that's why they've been trying to teach that to me for all these years.'" Quite independently, this student teacher's cooperating teacher also tells me, "This is a very difficult concept she's tackling. It's one I didn't understand until I was an adult."

The lesson begins. "Now children, I've written a 9 and a 2 and a 1 on the board. One number is here in the corner, one in the middle of the board, and just below that is the third number. Is this how to write the number 192?"

"Noooooo," sings the chorus of fourth graders.

"So, if I take the three numbers and write them like this [she writes 2, then 9, then 1, side by side], is that how you write the number 192?"

"Noooooo," again.

"No? But all the numbers are there. What's wrong with writing the number 192 that way?"

"Because you've written the number 291."

"What's the difference between 192 and the number 291?"

"The order."

"The order of what?"

"The order of the numbers."

"That's right. So how should it be? The number 192."

"Write a 1 first."

"So I write a 1 in the . . ."

"Hundreds' place," comes the voice of a subset of the original chorus.

"Uhhh, yes." The student teacher turns around seemingly to see who has answered, but more, I suspect, to see why *anyone* knew the answer already. They had not yet, this early in the year, gotten to the place in the text where they are supposed to learn about place value. "And then I put the 9 in the . . ."

"Tens' place." The chorus has grown as more students in the class remember these cues and the answers that are supposed to follow.

"That's right. And the 2 goes in the . . ."

"One's place." Everyone is participating now. Everyone says the answer, except for the teacher.

She could have been wondering, What do you teach when the students know the answer? It could have been an especially puzzling question this time since two adults in the room had agreed, in advance, that place value is an especially difficult concept that neither of them "got" until they were well beyond elementary school. And, here, right in front of them both, all of the *children* in this class knew the answer in a way that was sufficient to get them through all the questions in the book and on the work sheets about place value.

In fact, the student teacher conducting the lesson on place value did not experience the sense of losing a part of the lesson that the "biggest mammal" teacher did. She had plenty of material to fill the rest of the time. Actually, the lesson was not about place value per se. The lesson was about different ways of representing numbers. There was, the student teacher said, the "standard form," using those symbols—1, 2, 3, . . . 9, and 0—as numbers and putting those numbers in their proper places; there was a "written form," writing out the number using words; and there was "another way that I'm thinking of," she said, that involved the students grouping a set of objects whose cardinality was the number in question into groups of tens and ones to form so many piles of ten objects each and a small pile of leftover objects that were the "ones" of the number. She said, "So now you can get into groups and pick up some Unifix cubes. I'll come around to each group and give your group a magic number. Then, as a group, you should write this number in those three ways." So, this teacher never really had to face that question of what to teach when the students know the answer. Her job was just to keep them busy, each group with its own magic number. (And when they finished with one number, there were a million [or more] where that one came from.)

If I could work a hex on all student teachers, I would put into every class at least one child who knew the answer to every question.* That way no one could claim to be teaching anything when he or she was just filling time by asking leading questions. Everyone should always have to face that troubling question, What am I going to do if they know the answer? because in the case of most questions asked by most elementary school teachers, there is no reason that the children should not know the answers. I would work my hex not out of mean-spiritedness, but because I wish teachers would spend more time thinking carefully about just what they are teaching when they teach. If you teach as though every child will know the answer to every question you will ever ask, you might think more carefully about what you want students to learn and what you are teaching when you teach.

Another example involving the "place value" person: I watched her teach a lesson on "money." My strong suspicion was that almost all of the fourth graders in the class understood, in advance, what money is, what each coin is and how the various denominations of coins and bills add together to make a given amount of money. This would remain only a suspicion in this class since the teacher did not check the students' under-standing of money before she began the lesson. But that didn't matter because the lesson was only ostensibly about "money." The lesson was actually about how to work the money problems in the math workbooks. The lesson was almost entirely devoted to the "translation" of problems in the books, problems which used *pictures of money* (and not very good ones at that: the dollar bills were disproportionately small and the "engraving" on the coins was amateurish in the extreme), into the realm of actual, in-your-pocket, use-it-to-buy-stuff money.

"Now, students, these pictures are sometimes difficult to understand. How much money in this first picture? . . . Seventy-five cents? I thought it was only fifty cents. . . . Oh, I see. It *is* a fifty-cent piece. You're right. See, even I have trouble telling one coin from the other in these pictures." This was a mistake that the teacher, and most of the students, would never make with real coins. But that only convinced me that the lesson was geared to getting the students able to use their prior knowledge of money to solve the money problems in their math books. It was not a lesson about money per se.

---

* Every *illegitimate* question, that is. Legitimate questions—questions one asks because one does not know the answer—should always be allowed and accorded their moment of contemplative silence; they should never be hexed. Illegitimate questions—those one asks to show how smart one is or those one asks for purely pedagogical purposes—should always be answered quickly and dismissively, preferably with a sneer.

Now, there is nothing inherently wrong with students learning to work the problems in their books. But there is something wrong when a teacher thinks and insists that she is teaching about money when she is really teaching about how to solve these very peculiar (peculiar from the point of view of life outside the school) problems.* It makes one want to ask a teacher a question that sounds strange, *What* are you teaching? Are you teaching about whales or about the ways in which adults sometimes ask trick questions about the world to get you to spend time showing what you don't know? Or are you teaching that the schools find it hard to find anything but whales (and spiders) to teach about at the beginning of each school year? Are you teaching about place value or about three ways to write numbers? About money or about how to decode bad pictures of play money? About how to calculate the sums of coins and dollars or about the importance of testing in a student's life? About the importance of knowing the answer or the importance of inquiry beyond what you already know?

The physicist Richard Feynmann tells a story of the way his father approached teaching and learning. When Feynmann asked his father the name of a bird, his father told him. Feynmann suspected that the name was, in fact, incorrect. His suspicion was confirmed when his father went on to tell him the name of the same bird in several different languages, languages his father did not know. Finally, his father told him:

> You can know the name of that bird in all the languages of the world, but when you're finished, you'll know absolutely nothing whatever about the bird. You'll only know about humans in different places, and what they call the bird. So let's look at the bird and see what it's *doing*—that's what counts.
>
> For example, look: the bird pecks at its feathers all the time. See it walking around pecking at its feathers? . . . Why do you think birds peck at their feathers?[1]

If Feynmann asks his father about birds, then Feynmann's father decided that maybe the best thing to talk about was *birds*, not birds' *names*. Perhaps

---

* When I told this student teacher what I saw, she protested that it would be unfair if the students did not learn how to work the problems in the book or if they did not learn how to pass the standardized tests that they would all have to take at the end of their first quarter in the fourth grade, tests that would contain money problems just like these. I appreciated her concern, but it just reinforced my idea that this approach to the problem of money is peculiarly school bound and that the school is nothing if not essentially self-referential. That is, it ensures that its peculiar view of things—bad pictures of money standing in for money in this case—is not deemed "strange" or "weird" by referring the substance of its teaching not to anything outside of the school but to a test designed to assess how well the schools are doing in relation to national norms derived only from years of using those tests.

Feynmann's father did not have the best eye for what ought to be taught in any given circumstance, but Feynmann gives the impression that his father knew *what* he was talking about when he was talking pedagogically to his son.

Figuring out what, exactly, is to be taught seems to me a much more important question than how to teach. And yet most teachers spend most of their time troubling over the question of method: how to teach. And most of the rewards in the profession go to those with the most clever ideas about how to teach. But, to my mind, the best teachers are those who know their students and their subjects well enough that they always will be able to answer the question, *What* are you teaching? They will know what they are doing at any given moment and where a line of inquiry might lead. They will know the limits of their own knowledge and, within their field of inquiry, they will know which questions are the legitimate ones and which are the illegitimate ones. They will know when they are accommodating themselves to the demands of the school or the curriculum and when they are engaging the students in matters of substance. They are the teachers who will never face the question, What do you teach when the students know the answer?

CHAPTER 18

What Do You Expect?
Pamela Stewart

A friend of mine was unlucky. He isn't a friend in the usual way we think of friendship, but in a game with a gun, he was unlucky. I was Antoine's tutor. He was the kind of kid about whom we say, "He's got potential," to soften the fact of failing grades. Now, after what the medical people term a "brain injury," he's having to relearn everything. I'll be his tutor again, but he won't be the same. I don't know if he will ever be as much of a friend as he was before.

Antoine is back in school. Recently I saw him and his best friend at the bus stop across from their high school and pulled over. As he recognized me, Antoine raised his hand in greeting, but his face, so expressive in the past, was vacant now. "Where are you two headed?" I asked as they got in the car. "We're going home, to Ben's house," Antoine said with no affect.

I knew he didn't live with his aunt anymore, and his parents live in San Francisco. They had sent him to his aunt's in Tacoma three years ago to start high school. Now Antoine has left her, or she kicked him out, so we were going to Ben's house, Antoine's residence for now.

"Where's your house, Ben?"

"You remember where his house is," Antoine told me. "We used to go by it all the time and honk. Hey, Ben, this is the car I drove when I came by that one time." He wore a smile, but an empty one.

That I remember distinctly—teaching Antoine how to drive my car. Afterwards, whenever we got together he would hound me to let him drive. Even when I sat in the driver's seat, Antoine still drove, commanding the gearshift while riding shotgun. Now, on the way to Ben's house, he watched my hand move the stick shift from second to third gear. Maybe he was remembering how he used to place his big hand over mine in his efforts to drive from the passenger seat.

Antoine always liked to touch; he liked the sensation of it. I keep my hair short, and he used to run his hand through it like you would rub a dog's belly. His face would light up. He wrestled with me, and with girls at school. He was strong and flirtatious. He enjoyed himself. Now things are different. When I saw him a month ago he gave my hand a bone-crushing squeeze. His touches are not tempered with enjoyment but laced with anger.

The school hired someone to accompany him during classes, to help him with homework, and to pry him off girls whose breasts he wouldn't leave alone. He becomes unruly when there is a lot of noise in the room because he can't block it out anymore like everyone else can.

I began tutoring Antoine in math and English early in his sophomore year. We studied at his aunt's apartment tucked inside a labyrinth of others off Pearl Avenue. Or we studied at the library, or at the Antique Sandwich Shoppe. He made funny faces as we drilled vocabulary into our heads, and we laughed at the silly sentences he made up. He told me he never knew learning could be fun.

One November night I asked Antoine about gangs. I knew he was affiliated with the Bloods and I wondered if he would tell me anything.

"Gangs are baaad," he said. "They shoot every day, kill every night." "How does someone join one?" He looked at me with laughing eyes and said, "You just start hanging around them. After hanging with them awhile, you just want to be with them. Then you get courted in. And there are two ways. The first is to fight every member, one right after the other. You aren't supposed to win, but you're supposed to make it through. . . . And if you don't want to fight, you get a contract to fill. You usually have to shoot someone, a stranger."

"What about the girls?" I asked.

"The ladies?" He sized me up. "Well, it's called a train. They run a train on the girl. . . . Everyone gets into the engine, so to speak. . . . She has to lay with every guy, . . . sometimes two at once. You know, one in her mouth and one the usual way." He must have seen my pain because he stopped there. His face said this was a matter of course.

Antoine showed me the gangs' signs: B for Blood, C for Cripp, CK for Cripp Killer, BK for Blood Killer. He shaped my hands into the letters. Hands of a cripple, I thought. He ripped through them in a rhythmic performance of hot energy.

Then he told me about the best night of his life: "There were three Cripps with buckwheats in their hair—know what those are?" He saw I didn't. "Well, buckwheats are those little rubberbands, and you take a bit of hair and tie it up with a rubberband. You do this all over your head. Anyway, these Cripps were wearing blue rags. Me and four other homeys chased them and caught up with them at the top of the Dirt Hills. We beat one guy up real bad. He got it real bad." He said it without pride, without remorse, as if he were watching a movie. "Blood was coming out his nose and mouth, and one eye was swollen shut. We got these three down and tied our red rags around their heads. Then we burned their rags right in their faces." For me he explained, "You see, Cripps don't like red. They say red is like fire, that it burns them. They say Red Dead. The Bloods, they say that blue is like ice, that it freezes them. They say Blue Flu. . . . That one guy, he got it real bad. That was the best day of my life."

Six months later, in April, Antoine had the worst day of his life. You could say I should have seen it coming. When Antoine and I planned to meet for tutoring, he rarely showed. His aunt said he wasn't coming home after school anymore. She said when she asked him to help with the laundry or clean, he would storm out of the house, screaming at her about how he didn't need this kind of shit, that she was trying to run his life. The changes were easy to explain. He had been hanging with a gang.

One Tuesday afternoon Antoine and four friends were at an apartment on the Hilltop. They were playing cards when their host came out of his bedroom carrying a .22 pistol. He said he wanted to play, but not cards. He wanted to play Russian roulette, but he wanted to use their heads, not his. He unloaded all but one bullet. The kids were still. The man was drunk. "Okay. You." He pointed with his gun at one boy. "You're first." He raised the gun to the boy's head and pulled the trigger. Click. The man said to him, "You're lucky." He put the gun in the next boy's ear. Click. "Hah!" The man smiled. He went on to the next player. He rested the pistol against Antoine's temple and squeezed. As the gun fired, the man's hand slipped. Antoine was blown from his chair. The bullet cut through his right temple and went out the top of his head.

The first boy was, as the man said, lucky. He had a one-in-six chance of being shot. The second boy, with a one-in-five chance, was even luckier. Antoine was not lucky. It's so absurd to think of children's lives in terms of probabilities and luck. But that is what we do. Antoine was, even to the social service program that hired me, a "child at risk."

Antoine didn't become a typical "statistic" on that Tuesday afternoon in April; he is alive today, or at least he was last Monday. But he isn't the same. The guard no longer walks the school halls with him, and he has shed the helmet he once wore to protect his shattered, swollen skull. But his eyes are still empty like they were when I first saw him in his hospital bed. All Antoine has said about being shot is, "If I had been home, I wouldn't have been there." I wonder if he thinks he will eventually become lucky if he goes over that afternoon enough?

Last June, Antoine learned to tie his shoe; now, six months later, he is working on seventh grade math. "I'll be taking regular classes next semester," he told me as he and Ben got out of the car. "I may need some help," he said. "Alright. I'll give you a call."

Other high school students say they don't like him anymore: "He's not like he used to be." "Well," I say to them, "he's been shot in the head. What do you expect?"

Sometimes I dream that Antoine will rise from this a hero—that he will be a teen spokesman against violence, that he will give stirring speeches. I imagine all of Tacoma banding together to make the city a safer place, in the name of Antoine Batts. But I watch him go into Ben's house and say to myself, What do you expect? He's just another kid in Tacoma who's been shot in the head.

CHAPTER 19

Criticism of the Schools in the Schools

For at any price we must keep those who have a clear conscience from living and dying in peace.

E. M. Cioran, *The Temptation to Exist*

"There are a few problems, mostly related to her placement. You know, the situation in that school is not good: not so different from other schools, but not good anyway. *But I would never say anything about it on paper.* I know the effect of writing something down. It would stay with her forever. I just write down how well she's doing—and she is—and I'll talk to her about the rest."

This was a man supervising student teachers. He had been in the public schools for 35 years, a principal for many of them. By successfully completing a project to review 75 substitute teachers for possible permanent positions, he came to be recognized by the top-ranking personnel officer in his district as a skilled observer of student teachers, a helpful critic of the schools and of their agents, the teachers. But he would never write down his criticisms. Writing down a criticism might have an effect.

* * *

"I think you are at a real disadvantage. I think it's impossible for anyone to observe in the schools without having taught there. You can't know what you are seeing. You don't understand the reality of the schools."

That's what I was told by one teacher who was bothered by my critique—which I did write down—of the student teacher working in her classroom. I had written a long letter to the student about how she had conducted herself during "the usual morning stuff," how she had interacted with her first grade students, and about the way she had used a prepackaged scheme for the teaching of reading.

After hearing the cooperating teacher's worries on behalf of the student teacher, I asked the student teacher if she was upset by my letter to her. "No, but she [the cooperating teacher] didn't like what you said about the reading lesson. She attended a seminar this summer to learn how to use that reading package, and I was just following the scheme she taught me."

The student teacher knew, from spending the previous on-campus year around me, that I would write about what I saw—even if I didn't understand "the reality of the schools"—and that she could respond however she wished to my comments. I thought that she appreciated the value of my critical observations. (I say "thought," past tense, because in her evaluation of me at the end of the quarter, she wrote about how I was a little disadvantaged by not having taught in the schools and about how I didn't seem to understand the reality of the schools.)

* * *

Is there any place for criticism of the schools *in the schools*? The answer from well-schooled school people seems to be, clearly, No!

People in the schools, including outsiders like me who enter only for a particular purpose, are supposed to be positive. There is, after all, all that self-esteem to build up, and criticism of any sort, everybody knows, can do just the opposite of that. But beyond the self-esteem of the students and the teachers and the student teachers, there is the rest of the reality of the schools—the drug-numbed students, the victims of abuses of all sorts, the illiterates passed up from the lower grades, the parents who don't give a damn about anything, and "society" that makes too many "demands" on teachers. Teaching is hard work because of *that* reality of the schools.

The last thing the schools need to have added to their reality is criticism from someone who has not been schooled enough to understand what he or she is seeing. Perhaps a little "constructive criticism" can be permitted, but there's no need to write it down. Everyone can always improve—that, of course, is the premise of an age-graded curriculum stretched out over twelve or sixteen years, or, for teachers, over a career—and generally no one has to have his or her deficiencies pointed out; they are always obvious, even to the (more or less) deficient person. So, come in as the outsider and the guest that you always and forever will be in the schools and watch; don't expect to understand the reality of the schools; comment but don't criticize; bolster others' self-esteem; appreciate the reality of the schools; and never ever write any criticism down. It might have an effect.

Ivan Illich is a person who has understood for many years the obvious deficiencies of the schools. But he has not been a respecter of self-esteem problems or a gentle critic who would use his understanding of those deficiencies to suggest reforms. Neither has he been a man dissuaded from his critique by the facile assertion that he does not appreciate the reality of the schools.

Indeed, Illich thinks he understands the reality of modern schools quite well. Once that enduring value called "education" has become institutionalized as it has in the modern school, Illich argues, the schools become specifically and paradoxically counterproductive. Instead of producing educated people, schools produce ignorance. Instead of producing the sense of enlightenment that educated people have always known accompanies the difficult discipline of learning, schools produce a foreboding sense of failure, even in the most successful and well-schooled of students, i.e., those with high GPAs. Instead of producing a nation of readers who might use that skill to, among other things, participate in a democratic society, the schools produce illiteracy. This is what Illich has seen in the schools; this is the reality of the schools he thinks he understands very well; this is the unrelenting criticism of the schools that he has been writing down since the early 1970s in the hope of having an effect.

Actually, the Illich of *Deschooling Society* thought he only had to have the effect of a prophet. He was convinced that schools were getting so bad and absorbing so much more money in what would necessarily be futile efforts to continue doing more of the same paradoxically counterproductive stuff that the process could not continue. He thought that the only role a social critic had to play in the late-modern days of the 1970s was to warn people that the businesses of social institutions, including schools, could not continue as usual. Something was going to change, he thought, and the changes would be drastic, dramatic, and harmful to many people. So, *vox clamatis in deserto,* he tried to warn people as any good prophet would.

It turned out that Illich was wrong. He was wrong in his estimation of how many resources, human and fiscal, the schools and other institutions could command and absorb and, eventually, destroy; he was wrong in his estimation of how much ignorance the schools could produce and still be tolerated by citizenries. Illich had badly underestimated the resilience of schools, their amazing capacity to respond to the calls for reform that came from all quarters and thereby to sustain themselves even though the schools, better than any other agency or sector of society, kept on doing the studies and collecting the statistics that showed that they were bad for people. He had not understood the profound equilibrium-sustaining capacity of large social systems.

During the 1980s Illich realized that he had been wrong. He did not change his analysis of the schools. Instead, he deepened his criticism. No longer did he write just about the specific counterproductivity of the schools; he began to speak about "the present school system as one manifestation of a *mystery of evil*."[1] No longer the prophet but now a historian writing in a theologically informed language, Illich stopped warning of the inevitable collapse of the schools and began urging people to do things that they could actually do, even in the schools. In a lecture to a group of theologians he said, for example, "I want to motivate Christians, who claim a privileged understanding of *evil* to become leaders on behalf of the civil liberties of the . . . dropout." Instead of writing critical assessments of the way schools do what they do (inter alia, produce ignorance and senses of failure in graduates), Illich valorized those who escaped social institutions, those who had dropped out.

> These dropouts . . . are privileged: in school they have learned to fake almost anything, and to see the school system for what it really is: a world-wide soul-shredder that junks the majority and hardens an elite to govern it. They recognize the school system as an evil, no matter how good or effective or pleasant some schools might be for their pupils, and all schools, occasionally, for some kids. The reflective dropout learns to laugh about the pious platitudes praising modern education, when the enterprise which organizes it is by its very nature an instrument which compounds their truancy with psychological, social, and economic discriminations.[2]

Illich portrays many dropouts as streetwise and able to see what those of us who are well-schooled will never see, not "the reality of the schools" but "the school system for what it really is." This Illich, who understands the power of an educational system to redefine and sustain its work when it is obviously harmful (through its "psychological, social, and economic discriminations") to so many so often, distances himself from the Illich of *Deschooling,* who envisioned new, more convivial tools (sidewalks, computer networks, etc.) that could and would be institutionalized, more likely than not by the schools themselves. This more recent Illich calls on the people who would help the dropout remain *outside* not to think ever again in terms of substituting new institutionalizable "tools" for the old institutions. He calls on everyone simply to do what he or she can:

> Withdrawal from the school and detachment from the educational model of mediation ought to be welcomed as signs of social health. . . . Educational research in the U.S. swallows more money than biology and chemistry taken together. Yet none of it is focused on the transformation of the status of the dropout from that of an escapee who must be caught and brought back into the fold into that of a world-wise, reasonable person. I do not plead for some new form of institutional haven. I think of niches, free spaces, squatters' arrangements, spiritual tents which some of us might be capable to offer, not for "the dropout in general" but each of us for a small "list" of others who, through the experience of mutual obedience, have become able to renounce integration in the "system."[3]

Instead of heralding the news that the schools will crumble under their own weight, Illich moves from his understanding of the reality of the schools to a call to those who can to serve, however they may, "a small 'list' of others."

Illich got his notion of list from Thomas Keneally's *Schindler's List,* a report on the activities of Oskar Schindler, an industrialist during the rule of the National Socialists in Germany. Schindler was not, by most standards, a nice man. As Illich puts it, "The man . . . was, as we say, no saint. In the midst of hunger and murder and typhoid fever around him, he lived it up. Every one of his Jews remembers his partying and wenching." "His Jews" refers to the 1,700 Jews that Schindler saved from the ovens of the death camps. They call themselves "Schindler's Jews." They were Schindler's small list of others, people whom Schindler obtained from the camps and put to work in his factory where he fed them a few hundred more calories a day and offered them a little more protection than the other industrialists of that horrid time and place. Schindler was no reformer. He never once tried to make the Nazis behave better; he never once tried to humanize the Nazi machine. He did, simply, what he could: He saved only a few Jews from the certain death of the totalizing machine of the camps.

Even though Keneally arranges his biography so that it suggests reasons for Schindler's behavior, no one knows why Schindler did what he did. Schindler himself gave no reasons. But who should need a reason for saving a few people if one is in a position to do so? Indeed, if anyone ever gives a reason for doing something good, you can be pretty sure that that act is the start of a new process of institutionalizing "good actions" or new "values." Schindler did what he did—just and only that—we cannot fully understand his actions but we can reflect on them. Illich says, "For me, Schindlers and McDonalds [McDonald was a principal in a particularly tough Chicago school; he saved his own small list of others, his students] and their brand of anarchists have something about them that makes them 'Christlike.' More than any of them, Jesus was an anarchist savior. That's what the Gospels tell us." We are left to reflect on the actions—obviously, blatantly, palpably *good* actions—of people who came not to change the law, not to reform institutions, not to establish programs to "help" a general class of people or, megalomaniacally, a whole population, but who, through simple actions, served and saved a small list of others. We are left to reflect in the face of actions that are obviously good even though they are not done for any good reason.

Illich's critique of schools is complete and unyielding. By talking of Schindler, Illich links, in a very specific and careful way, the work of the schools with that most extreme manifestation of evil in our times, the Holocaust:

> In a sense there is no way of comparing the class of historical events that go under the name of Hiroshima, Pol Pot Cambodia, Armenian Massacre, Nazi Holocaust, ABC-stocks and/or human gene-line engineering on the one hand and, on the other, the treatment meted out to people in our schoolrooms, hospital wards, prisons, slums or welfare shelters. But, in another sense, both kinds of horrors are manifestations of the same epochal spirit. We need the

courage and the discipline of heart and mind to let these two classes of events interpret each other.[4]

It is laughably obvious that this kind of criticism of the schools would not face a warm reception in the schools, but perhaps someone could muster the courage to take it there anyway. I should think that such a critique might be liberating, at least for a small list of teachers.

You do not have to be an expert critic to know that schools are failing. The teachers are the first to tell you that they are. Second to say so are the educational researchers who document the failure of schools in their statistics. Third are the politicians and members of the media. And if anyone dares to ask them, the students will say so, too. But none of these critics seems inclined to follow Illich because most of them are so absolutely committed to the reform of the schools, to the improvement of the beast, to the refinement of the schools' techniques of restraint and confinement, that they are unable to see the work of the schools "as one manifestation of a *mystery of evil*." People are inclined to criticize the schools only if they can accompany that criticism with a scheme for making it, that system called schooling, better.

Raymond Williams's *Keywords* says that the word *criticism* "has become a difficult word, because although its predominant general sense is of fault finding, it has an underlying sense of judgment and a very confusing specialized sense, in relation to arts and literature." But he concludes his assessment of this word with a hope that instead of retreating to the use of "criticism" as, simply, faultfinding or, more elaborately, as "an apparently general process of judging," criticism could refer, in any situation, to "the specificity of the response, which is not an abstract 'judgment' but even where including, as often necessarily, positive or negative responses, a definite practice, in active and complex relations with its whole situation and context."[5] Criticism could be made to mean *saying what one sees*—in the schools, for example—using a language that forms a judgmental matrix but that strives always and only for precision of description that can move one to respond well in a set of specific circumstances.

An example: In a seminar I gave on teaching practices, a woman described an interaction she had in a fourth grade class.

> I knew she could do these math problems. But she said she couldn't. The only thing she was interested in was getting the right answer. She was not interested in finding a way, her way, to get an answer. She was set on getting the right answer. My problem was that I was watching a young girl—another one—being shown that she could not do math. All in the name of the right answer. And I knew that with my help she could do the problem. But she wouldn't.

At this point, another person interrupted: "Excuse me, but why didn't you give her the right answer?" "Because I knew she could work the problem and I didn't want to participate in tagging another girl as a failure in math." "Yes, but you said that all she wanted was the right answer. Why didn't *you* give it to her?" "I thought I just told you." "You told me that you thought she could do the problem. I just thought that if you gave her what she wanted—the right answer—you might, then, have the chance of teaching her how to do the math to get the answer herself. So I was wondering why you didn't give her the right answer?" A very large smile broke on the woman's face: "Oh, you mean, because I'm sadistic and like to see children suffer in math class?" A big smile in return.

Saying what you see—making critical observations—can be powerfully liberating sometimes. Having the courage to recognize the violence of acts of teaching, even good teaching done for "good reasons," can be valuable, not because it might suggest any specific change in the practice of teaching but because it can make even teachers attentive to the evil of which they are a part.

But being attentive to the harshness of one's own actions would not necessarily drive one away from the schools. Embracing wholly the fact that schools are failing can be freeing. It seems to me that if a teacher or a parent or a student kept repeating, like a mantra, "The schools are failing. The schools are failing. The schools are failing," it could occur to that person, finally, that maybe *that* is the point: The schools are failing! And at that precise moment of insight into this banality of our time, a teacher or a parent or a student could be freed from the burden of the cognition that the schools are failing, the burden that settles itself in the impulse to offer programs of reform. Precisely at that moment, it could occur to anyone associated with the schools that, because the schools are failing with respect to almost any conceivable educational agenda, it doesn't really matter what one does in the schools. No matter what anyone does in the schools, he or she will probably fail, too. No matter what sort of reform program one might mount, it will probably fail. No matter how kind one is or how many times one works the word "humane" into policies and procedures, the schools will probably continue to be essentially violent places. But then one would be free, free of the schools' efforts to reform and reframe themselves, free to try *absolutely anything* new—in the schools.

Why "in the schools"? Illich says, "One thing which makes the Schindlers of the world alike is this: they expect nothing from an evil system in which they have made their career but the chance to make its total victims feel that they can beat it." Not for any good reason, not because, for example, "thereby, the system will be better," not to improve the efficiency or the humanity of the system that is evil. One does not help others *because* helping them will improve things in general. The terms of the sentence are reversed: *if* one helps others in this way, then one might be seen by critics such as Illich—perhaps by others as well—as "Schindler-like."

But one can never become free of the schools, free to try anything new, unless one is willing to see the schools for what they are. To see the schools for what they are does not mean to develop a well-schooled understanding of the reality of the schools. It does not require even the provisional acceptance of the schools' explanations for what they do because explanations sometimes simply serve to permit one to look at bad acts with a clear conscience. It means a willingness to look at the schools in search of a harsh clarity. It means a willingness to engage in constant criticism. It means constantly making acute critical observations. But this discipline would require everyone in the schools to say what he or she sees, perhaps even to write it down, perhaps even with the intention of having an effect.

Illich says that only those willing and able to *renounce* their integration in the "system" that is schooling stand a chance of serving "a small 'list' of others." Renunciation is an act that begins in clear-eyed recognition and awareness of that which is to be renounced. To renounce integration into the system of schooling, one would have to begin with a recognition of the work of schools and an acknowledgment of the power of that system to command the souls of those who come under its sway. Those who would use their critiques to reform the schools and refine practices within them ("I just write down how well she's doing—and she is—and I'll talk to her about the rest") are unable to see the schools for what they are. They are too much turned toward the future. To become free of the schools in the schools, to have the opportunity of serving a small list of others drawn from the lists generated by multiple administrative apparatuses and spewed out by the computers that organize the school's work better than a simple functionary like Eichmann could ever have imagined, one must be able to see that the schools are, for example, "one manifestation of a *mystery of evil*." Then one must say this and write it down—so that one can move on.

CHAPTER 20

Praise in Place of Accomplishment

In the mail a letter from a twelve-year-old child, enclosing poems, her mother having pushed her to ask my opinion. This child does really look at things, and I can write something helpful, I think. But it is troubling how many people expect applause, recognition, when they have not even begun to learn an art or a craft. Instant success is the order of the day; "I want it now!"

May Sarton, *Journal of a Solitude*

"Strike three. Out." This is said with little emotion because in third-grade Little Baseball even the umpire hates to see a kid strike out.

"Great swings, Tommy!" "Yeah, Tommy. Way to swing." This, with much emotion, from the parents' gallery behind the fence.

Great swings?! *But they weren't*, I say to myself. Every one of them was late. And none of them had any power because Tommy didn't step into the pitch. And the kid swings from his wrists.

At times like this, when you are a parent among parents handing out praise even when there has been no accomplishment, the touchstone of one's sanity becomes the kids themselves. I look at Tommy as he walks back to the dugout behind the fence. I know from that walk and from the way he hangs his head that *he* knows he has done poorly. How could he not? He's been on the bench watching his teammates get a hit here and a hit there; he's seen others when they strike out. Tommy knows what an accomplishment is in baseball. And he knows he didn't accomplish anything this time at bat. He knows, I suspect, that his swings weren't great. Tommy has not yet lost the power of discernment, the ability to discriminate success from failure, as the parents behind the fence seemingly have. If Tommy is lucky enough not to hear the parents' praise for his "great swings," he'll have a reason to practice tomorrow. He won't be one of the many who expect applause and recognition before they have learned to play the game. And when his bat, swung with the body and not just the wrists, makes its first solid contact with the ball in the next game or the next, or maybe next season, he will be able to experience the pride of actual accomplishment. But only if he doesn't become dependent on the parents' praise first.

Just because third-grade Little Baseball doesn't look very much like baseball doesn't mean that people—the parents and the coaches—have to make it look like school. But that's just what they do. By shouting praise for every effort—what they would call being supportive and bolstering the self-esteem of the players—they distract children from the direct rewards that accomplishments in any activity automatically bring. Parents at the park have come under the sway of the rhetoric and practices of the schools that produce, according to report after report, American children who score at or near the bottom on internationally comparative tests of knowledge and yet who feel very good about themselves and their abilities. The parents at the ballpark, like teachers in schools, would never risk letting a child feel bad about a poor performance. It used to be that it wasn't whether you won or lost but how you played the game. Now it's not a matter of how you play the game but whether or not you feel good about yourself when the parents pass out the non-sweet, wholewheat snacks after the game.

There is one big difference between school and baseball. Most people, kids included, can tell the difference between good baseball players and poor ones. Good coaches at all levels know the difference and they take it upon themselves to teach children how to become better. They work with individual talents as they come packaged in each individual kid, design drills, teach fundamentals, and practice, practice, practice. The kids improve. The kids don't have to be told they've improved; they know it because their throws are straighter, their arms are stronger, their hits are longer, their strategies are wiser.

Not many people I've met in schools would ever venture to utter a word about what it means to be well educated. Perhaps they don't know; perhaps they are afraid that someone might have a different idea; perhaps thinking substantively about education would endanger the rest of their efforts in the schools. Whatever the reason, workers in the schools—those we persist in calling "teachers"—will spend many, many hours of their time and of our children's time "providing opportunities" and designing worksheets and going on fieldtrips (in the richer districts) and individualizing instruction, but pitifully few of them will ever make a judgment that Sally is better educated than Juan. They wrap themselves in vague words and utterances about the uniqueness of every child (every one of whom gets processed through more or less the same curriculum) and about the way learning is not something that ever stops but continues throughout life (despite the fact that one of the most important functions of schools at every level is to decide when each child's formal education will end, which children will be allowed to go on to universities, medical schools, technical schools, business schools and the like, and which will be forced off the formal-schooling track into low-paying jobs) and about the way a child's culture influences the way she/he learns (when the only bows to cultural difference in most classrooms are pictures of people of different tints and stories from other cultures introduced and read in the same "school reading" monotone in which *Silas Marner* was read to us decades ago). They will tell you that what's important is that the kids *feel good* about who they are. Schools act as if they are the last places that will be concerned with just who children are; they ought to be first, they seem to think, in providing the praise that will make kids happy, comfortable, and safe, even when they feel like hanging their heads and walking slowly back to the bench because they know they've not done a good job.

What would it mean for schools to concern themselves with who the children in their charge are?

First, it would mean renouncing any concern for the "social problems" that "plague" all children and turn them all, more or less, into "victims" of this or that modern ill. I am not suggesting that schools ought to operate in ignorance of the modern facts of life in the cities, the suburbs, and the countryside. But I would suggest that the schools' overwhelming concern for finding solutions to modern social problems has led them to look at children generically (as, for example, the victims or, on the other side, the fortunate and the lucky) or to see each child as another instance of more general phenomena that can be understood using categorical problems provided by contemporary politics: drugs, broken homes, child abuse, sex, etc.

Even in third-grade Little Baseball, the coaches don't try to do anything about "hitting problems" or "catching problems." They work with each child on his or her hitting or catching or throwing or game strategy.[*] Of course, there are the fundamentals of hitting, catching, and so on, and coaches always remind players of the value of fundamentals. (And the players know the litany of fundamentals, usually well before they start playing on teams where ability matters.) But finally, it is the player's own individual approach to hitting or catching that matters and, finally, it is to that that the coach must attend. It is possible for a coach to be interested in individuals and their own, individual approaches to the play of the game because coaches know that the final arbiter of success is the game itself.

Schoolchildren know the fundamentals of the social problems curriculum. Most second graders will tell you that drugs are bad. By the eighth grade most students know that sex involves risks. The schools' curricula don't build on students' knowledge of these fundamentals and then attend to the individual students, their particular knowledges and circumstances, and what each one might need to know to live his or her life better. Indeed, schools just keep hammering away at the drug problem and the sex problem and family problems and so on. Teachers get burned out

---

[*] And very few of them would ever use a phrase like "hitting *skills*." The schoolish addition of "skills" would suggest that there is something generic about hitting that can be reduced to a set of skills.

because they are expected by society to be concerned about so much more than academics. But by constantly addressing the general problems and questing after the grail of solutions to these modern social facts, schools make it nearly impossible for anyone to pay attention to the students themselves, as if they were individual people.

Second, if schools are to concern themselves with children they must make it possible for those children to feel failure. We know, of course, that the history of schools can be written as the history of an institution designed to *create failures*. Indeed, I suspect that many contemporary school practices, including more "humane management" techniques and (over-) reliance on praise, are very much the schools' reaction to this well-known history. But as often happens with reactive behaviors, this one has become an overreaction. By moving away from imposing judgments of failure and away from organizing themselves around the "marks" that schools make on each student's documentary body and by moving toward practices that ensure that every child will feel himself or herself to be a success, the schools have made sure that children will not *feel failure*.

Children in schools know that no project or paper will come back without an acknowledgment of some success or other, no matter how low the teacher has to go to find some little something that the child actually did. Teachers have come to believe that if they are going to make a criticism or offer a suggestion, they have got to search around for some tempering praise. But always trying for a balanced commentary never allows the teacher to take the true measure of the child, and the child never comes to appreciate the fact that no one is good, even pretty good, at everything.

For children to be able to appreciate their abilities, they have to have the chance to learn their limits. For teachers to pay attention to students, they have to allow themselves simply to watch children approaching their limits, and they have to watch them be stopped there by their limits. It is only in the face of failures that accomplishments come to mean anything. Big people will be able to look at little people with open and attentive eyes when "Strike three!" is allowed to mean what it means: "You're out." Adults are being irresponsible when they lead a child to think it means anything else.

Children can only come to feel failure, however, when there is a fairly clear goal that lies just beyond their reach. On the ballfield, the goals are built into the game: get hits, score runs, win games. But in those same children's schools, it's a different story. In response to a simple question like, "What's the point of this lesson?" few teachers will tell you what they expect the children to learn or what they are trying to teach. They will reply with phrases about "providing opportunities" and "allowing the children to make choices" and "encouraging them to work in groups" and so on. And that's the third thing schools would have to do if they wanted to concern themselves with children: They would have to articulate and make manifest a view of what it might mean to be an educated person.

An activity like baseball is self-rewarding because it is clear what the game is about and what success looks like. Of course, success comes in different forms, but that only makes the self-rewarding character of the sport more interesting: People of different shapes and different abilities can all experience success in the game. Coaches can pay attention to individuals and help each one strive toward the accomplishments that are possible within all the constraints that any individual brings to the game. They can be spare with their praise because accomplishments are palpable and sensible, all because the goal of the game is clear.

In today's seemingly standardless schools, children are graded only relative to themselves. Teachers spending their time deciding what each student might be able to accomplish are saved the trouble of having to say what they think any given student *ought* to be able to accomplish. And it keeps them from having to design lessons that will allow children to experience the thrill of accomplishment with respect to a goal that is sensible. If teachers ever decided to articulate a view of an educated person, they would then face the problem of making that view manifest. They would have to show students what it means to be a "reader," a "mathematician," a serious student of and practitioner of citizenship, and they would have to demonstrate the joy that accompanies some measure of accomplishment in each of these areas that the schools seem to think are important. Schools would be very interesting places if the teachers there read real books, applied real mathematics to real life situations, and demonstrated the real dilemmas of real democratic citizenship as often as a batting coach steps up to the plate to show his players what all his words are about. To make school material real, teachers would have to stop praising their students for their efforts and demonstrate what real accomplishments really look like. If they did that, children would be able to decide for themselves, every day, if schools were offering them anything worth learning.

As Tommy takes that painful walk back to the bench, he's in danger. He could be seduced into believing that he has done something that merits praise from adults. If he falls for their praise—"Great swings!" indeed—he will never have any reason to become a better baseball player. He will move quickly from third-grade Little Baseball to video games that reward him a little for every meaningless move he makes. He will tell his parents that he enjoys school but he will be, through no fault of his own, at an honest loss for words when they ask him what he is learning there. He will be another member of the masses dependent on praise but for whom the taste of genuine accomplishment is foreign. And he will never frequent a venue that makes him uncomfortable, that tests his measure, that pushes him to his limits. Those around him, those who protest that their unending praise is the truest sign that they really care for Tommy, will never understand that even though Tommy is involved in a blizzard of activities he is engaged by none of them.

Until schools make it possible for themselves to pay attention to children, they had better keep on praising them. Unless students are made to feel good about what they do in the schools, they might decide to skip school and undertake an activity that is rewarding.

CHAPTER 21

Who Will Manage the Self-Managers? Four Scenes from a Post-Quality School

In 1990 William Glasser, M.D., continued his decades-long efforts to reform schooling with the publication of *The Quality School: Managing Students without Coercion.*[1] Glasser imagines schools in which teachers stop bossing students around and, instead, get them to do things that satisfy what he claims are their biologically given needs for survival, love, power, fun, and freedom. Teachers who become "lead-managers" instead of "bosses" will be in a better position to persuade students to do quality work, work that "feels good" and that, over the long run, is good.

By 1990 there were some schools that had gone beyond Glasser. Teachers in them acted as if they had spent their time in human relations courses learning how to handle clients instead of in teacher education programs learning how to discipline and teach students. They adopted Glasser's rhetoric, perhaps even his logic, but they went Glasser one better. While Glasser insisted that teachers still had to see themselves as "in charge" of the classroom, i.e., that they were still the "managers," these "post-quality schools" slathered the managerial idiom everywhere. Why not make the students into managers, too, and get them to manage themselves? Why not aim education not at the development of the child but at the creation of "self-managers" out of what used to be called students?

Glasser's interest in the production of quality work relies heavily on the work of W. Edwards Deming, the American statistician who helped post-war Japanese businesses produce high-quality goods. It was almost inevitable that someone would Americanize the discipline of Japanese managerial severity and try to out-Glasser Glasser. The logic goes like this: If teachers can become friendly managers who can persuade children to think that schoolwork actually satisfies their innate biological needs, why can't the students be taught to become managers of themselves? Instead of conceiving of students only as workers and instead of having teachers constantly worry about having to manage students to get them to do what is good for them, why not try to eliminate the middleman-manager; why not eliminate the manager-worker relationship altogether? To make students into self-managers would be to drag Glasser and Deming out of the post-war rubble where something had to be done and someone (the managers) had to make sure it got done into the post-me decade of autonomous-but-interdependent, empowered, and supported people who can do anything, including being all they can be. It just sounds right.

I observed one of our students who worked in one of those post-quality schools of self-management. To hear the administrators and the teachers talk, it sounded like they had adopted Glasser's scheme wholesale. They had bought the book, Xeroxed the supplementary materials, and held the suggested seminars and discussion sessions. It didn't matter to them that they had adulterated Glasser's scheme into something he could never abide. But they were adamant and, with our student at least, they were effective. Two weeks after the start of school, I received a letter from the student-teacher telling me what he would like me to watch for as I conducted my first site visit: "Tell me if I am enabling the students to become effective self-managers."

Not even a school of self-management could answer such a question because, as Deming would be the first to point out, to tell whether a student was an effective self-manager or not would require an operational definition of just what that might be. This school was too adamant in prosecuting its mission to slow down enough to ask exactly what a good self-manager looks like. But observing the work in this school did give me an indication of how the managers of the would-be self-managers managed themselves.

Scene I

Our student's supervising teacher agrees to take the student teacher's playground duty so that we can have a post-observation discussion of his work. Ten minutes later, she returns. "Can I see both of you in the classroom? Now?!" The boss-like "Now?!" was not necessary to make me wonder if this was an exemplar of Glasser's "lead-teachers [who] add kindness, courtesy, and humor to whatever they ask students to do."[2] She was mad, and she had some law to lay down.

She said to me: "Two children, quite independently, said that you acted mean during your observation today. What did you do?"

"Actually, I just observed. I don't recall saying anything."

The student teacher looked puzzled, probably for several reasons.

"Well, these students don't make things up. I want you to be sure that you don't act mean while you are here. If you have something to say to Mr. ———— that is critical of his work, you should probably do it elsewhere."

As Mr. ———— and I pieced together the problem over the next several days, we remembered one student who had helped clean up the manipulatives after the math lesson. She had watched as I showed Mr. ———— how he had confused part of the group during his lesson on adding fractions. As she was cleaning up, I had put some of the fraction bars on the table in a configuration Mr. ———— had used and then said, "Look at this and tell me why three-sixths plus four-sixths is not seven-twelfths, like the blond girl at the end of the table said." The young student-helper had taken her report of this incident to a friend on the playground, they had laughed about it with their friends and the story made its way, quickly and through two by-then "quite independent" routes, to the supervising teacher. My encouraging Mr. ———— to see the logic of his students' errors, which were caused, at least in part, by his presentation of the problem, was, in the context of this school which insisted on overlaying a veneer of friendliness on every comment, "mean." Even though Mr. ———— saw his problem immediately, I had not added what passed for "kindness, courtesy, and humor" to my encouragement that he teach better.

As we talked about this incident, Mr. ———— came to appreciate his supervising teacher's position.

"I think we probably should have gone elsewhere, or at least we could have waited until all the students were outside. That way they wouldn't have to see anything that they might interpret as 'critical,'" he said. "It's important not to be critical or even *seem* critical if you want someone to be a self-manager. They think that being critical is 'mean' and it upsets them."

"What are you trying to teach them?"

"To be self-managers."

"And when they fall short of being a self-manager? What then?"

"I encourage them to see that it's really in their best interests."

"You're critical of them, right?"

"I wouldn't put it that way."

"I know you wouldn't because, in the name of making little self-managers, no one has ever taught your students the difference between someone being constructively critical and someone being mean."

"But I would call this an *exercise of discretion*, something you've urged on us since we started in teacher training. We should have conducted *our* business elsewhere, in private. I can be critical of students, but I can be discreet in my criticism."

"It seems to me that in this case discretion has turned into deception. And that's mostly because anytime you think it's time to be critical of a student's work, someone—or some part of your conscience—is there to tell you to do that elsewhere. Remember when Mrs. ———— was critical of my being critical of you? She took us into an empty classroom and made sure there were no students playing hooky from recess before she unloaded her anger. Why not be critical in public so that students can see it's possible to be critical, perhaps even helpful, without being mean?"

"I don't think you and I are going to agree on this."

"Especially since your getting a job here depends on your discretion."

Scene II

I arrive at the school just in time for an all-school assembly. Five hundred children are packed in the multipurpose room (a large room with a stage, basketball hoops, and gymnasium-grade carpeting with inlaid foul-shot circles and half-court lines). In front of the stage is a smaller stage set up for the occasion.

The clock sweeps past the appointed starting time for the assembly. A young man starts disassembling the portable stage on the gym floor and reassembling it on the larger stage as teachers open the curtain-like stage doors and change the lights. The hum of the children increases. Some of the teachers who have stayed with their classes stand and start looking a little more stern. Finally, the principal goes to the front of the room.

The principal raises her hand, fingers spread. About four hundred hands go up in a gesture of mass reciprocity. The principal speaks: "If your hand is up, you're ready. If your hand is not up in the air, you're not ready." The other hundred hands comply with the coded order to discipline oneself into silence. The principal says, "You can help now by being on your bottom and being quiet." The teachers who stood to communicate their sternness now help by putting themselves on their bottoms. Still there is shuffling. "It's my turn now. . . . Excuse me. . . . No. Excuse me," says the principal with increasing but controlled shrillness.

The principal begins: "Because of some teamwork that didn't occur this morning, our guest is having to set up his stage right now. It's very hard to entertain 500 kids, but that is the problem here this morning. So we're going to take a little time. I want you to take five seconds now and think about what it is that might be happening here this morning."

Just as the order to "think" is given, the guest, a puppeteer, slings an embroidered cloth over the back of his stage. "Sleeping Beauty," it reads. The kids who can read start to say to one another, "'Sleeping Beauty.' We're gonna see 'Sleeping Beauty.'" It quickly becomes like a mass mantra: "Sleeping Beauty."

"Excuse me," the principal shouts. "I'm going to count to five. You're not supposed to be talking now. I want you to think," she says, putting her two index fingers to her temples in the same way women of a former time were pictured with their fingers in their dimples, "think for five seconds now about what you *think* is going to happen here this morning. Then raise your hand." Two seconds later she says, "Yes, Jason."

"I think we are going to see a show called 'Sleeping Beauty.'"

Muted laughter.

The principal doesn't get the joke, or at least she doesn't seem to get it because next she says, "Okay. Jason has the *idea*," with that word stretched out like Jason had taken a full five seconds to think it up, "that we are going to see a show called 'Sleeping Beauty.' Can someone pick up on that *idea* and make it bigger? . . . Yes, Martha."

"It's going to have puppets."

"Martha thinks this show called 'Sleeping Beauty' is going to have puppets. Is there another name for puppets?"

"Marionettes"

"Raise your hands. Yes, Carl."

"Marionettes."

"Very good, Carl. It's going to have puppets, or marionettes. Can someone expand on that idea? What is a marionette? This will take some time. Take ten seconds and think about that. Ten *quiet* seconds . . ."

The puppet show started. It was called "Sleeping Beauty" and it did have puppets, or marionettes. And the principal's shrillness never spilled over into the hysteria on which it constantly verged. She was, after all, the head self-manager of this post-quality school.

Scene III

I leave "Sleeping Beauty" and walk to our student teacher's classroom. The lights click on as I enter the room. The principal had motion sensors installed the week before. Even the classrooms self-manage themselves.

On the far wall, there is a poster:

My Job (Students')	Teacher's Job
To Listen	To Teach and to Learn
To Teach and to Learn	To Listen and Hear
Be a Self-Manager	
Be Respectful	
Respect Property	
Take Care of Self	
Be Courteous	
Be Helpful	
Be Friendly	
Be Caring	
Be Responsible	
Gum Free School	
DO YOUR WORK!	

What struck me about this poster was not the obvious disparity in the lists nor the humor of both student and teacher being obliged to listen while only the teacher must hear. What struck me was the way the poster could not maintain its point of view. By reading the poster, one cannot tell if we are in the land of boss-managers, lead-managers, or self-managers—or of people who are simply confused.

There is in that "*My* Job" list an opening bow to self-management, a recognition that the students, who probably had a hand in the construction of these lists, might come to own these sentiments and see their responsibilities reflected there. But the parentheses make it clear that these are rules governing a division of labor between students and teacher, not a set of responsibilities to be individually honored because they were claimed collectively by the class. The first entries on the list shift back to a point of view that permits the student to see himself or herself as the actor: "My job [is] to listen. My job [is] to teach and to learn." Then, only three steps deep, we are back to a list of school rules that seem all too familiar: Be this; be that; be yourself; don't be a brat; thanks very much; I know where I'm at. All this concluding with a line that is better understood as a commentary on the exercise of constructing the poster itself ("Be Reasonable"), a line that would be more entertainingly expressed with one of those circle-and-slash international signs ("Gum Free School"), and the final excrescence that reminds the students of their real position in a school so enamored of a kinder and gentler rhetoric ("DO YOUR WORK!").

On the wall opposite this poster is another poster. This one is headed "Self-Managers." Down the side is a list of 25 names, all the members of the class. Opposite each name are multiple numerical entries: 50, 100, 200, 100, 500, etc. The sums awarded to the top scorers would easily be four-, if not five-digit numbers. Earlier I had seen the points being awarded to members of groups who obeyed the dictum DO YOUR WORK! and I had sensed the depth of the dispute between the supervising teacher and the student teacher when the latter awarded 200 points to all members of a group just for sitting through his math lesson. This poster was obviously an axis around which the practice of teaching "self-management" turned. I looked at it more closely. Names with many points beside them were circled. These were obviously the real self-managers of the class. As I scanned the circles, I saw that the children I knew to be the good classroom citizens were the ones recognized by a circle on this list.

Then I laughed. There, fourth from the bottom, was the teacher's name, Mrs. ———. Beside it were only two entries: 50, 200. Her name was not circled. "Definitely not a self-manager," I thought to myself. Sad.

Scene IV

Just after noon, as I am signing out on the visitors log, I overhear a conversation, half of which is carried on with a recognizable shrillness-on-the-edge-of-hysteria. It's a conference between a teacher and the principal about placing a child in this class or that one next year. Just as they are about to reach the decision point, there comes a loud eruption from the multipurpose room down the hall.

"Are they done already? They shouldn't be done already." The principal breaks away just as the teacher tries to say that it's probably just a part of the story where the audience has to warn Sleeping Beauty not to do whatever it is that Sleeping Beauty has to do if she is going to get into the fix that Sleeping Beauties get into.

A few second later, the principal is back, a little more breathless now. "No, it was just something in the story, some audience participation thing."

Now I notice something that doesn't go with the head self-manager's business person's wool suit. Scotch taped to the principal's lapel is a five-by-eight-inch piece of note paper. On the paper is her schedule for the day. Each of the entries through 12:15 P.M. are roughly scratched out. At the bottom of the page, penciled in, is the question, "And how is your day?"

Someone has to be in charge of a school of self-managers.

* * *

It is a little strange, at first, to read Glasser's recasting of the student teacher relationship in a managerial idiom. "Teachers are people managers, and almost everyone will agree that students as workers seem to be most resistant of all to being managed." "For workers, including students, to do quality work, they must be managed in a way that convinces them that the work they are asked to do satisfies their needs." "[S]tudents are not only the workers in the school, they are also the products."[3] Once the shock of these statements wears off, their banality sets in, and anyone who breathes the contemporary cultural air will find it hard to fault Glasser's push for quality schools. It makes good, almost common sense. And the writing has a certain integrity to it. At least Glasser never loses sight of the fact that, while students may have certain "jobs" in schools, it is the responsibility of teachers (and administrators and superintendents and so forth) to manage the schools so that students can learn.

In contrast, the hyper-Glasserized, post-quality school of self-management puts almost all responsibility for almost everything (see the poster, scene III), first, on students. Once the students are engaged in the job of monitoring their own self-management practices, the wardens of the school can go on doing what they have always done, but they do it under a cloying veil of self-serving rhetoric and sappy, institutionalized friendliness and kindness.

Children in the school may be taught to be self-managers. What they will necessarily learn—unless they are lucky enough to first learn cunning, evasion, and resistance—is hypocrisy.

CHAPTER 22

"I Learned Everything I Know about Teaching in the Classroom":
An Open Letter to Student Teachers

The Pupil: To comfort myself, I hit upon the thought that there must be a trick somewhere which the Master for some reason would not divulge, and I staked my ambition on its discovery.
The Master: What stands in your way is that you have a much too willful will. You think that what you do not do yourself does not happen.

Eugen Herrigel, *Zen in the Art of Archery*

"I learned everything I know about teaching in the classroom." "Those methods courses were so Mickey Mouse. In fact, that's why they invented the term. 'Mickey Mouse' means 'Methods Course.'" "All that theory . . . [pregnant pause]; there's absolutely no substitute for practice." How many times and in how many ways have I heard from teachers that line?

But there's the other side. I've heard it, too, often from the same person. "I don't know about a program that would send students into classes without a few tricks. Call them 'methods' or call them 'tricks.' You've got to have some." "I've talked to all the young teachers in the building. None of them has anything good to say about their methods courses. But they all admit that they use them." "And you're going to give them a *master's* in teaching with no *methods*?!"

I have not talked to one person in the schools who is not ambivalent about his or her training in methods. No, it's not ambivalence; it's almost always a passionate love-hate. It's enough to make some of them start to think about their "inner child" again and to say things like, "Teachers need a twelve-step program. They need to see themselves in need of recovery from methods" (a true quote). And I hear it popping up in seminars and in casual discussions with you, now that you've tasted several weeks of student teaching. It's enough to make me wonder whether we did you a disservice by not teaching at least a little methods.

I've been able to console myself a little by remembering Don Finkel's lecture on the practical implications of his understanding of Piaget, suggestions that you might take into your student teaching. Don said something like, "The implication is that there is only one thing you have to do to be a good teacher: remain intellectually alive. The schools will conspire to keep you from doing this. But you have to do it. You've got to carve out a space for reflection." And he did say *only*—"the only thing." He said you don't need *any* methods courses, period. You only have to keep your mind alive.

I hear a lot of talk about "just surviving" student teaching. That's not what Don meant by "keeping alive." He meant that in order to learn anything from student teaching you have to (a) have experiences and (b) reflect on them. You can't help but have experiences in your student teaching. But you can find ways *not* to reflect on them. There are few experiences in teaching that you cannot "survive." But if I understood Don correctly, if you focus on surviving experiences, you will surely avoid reflecting on them; by surviving, you will avoid "keeping alive."

When I mention this to some people, they offer some variation on the theme: "Student teaching in itself is where the greatest amount of reflectiveness has happened within me since first entering this program" (another true quote). And then they tell me how their talks with teachers help them think through lesson plans, anticipate difficulties, flesh out strategies, and so on. Or they tell me how valuable the debriefings are. "If only I had. . ." "Next time I will . . ." "I've learned so much from . . ." I would put most of this into a category I would call "the busyness of teaching," the strategizing, the second-guessing, the planning, and so on. These busynesses are all ways in which teachers, both novices and long-timers, avoid reflection.

As I understood Don, reflection involves setting to the side all commonsense understandings of what it might mean for a technique to have "worked." It means setting aside school-based notions of "good" and "bad" work in the classroom. It means not stopping too soon when thinking about a classroom experience that was particularly pleasurable for you and not being too quick to find a reason (let's call it an excuse) for something that was particularly troublesome. It means asking a peculiar question about a particular experience, "*What* did I do as I did that?" To reflect means, for me, answering *that* question courageously. "I made that comment, I think, to make a little joke, to make a transition, to build a little rapport. But in the back Cathy winced. Was my comment humiliating to her? I know that jokes can hurt. Was I, maybe, a little angry with the whole class and did I want to just niggle them a bit? Why did I take on the whole group when it was really those jerks next to Cathy that I was angry with for what they did when . . . ? But maybe I was genuinely interested in building rapport. Why is rapport important to me? How have I justified this interest in 'rapport' in my own philosophy of education?" If you can find a way to do this kind of work, and to do it regularly, rigorously, and honestly, I suspect that you will learn quite a lot about what you can and can't do as a teacher.

I don't know if this kind of work—this hard work of reflection that most theorists say is the essential half of true learning—will make you good teachers. Don said it will. I am willing to take his word, but I can also wait the five or ten years it will take for you to start providing me with your own answers. I should tell you, though, that when I talk to you those several years from now, I really hope you don't tell me, "I learned everything I know about teaching in the classroom."

CHAPTER 23

Reading

Reading can still happen in schools. I am convinced of this because I have seen it, twice.

The first time was in a kindergarten class. Keiko was student teaching there. After lunch, the students were to come back into the room and "read." For some of the students this meant holding books in their laps; others looked at picture books; some sat around as a teacher or a visiting parent read aloud. The schools unashamedly and indiscriminately call so many activities reading. In fact, this "reading time" was designed, so the teacher told me, to give the wee ones in her charge a time to calm down from their time on the playground. "They just need the chance to unwind," she said.

Keiko was so young, so new to her profession, that she did not understand. She had been in the schools for so short a time that she still thought that "reading" meant reading and that reading time was a time to read, really.

Keiko came in from lunch, grabbed a book, sat on the rug in the front of the room and began reading, out loud. Some of the children gathered around her. They listened because children who are not yet well-schooled are still able to recognize reading. They had not yet learned to be embarrassed in the presence of someone interested in a book or excited by words. Keiko read the words and showed she was engaged by the text. "Look at that picture. That guy's all green. Saying that he ate something that didn't agree with him is really an understatement, isn't it?" "I don't like the way she's going about this. I think she's going to be in big trouble." Soon the children joined in. They commented on the characters and the pictures. Keiko responded, "You think so? Could be that he's the bad guy. Could be he's just trying to help and he's a klutz." She didn't shape her responses to some expert's idea of the kindergarten mind. She didn't choose her words from the approved kindergarten lexicon. She was reading.

As Keiko read, she was thinking, and talking back to the book, and interacting with those around her. She showed that reading is not just the decoding of information on the page. She showed that reading is the book's momentary appropriation of one's soul.

Of course, the children did not calm down as they were supposed to do during reading time. Those off in the corners took the books from their laps and put them back on the shelves because they saw, up there on the rug, something real happening, and they became greedy. The group enlarged around Keiko and became feisty, with the author, with the text, with Keiko. Their exchanges were as electric as any that occur on playgrounds. And finally they all had a little difficulty settling in for the math lesson scheduled to begin immediately after the 15-minute reading time because they had been reading.

Before coming to Keiko's class, I had seen what passes for reading in the schools. It happened during almost every observation I made.

During a ninth-grade civics lesson, a teacher said, "The words of the Declaration of Independence always move me. Even as I was reading them out of the textbook again last night, they moved me. I cannot begin to tell you how much they moved me. Well, here, let's just read them. Read them quietly to yourself and see how much they move you. They really move me."

Of course, the only movement that occurred was the silent turning of heads this way and that, in any direction but toward the books. Students looked out the windows or rolled their eyes at their friends, anything to avoid the possibility of actually being moved by words on the page. But that's hardly the students' fault. This teacher was so interested in *telling* the students that these words moved him that he was unable to *show* them that the words moved him. To show students that words are moving would require the teacher to read the words in a moving way (or to teach students how to read so that they might be moved). If this teacher actually read the words, words that were, in this case, originally written to move people to action, everyone might be moved to act, even though they were in a school—better to read in silence.

I don't mean that reading aloud is necessarily better. Reading aloud in the schools seems to lead inevitably to schoolish reading. Anyone can recognize schoolish reading by the machine-like monotone—the cadence of which is broken only by silent, implicit requests for rescue from having to pronounce words of several syllables—that is imposed on even the greatest passages of literature.

I happened to observe a senior English class on the day they were studying "the Bible as literature." The textbook chapter consisted of a three-paragraph introduction to the King James Version of the Bible and two passages—the Twenty-third Psalm and the parable of the prodigal son—followed by questions. ("What is the function of the word 'Yea' in the middle of the psalm?" "What is a parable?") I didn't know they did this anymore, but, sure enough, the teacher selected three students and asked the first to read the first paragraph, the second to read the second, the third to read the third. Then they read the psalm, and then they read the parable. And then they answered the questions. And then they went on to some other piece of literature, something that came a little later than James. The lesson that got taught that day? That reading, even reading the greatest works of literature, is monotonous.

After class I asked our student teacher why he hadn't encouraged the students to read with feeling. "They don't get it." "But if they don't get it, at least you could read it for them, with feeling. Here, how would you read this psalm to them?" He read in a schoolish monotone, but from deeper in his chest and with angst. I reminded him that psalms were hymns of praise. "Could you possibly read it again, with some feeling of praising?" I asked. "Yes," he said. He read it louder.

Schools are not good places for books. At school, books and other reading material get subjected to the "reading process" and become only devices around which students can "enhance reading skills." In the hands of the experts, reading has become something different from what Keiko did with her students around a book that they all found interesting.

For example, experts dissect reading into its constituent parts. And there are many. The Comprehensive Test of Basic Skills, a commonly used standardized test, divides reading into 40 different skills collected into seven "objective statement groups." Thus, a reader is someone who has developed skills in "Visual Recognition, Word Analysis, Vocabulary, Comprehension, Spelling, Language Mechanics, and Language Expression." In each of these areas there are multiple teachable and testable skills. So, among other things, fourth graders are tested to see if they can "identify the meaning of sentences or recall details and other information stated in passages" or "critically assess information to form hypotheses and make predictions and other judgments related to passages" or "identify the correct use of nouns and pronouns." Or—my favorite—they should be able to "identify multimeaning words [whatever that means] by inferring the missing word in sentences."[1] When it becomes reasonable and necessary to ask anyone to read sentences with missing words, we know we are no longer in the realm of reading. But I know that whenever something is dissected into 40 parts, whether it is a frog in biology class or reading in the hands of the educationists, there is not much of the thing itself left at the end of the lesson. Perhaps the monotone of schoolish reading is really a dirge that students sing at the passing of something they thought in their early days they could come to love.

Keiko has not yet faced a parent whose child has performed poorly on these sorts of tests. Many of her students will not score high, or, if they do, it will not be Keiko's fault. That's because Keiko, by conscious and rebellious choice or by unschooled intuition, has decided to show her students what reading can be instead of teaching them what they are supposed to learn. If she persists, she will pay a price. But her students will have the chance to remember the way the discipline of reading vitalized them after their undisciplined and tiring romps on the playground.

I remember the time I left Illich's house near Penn State University with the manuscript of his *In the Vineyard of the Text* in my bag, 126 double-spaced pages, many of them not even full pages because of the many, many footnotes, in a tiny font, at their bottoms. Perfect for the plane ride across the country, I thought. When I landed in Seattle some six hours later I was on page 27, not yet a quarter of the way through Illich's text. Over the next days I completed my first reading of this commentary on Hugh of St. Victor's *Didascalicon,* and I began to understand something when, around page 90, I read that Illich had written this book to introduce his readers to a different way of reading. I began to understand that reading sometimes requires a discipline that even an experienced reader like me is not used to.

When I saw Illich next, some three months later, I apologized for not being ready, even after several readings, to comment on his commentary. He got this wise grin on his face and said simply, "Some of my best readers are in prison." Of course, people in prison have more empty time before them than the mere six hours it takes to get from University Park to Seattle in an extruded aluminum tube moving at 500 mph. Prisoners are sufficiently settled and enough ignored that they might achieve the discipline that real reading requires.

Schools, despite their similarity to prisons, are not good places for reading because schools often expect something from their inmates. If only schools could cultivate the indifference toward students that prisons are mandated to practice with regard to prisoners!

But that brings me to the second time that I saw reading happening in a school.

Late one afternoon in the fall I walked into my son's classroom. Two steps in, I stopped. In six weeks of traveling around the region to observe student teaching in a dozen or so schools, I had not seen anything like what I saw there, so close to home: My son's teacher was at her desk doing her work, and most of the children in the class were at their desks doing their work. The teacher was reading. I knew she was reading because she was as oblivious to my arrival as she was to the various activities occurring around her. She was completely involved in her book, and her indifference to what was happening in her classroom gave the children the chance to work. Some were reading, some were drawing, some were walking around talking to their friends. This was not another instance of "sustained silent reading," that institutional transmogrification of reading where the teacher gets to show off the fact that she too can be quietly interested in a book and where children, again, are encouraged to copy the teacher's actions in their various childish ways. This was something I was able to recognize without knowing any gibberish perpetrated by schools to ensure a nervous public that their children's days are programmatically diverse and interesting. Here, right in the middle of a school, was a bunch of young people doing a bunch of different things. And off to the side was the teacher, reading.

CHAPTER 24

Gimme My Gun, I'm Working on My Self-Esteem

May 8, I'm on the interstate to Tacoma to watch another session of student teaching. I'll be observing a student who, echoing an idealism from thirty years before, wants to teach in the poorer districts in our state. On the radio is a blurb from a convention being held in Seattle: Researchers from something called the Gun Safety Institute somewhere in Ohio "reported today that they have discovered one reason students carry loaded guns at schools—carrying a gun enhances self-esteem." The story to follow, as they put it, nine minutes from now, after the weather.

Self-Esteem

The real headline behind this bulletin has nothing to do with guns. The real headline reads, "Schools Score Success: Self-Esteem Way Up."

It was only about thirty years ago that schools tried hard to teach students math, writing, history, civics, and so on. There were debates about whether other topics—sexuality, for example—ought to be taught, but the debates were about the propriety of this or that subject matter. The debates always had the potential of being substantive.

Around 1970 a number of reports started to suggest that the schools were not doing a very good job at what they conceived of as their primary mission: teaching students matters of substance that children might find useful as they grew older. Some schools tried harder to teach what older people thought younger people should know.

Other schools, the enterprising ones, found other things to do. Many schools decided that if they could convince children (and their parents) that everyone *needs* a high self-esteem, they could step to the side of the embarrassing fact that they were failing to teach math, writing, history, civics, and so on. Forget the fact that "self-esteem" was completely without substance. (No one knew of what one's self-esteem consists and no one knew how to enhance it through teaching.) The self-esteem movement was to be, first, a public relations effort. If people could be convinced that self-esteem was crucial to the living of a good life, the schools could find people to invent the curricula and research the concept later. The schools took the lead in nurturing this new need for self-esteem.

The schools succeeded.

Not only is the importance of self-esteem part of our cultural cant, self-esteem enhancement finds its way easily and routinely into the strategic plans of school districts. Our local district prefaces its plan with a set of fifteen "beliefs." Belief Eleven reads: "Students' self-esteem is important; they must feel valued as human beings and successful as learners."[1]

Christopher Lasch writes, in a review article on "shame," that this word that used to be such a powerful word "has lost its moral resonance." He continues,

> [S]hame, these days, refers to whatever prevents us from "feeling good about ourselves." Disgrace implies a failure to live up to internalized codes of honor. Today it is widely believed that people come to grief when they adopt "society's" standards as their own. They are advised to set their own goals instead of conforming to what others expect of them. Formerly shame was the fate of those whose conduct fell short of cherished ideals. Now that ideals are suspect, it refers only to a loss of self-esteem.[2]

The title of a Gloria Steinem book links "revolution" and "self-esteem."[3] These two words could have not been put together thirty years ago, not even ten years ago. Thirty years ago, as Steinem's work showed us then, politics was a public matter, not a private project of self-enhancement.

A sure sign that the schools have been successful in convincing students that their self-esteem is important is that students now can use their self-esteem as a basis for criticizing the work of their teachers. Zack approached one of our student teachers and asked, "Ms. Ruppert, what did you think of the scripts you had us write." "Honestly?" she asked, for she knew the value of discretion. "Yeah." "I thought they were awful." Zack replied, "Now, Ms. Ruppert, what do you think a comment like that is going to do to my self-esteem?" Ms. Ruppert got zapped by Zack, but that's only because Zack, a suspect student in every other way, had learned his lessons about the importance of self-esteem well. He knew that the schools were more concerned about injuries to his self-esteem than about whether he knew how to write well or calculate or reflect on his present circumstances in light of history.

Schools have heightened our cultural and individual consciousnesses about the importance of self-esteem, but more important for present purposes, they have been wildly successful in building up the self-esteem of their charges. One of Charles Krauthammer's columns begins,

> A standardized math test was given to 13-year olds in six countries last year. Koreans did the best. Americans did the worst, coming in behind Spain,

Britain, Ireland, and Canada. Now the bad news. Besides being shown triangles and equations, the kids were shown the statement "I am good at mathematics." Koreans came in last in this category. Only 23% answered yes. Americans were No. 1, with an impressive 68% in agreement.[4]

Krauthammer's column was titled "Education: Doing Bad and Feeling Good." Students in our schools feel great about themselves and their work, even when their work is of a standard that thirty years ago would have been called "failing."

Krauthammer is old-fashioned enough to conclude, "The pursuit of good feeling in education is a dead end. The way to true self-esteem is through real achievement and real learning."[5] Poor Charles, he writes like a man inclined to examine the alternatives. Far from being a "dead end," the pursuit of good feeling in education has opened up new and unusual possibilities. The young people who responded to the Gun Safety Institute's inquiries found an obvious alternative to gaining self-esteem through the hard work of "real achievement and real learning": they carry guns.

Gimme My Gun

Harborview Medical Center surveyed 11th graders in Seattle and found that 34% said they already have a gun or "could get one in a few days." A local health care magazine commented on this study: "Such reports are 'not an indictment of the schools,' says Dr. Charlie Callahan, author of the Harborview study. They simply reflect what's happening in society at large."[6] But Dr. Callahan is wrong. We know, from the Gun Safety Institute, that many children carry guns to school to enhance their self-esteem,* and we know that the schools have had a heavy hand in teaching children that their self-esteem is very important. Such reports *are* an indictment of the schools—an indictment of their *success*.

When I heard that schoolchildren carried guns so that they would never have to feel bad about themselves when confronted with a difficult situation, so that they would be able to respond positively and effectively to just about any challenge, so that they could keep their fragile egos intact by blowing away teachers and fellow students who did not share Belief Eleven states that they "must feel valued as human beings and successful as learners," I jumped to a logical conclusion. Now, I thought, the schools will see the errors of their ways. They will abandon the self-esteem curricula. They will burn the books and the work sheets. They will cancel all the workshops. They will send the teachers to continuing education programs

---

* A 15-year-old in the Federal Way, Washington, school district was found to be carrying an Uzi in his gym bag. He must have felt especially good about himself.

on teaching matters of substance instead of sending them to sensitivity training sessions. And they will begin this process of undoing the self-esteem movement with an apology. Some elder educationist will, without a doubt, appear on television and say, "Students of America, we are sorry for making you think that you should feel good about yourselves. We have concluded that we really should have stayed the course, difficult though it is, and tried to teach you math, writing, history, civics, and so on. And beginning tomorrow, that is what we will do. And if you feel good about your accomplishments, that will be, from this moment on, your business. We will no longer be concerned with anything but substantive matters."

That didn't happen. Not even the spokesperson for the Gun Safety Institute said, "You see, the real problem is not guns, but all those self-esteem curricula the schools have foisted on us and our children for the last thirty years." No, her reading of her study's results led in a completely different direction. Instead of thinking that we should dismantle institutional interest in self-esteem, her conclusion was that *in addition to teaching students to feel good, schools also need to offer curricula on gun safety.* And even if she didn't say it, I heard, rumbling around behind this report from the convention center something like, "And we at the Gun Safety Institute have just such curricula available for use in your local schools. Call our 800 number. Have your school district's credit card ready. Operators are standing by."

Frankly, the problem has expanded beyond the possibility of a simple apology from the educationists for making our children so concerned about feeling good that they will carry guns to school. There are too many institutions and egos already involved to proceed that logically. The health magazine in which the story "Kids and Guns" appears is published by Group Health Cooperative, an HMO second in size only to Kaiser. Group Health's article urges its readers to work with local law enforcement agencies to set up "neighborhood watch" programs, and it lists local groups devoted to buying guns back from youth, to teaching people how to resolve conflicts without resorting to self-esteem enhancing violence, and, naturally, to providing violence prevention programs for use in the schools (programs that have been pretested in Los Angeles). It will be darned difficult to keep something like gun safety curricula out of the schools when the health care industry, the media, and policy makers have all discovered this problem that the simple addition of yet another new curriculum might help solve.

I suppose that the rest of us, parents and taxpayers, can take some comfort from the likelihood that the National Rifle Association might initiate a grant program to pay for the purchase of the Gun Safety Institute's curricular material so that even the poorest districts can teach their students how to handle their Uzis safely. The NRA might even supply speakers. Research has shown that NRA members feel very good about themselves.

CHAPTER 25

Why I Won't Believe in Developmentalism

"Development" is primarily a concept, or to use an expression from the natural science of Goethe and Lichtenberg, a "way of imagining."

Uwe Pörksen, *Plastickwörter*

"What do you mean you don't believe in developmentalism? It's not a matter of belief."

"I have a friend who's a developmentalist through and through. What I mean is that I won't imagine how he sees things—everything—that he looks at. He sees children developing all the time. I won't. It's like trying to imagine what a fly sees. Seeing children developing can be hard on the imagination. So I refuse to try."

"But children *do* develop."

"You see them doing this?"

"Yeah."

"Proving once again that you can see whatever you believe."

* * *

It is time, once again, to listen to the voice of an expert. This, once again, from an interview on the local "news radio" station: "I studied children in 37 families headed by lesbians. I studied their intellectual development, the development of their sex-role identification, their psychosocial development, and so on. In all important respects, children in these families were indistinguishable from other children."

When anyone, even an expert deluded by her expertise into thinking that she can be helpful to a cause, finds some children *indistinguishable from other children* "in all important respects," we know we are wading in dangerous waters. We must proceed cautiously.

There is nothing inherently wrong with seeing children develop. Jean Piaget adopted a peculiar (but not, for that, bad) parental point of view that allowed him to watch his children carefully, observe the errors they made in their reasoning, figure out the actual "reasoning" that led to these "errors," and then write about the general implications of his observations and inferences. Piaget knew what "development" meant because he made the effort to say, over several decades, precisely what it meant. Perhaps *his* children did develop.

Very quickly, development became a scheme under which all sorts of activities could be studied. Kohlberg studied moral development.[1] A host of people expanded Piagetian thinking into the study of psycho-social development. And, of course, sexuality develops and sex-role identification develops. So many aspects of living develop—at least, all the important ones do—that one can now be a developmentalist without being concerned with or even particularly knowledgeable about some particular aspect of child development.

We are, in fact, well into the second generation of professors of development. Good students like Carol Gilligan and Belenky, et al., respectfully but defiantly take on the first-generation masters to assert that some people develop differently from other people.[2] There are, they say, different stages of development, different orders in which the stages appear, no necessary order to the stages, etc. But these good students of the original developmentalists don't dispute the indisputable fact that everyone develops, at least in all important respects.

The developmentalists are so advanced in their thinking that they can now define "development" in general. Life—the important aspects of it—proceeds in stages, they will tell you. Progress from one stage to another is characterized by a double movement: There is greater differentiation accompanied by greater integration at a higher stage. So they tell us, pointing back to that first great development—the development of "life itself"—the embryo *develops* from that first, undifferentiated cell by generating cells of specialized types (liver cells, brain cells, blood cells, etc.) and integrating them into ever more complicated wholes. Through this differentiation and integration, the embryo *develops*, eventually, into a baby. In exactly the same way, or so they say, the child who makes the classic "conservation of volume" error when the same amounts of liquid are poured into beakers of different radii and reports that the beaker in which the liquid rises to the higher level has more will eventually *develop* in cognition. The concept of "more" will, like that original embryo cell, become differentiated into concepts of "higher" and "more voluminous," among others, and these many versions of "more" will be integrated into a higher-order, more-developed sense of measurement. In exactly the same way, or so they say, the child whose morality is based on the application of a clear rule of "that is right and that is wrong" will eventually develop a sense of morality based on an ability to make sophisticated "judgments in context." In exactly the same way, many things happen to children throughout their development, and they come to be, eventually, grown up—well developed in all important respects.

Uwe Pörksen calls "development" a "plastic word," one of a transnational set of words creating a "new dictatorship of language." He says of the history of "development,"

> The original bold and strong image—in the 17th century one still "developed" scrolls, and from this image the concept of development was originally nourished—has long paled. The word no longer transmits an image; on the contrary, it withdraws images from the historical world. It is an apparently neutral abstraction and describes a process. This meaning is not yet very old. The original active and transitive verb does not become intransitive until about 1800. "A develops B" now become "something develops." The concept of "self-development" comes into use at the same time. I can only hint at this history of the concept . . . : from "development" as an *action*, it changed around 1800 into an *alteration*, whose original cause and object remains unnamed. These alterations—this lies in the nature of the intransitive—often have attributed to them elements of a natural law and also a built-in goal. Development appears as a natural process.[3]

Development came to be something that happened to children. Adults were no longer responsible for the development of their child and, therefore, they were no longer responsible for undertaking all the actions that might be necessary to encourage the young to become worthy of the world they receive as a fact of their birth. Children simply had to wait for development to overcome them. Off to the side might be a fatherly figure not unlike Piaget ready to assess and to infer the reasoning behind developmentally induced errors, but no one in the room would be responsible for actions any more. Assessors replaced teachers and the single abstraction "developmental disability" subsumed both a host of pathological conditions and what used to be called "behaviors" for which one might be held accountable.

The transformation of development into something that children must pass through more or less passively was actually the second stage in the appearance of this new "way of imagining." The first occurred when life was reconceived in terms of "life processes."[4] In the same way that birth became an element in "the birthing process" and death became an element in "dying" (the process),[5] growing up, learning, deciding who one was like and whom one wanted to be like as well as whom one liked, and making mistakes all became elements in the process of development. All of the things children used to do as they lived became elements of a process that happened to them as they proceeded through the aging process.

Conceiving development as a process encourages a certain kind of hubris. "Process," Hannah Arendt shows, stands at the service of *animal laborans*. Once one grasps the particulars of a process, one is led to think in terms of control, of improvement, of efficiencies, of pedagogies. Even natural processes can be helped along by a proper therapist. The Piagetian assessor sent to schools to do developmental checkups now arrives with a new bag of tricks. The alphabet soup of disabilities spawned by developmentalism brings in its tow programs of assistance, not to mention federal and state grants to assist the school that can demonstrate it is burdened with more than its fair share of ADDs, BDs, Title I readers, etc. Programs proliferate and the processes through which children proceed are helped along so that children might follow their optimal life-course trajectories.

The students who happen to get caught in a developmentalist's web of well-meaning programs have a peculiar disability inflicted upon them. When children were just students being taught by a teacher whose authority rested "on his assumption of responsibility for [the] world,"[6] they could always rebel. Students might claim, for example, "This curriculum is not the course that we new people, citizens of the future, ought to follow. We prefer a different course." And such a protest had a chance of being heard if the teacher acted responsibly, as a responsible person does. Now, children developing have no avenue of protest against those who would either observe them or help them. How can they protest against a natural process? The thought of rebelling and protesting against the development of their cognition, the development of their moral sense, the development of their sex role identification or any of the other important respects in which they develop is as absurd as protesting against the differentiation of stomach cells and their integration into the embryo's developing gastrointestinal system. A protest against development cannot be heard by anyone; it can only be noted by an assessor or integrated into a development enhancement plan by a therapist. The children who develop cannot speak their own minds; they can only provide input to those charged with having a professional interest in them.

Because it is silly to protest against development, I simply refuse to believe in developmentalism. That's not to say that young people don't develop. Some of my best friends tell me that they do. I respect my friends, but I refuse to look at children *as if* they are developing. Through my refusal to believe in developmentalism and to see as instructed, I am struggling to reserve for myself the possibility of being able to distinguish among the young, small people around me. At least I want to be able to distinguish them one from the other in *some* important respects.

CHAPTER 26

Halloween
Alison Roth

Halloween is a night unlike any other. When I was a child, it was a night to dress up as something horrible or frightening, stay up later than usual, run around asking for candy, and let loose a bit. We wore our costumes to school, and all the students paraded around the playground at lunch to show them off. We had parties in our classrooms and spent more than one day on art projects associated with this holiday. We could taste something wild about this night, even under the tight reins of strict parents and concerned teachers.

At college I fell under the spell of this night's wildness. One year a friend and I dressed in sheets and went spooking through the library throwing candy at the overly serious students trying their hardest not to acknowledge the power of dark nights. We ran around the campus screaming and cackling—outrageous fun. Another year, another friend, and another costume: We went through the science labs and private study places dressed as swamp creatures with moss in our hair and with dirt and leaves glued to our skin with Karo syrup.

In the mid-seventies the place to celebrate Halloween with abandon was on Polk Street in San Francisco. Outlandishly dressed characters filled the street; there were no cars or buses, just masses of anonymous people. I was there in a gorilla head mask and a tuxedo and blended in fine. Strangers kissed my rubber cheeks and danced me around. Men in drag and in the scantiest of loincloths, women in every imaginable costume all mixed together in a moving throng. It was a good way to enter into the spirit of the night of all souls.

When Christianity met old pagan religion, religion premised in an awe of nature and a reverence for the darker, passionate aspects of human life, it incorporated this pagan reverence by carrying on some rituals of abandon. All Saints Day was preceded by the Night of All Souls—All Hallows' Eve—Halloween. The night was given over to the spirits of the dead. There was a recognition of the need for transcending the ordinary, at least for one night.

Yet, as Georges Bataille writes, "The ridiculous thing about this urge towards transcendence in which concern for the preservation of life is scorned is the almost immediate transition to the wish to organize it in a lasting way."[1] We teachers are proving his point with a vengeance.

I spent nine weeks student teaching in a fifth-grade class. Halloween came on the Thursday of my final week, and we teachers had to make the holiday have as little impact as possible on the way the day went at school. We did not mention it. No art, no costumes, and no party. I was asked not to read students any poetry or stories having to do with this holiday. There was to be no lifting the weight of control from this particular group of children.

At the end of the school day, my supervising teacher conducted one of his friendly discussions with the class and asked them how they felt about the day. One child remarked that he had forgotten it was Halloween. Others, when prompted, happily interjected that they had enjoyed being "in control" and proceeding through the day in a normal, orderly way.

After getting from the children this support for his plan to "make it through Halloween smoothly," the teacher began soliciting comments on how the children were planning to behave during the night. Not a single child expressed any desire to run wild, to let loose, to celebrate the dark night. All told of how much better they felt when they and their friends remained "in control." They had nothing to be frightened of, except the possibility that someone might tempt them to take off this cloak of domesticity.

What of the deliciousness of a little bit of fear? What about fun? What about play? What about the illusion that the world is a rational place? What about the fact that we hammer in the notion that the world is not safe for children unless they behave in the circumscribed ways that we tell them create safety? Secretly I hoped, after contributing to their enforced docility that day, that once these students left the classroom they would not remain totally convinced of their need to be in control, that they would shed the cloak with their school clothes.

I do not know what they did on that night. The next day they brought their candy to school, but they did not tell any stories, and I suspect their evenings were tame. Not much to talk about.

The school probably will soon recognize that it has to teach these children how to play. Having stripped them of every impulse to wildness, the school will have to feed it back to them, and when such food proves unpalatable, the schools will blame the students for lacking creativity. Pablum instead of meat. Values instead of religion. Art becomes a school project that looks nice on the refrigerator door. And creativity becomes a project for psychologists to study. Wild.

CHAPTER 27

Saying vs. Knowing: A Sermon

Jeremiah 1:4-10
Luke 4:21-30

This is higher-education Sunday. I am employed by one of the local institutions of higher education and it is my pleasure to speak about that place—that *kind* of place—where I spend some of my time.

People look to our universities and colleges for a lot. Some people think that higher education should train youth for the world they will enter. Some especially hysterical people think that we in the academy should take on the problem of training people to the point where we, the universities and colleges, are helping out with economic development and long-term prosperity and competing with Japan. The demand that we train anybody for anything, especially for effective participation in the economy, is a very easy demand for us in the academy to mumble around: We realize, as probably most of you realize, that almost everyone in higher education is especially unsuited for training youth to do anything. So we mumble when some student looks to us for training, and we send the president to mumble to the legislature when they, our representatives in the prevailing hysteria, suggest that we start training people to do something in particular.

Some people look to universities and colleges as a source of knowledge. This expectation is more difficult to head off because there are significant numbers of my colleagues in higher education who believe that we are in the business of knowledge and that we can actually deliver knowledge to those who want it. I don't, and I wish those who keep expecting knowledge to come from the universities would just stop.

And that is my topic: If it is knowledge you want, please don't go to college or to my college—at least to my *ideal* college—looking for it. The colleges and universities, in my view, are not there for knowledge; they have an altogether different purpose, which I will get to, but let me take a couple of swipes at what we call "knowledge" itself, first.

There is a telling and instructive line near the end of E. L. Doctorow's *Billy Bathgate*. Billy, after having grown up with gangsters, hides in a closet in Dutch's hospital room as Dutch, the *capo* of the gang and Billy's father figure, is dying. Dutch rants through his deathbed delirium and Billy listens.

Finally Billy realizes that he understands where Dutch has hidden all his wealth. Then Billy says this: "So I knew everything, and everything brings with it an exacting discretion, I went back to school to stay."[1]

This line gave me an idea for an admissions test for college. The first question would be, "Do you know anything yet?" It wouldn't matter how you answered this question because it would branch and then we'd see if you would get in. If you said "Yes, I know something," then you would answer the question, "Well then, do you know everything?" If you answered yes to that, you'd get into college and you'd get to stay as long as you liked. If you said "No, I don't know everything" (after admitting that you know something), you would be mercilessly rejected for admission. If, in response to the first question, you said, "No, I don't know anything yet," then, on the other branch, you would have to answer the question, "Do you expect to know anything as a direct result of going to this college?" If you said "No, I don't expect to know anything," you'd get in and be given a scholarship because you would be the best of students; if you said you did have expectations for gaining knowledge, you'd be rejected.

I am not opposed to knowledge, and I am the first to listen very carefully when someone claims to have it. But I am cautious around it. One of the things I have learned from studies of history is the extraordinary mischief done by people who claim to know, the violence done by those who rush ahead thoughtlessly once they think they know something. (I will only mention in passing that I have written a book that is, in large part, about the people who built the first atomic bombs.) The Old Testament reading begins, "Before I formed you in the womb, I *knew* you" (Jer. 1:5). I think it is fine for God to claim knowledge. For the rest of us, we are told in Micah (6:8) what the Lord requires of us: not that we come to know anything, but that we seek justice, love kindness, and walk humbly with our God. My own view is that a certain cautiousness about claiming knowledge, even about seeking knowledge, is part of walking humbly with my God.

The rest of the reading from Jeremiah suggests what we can do instead of seeking knowledge or claiming to know. Jeremiah, a descendant of a banished priest, first speaks out of seeming humility: "Behold, I do not know how to speak for I am only a youth" (1:6). The Lord replies, "Do not say, 'I am only a youth,' for to all to whom I send you you shall go, and whatever I command you you shall speak" (1:7). If we should not presume to know, that does not keep us from speaking; just because we cannot have knowledge does not mean that we should cease saying what we see. In fact, as a professor in an institution of higher education, that is what I think is my one and only calling: to say what I see, to do so publicly, to do so carefully, to do so as precisely as I can, and then wait for others to speak back, to wait for them to say what they see also.

Last Sunday a review of a new biography of Niels Bohr, one of the men whose work I studied as I wrote about the building of the bomb, reminded me that Bohr's great philosophical contribution was to recognize that science is not about what we can *know* about nature. "It is wrong," Bohr said, "to think that the task of physics is to find out how nature *is*. Physics concerns what we can *say* about nature." Bohr was perhaps the first in physics to recognize that if we are to grasp anything about nature, we must say what we see and, more important, we should expect what any one of us says to be partial, incomplete, tentative, probabilistic, even contradictory to what others see. It is only, Bohr said, in the complementarity of contradictory descriptions that we have a chance of coming to understand anything. Hence we must say, for example, that light behaves like both a particle and a wave—contradictory descriptions of light—if we are to be able to describe the behavior as best we can.

The one thing that a university can responsibly do is provide a place where thoughtful and learned people can say, in the presence of other thoughtful and learned people, what they see. The university can be a place that allows people who see things differently to speak to one another. It can be a place where people can enter into careful, deliberate conversations. Michael Oakeshott, a British educator, says,

> In a conversation the participants are not engaged in an inquiry or a debate; there is no "truth" to be discovered, no proposition to be proved, no conclusion sought. They are not concerned to inform, or to refute one another, and therefore the cogency of their utterance does not depend upon their all speaking in the same idiom; they may differ without disagreeing.[2]

It sounds simple; perhaps it is much too simple an activity on which to spend so much of the public purse. But if you have read the popular press reports about the state of the university today, you know that it is very difficult for people even there to enter into such things as conversations where people may simply "differ without disagreeing."

I am quick to say that I think Oakeshott's idea conveys much too polite an understanding of conversation. Conversations—serious conversations of the sort he is describing—are politically volatile and are to be sought out precisely because they might change things fundamentally, in ways one can never anticipate. Martin Buber tells the story of meeting with a group of people of several faiths on Easter, 1914. He writes, "Some men from different European countries had met in an undefined presentiment of the catastrophe, in order to make preparations for an attempt to establish a supra-national authority." The men made a list of others who would constitute the core of a public initiative. Finally, with the list complete, one man spoke to say that he thought there were too many Jews on the list. Buber writes,

> Obstinate Jew that I am, I protested against the protest. I no longer know how from that I came to speak of Jesus and to say that we Jews knew him from within, in the impulses and stirrings of his Jewish being, in a way that remains inaccessible to the peoples submissive to him. "In a way that remains inaccessible to you"—so I directly addressed the former clergyman. He stood up, I too stood, we looked into the heart of one another's eyes. "It is gone," he said, and before everyone we gave one another the kiss of brotherhood.

> The discussion of the situation between Jews and Christians had been transformed into a bond between Christian and Jew. In this transformation dialogue was fulfilled. Opinions were gone, in a bodily way the factual took place.[3]

Saying what one sees, then having another say what he sees, having each one listen obediently to the other, mutually recognizing that each sees in a way that is inaccessible to the other—this is a situation that often leads to war. It can lead to exclusion. Remember what happened to Jesus in the synagogue, according to Luke (4:21–30): As the power of his message sank in, all those in the synagogue who had talked casually and politely about the "graciousness of his words" were eventually "filled with wrath." They wanted to throw him from the hill. Jesus, "passing through the midst of them, went away." But as Buber's story shows, saying, listening, and accepting that others see what is unacceptable to us is also a situation that can lead to an embrace in brotherhood by which everyone and, potentially, everything is transformed.

I have been speaking principally of the academy where I spend a lot of my time. But nothing I have said is essential only to the academy. Saying what you see and listening obediently when others say what they see is not the privileged work of colleges and universities. It is possible to engage in this kind of behavior anywhere, even in the church.

Many of you know that I am serving on the study committee on Resolution 90-06, the resolution concerning churches that are open and affirming of gay, lesbian, and bisexual people. Many people told the committee that we should not even be talking about this issue in the church. In fact, there is no better way to impoverish the church than by refusing to speak about what we see in our midst, than by refusing to speak conscientiously about issues that well-meaning people, people who seem to understand things in a way inaccessible to me, bring before us out of their experience. But we, those on the committee at least, have gotten to the point where we are talking about the issue. And I can tell you, from my experience there, that I begin to appreciate the church more fully when people who see the world in absolutely incomparable ways sit at a table together and begin to speak to one another about what they see. It is only when I listen to my sisters who are on the committee and who identify themselves as lesbians speak about their lives, lives I cannot ever hope to know, and when I listen to my brother who appeals at every turn to a literal interpretation of biblical text, and when I listen to the tangle into which others get because they are filled with emotions and opinions that, to me, are unknowably contradictory—it is in that company that I come to appreciate what it means to accept the word of another on faith, something that requires me to renounce any impulse to know the other fully, something that requires me to confront the ungraspable mystery of the other.

We are a people created of the spoken word of God. We are baptized in the word and, through the traditional function of the church, we are, like Jeremiah, called to prophecy. By tradition we are people of the book, but we are not slaves of the book. Ours is a noble, interpretive tradition in which it is the duty of each of us to construct our utterances according to the rabbinical formula, "It is written that . . . , but I *say* unto you . . ." It is a tradition in which those who accept their duty to say what they see are called, very simply, teachers.

CHAPTER 28

Experts and Critics and the "Eco-cratic Discourse"

"In any case," said the Frenchman, "it is not systems but their excesses that dehumanize history."

Gabriel García Márquez, *The General in His Labyrinth*

My son, tired from football practice, sent me back to his classroom to retrieve his coat. "It's in the first closet right inside the door. The closet has a picture of a globe and some 'Save the Earth' things all over it." Sure enough, the coat was there, right behind the earth.

Saving the earth is very big in schools. It's right up there with enhancing self-esteem. Almost every classroom has the obligatory picture of the earth seen from space. And inevitably there's a lesson on things— always "simple things" and usually 50 of them—that the students can do to and/or for the environment to save the earth. Frankly, I don't mind this sort of instruction because most of the students know it has as much to do with their immediate lives as their math. Enduring these lessons is easy because they often involve field trips or visits from guest experts (who sometimes bring real things, like an eagle, to class). They also give students another opportunity to pester their parents ("Mom, why don't you clean the stove so the reflectors under the heating elements can reflect the heat?" or "Dad, have you put aerators on the faucets yet?"). But, like most of what schools do, these lessons are harmless. A picture of the globe with some "Save the Earth" things is a fine way to distinguish one closet from another.

What concerns me is the possibility that our children may someday run into a teacher who sees through the silliness of this sort of globalism and who is thoughtfully critical of naive environmentalism, for just below the surface of the purchasable globalism on display in most classrooms is a set of sophistications of thought that have real and dangerous implications for life together. If anyone in the schools ever thinks beyond those glossy pictures of the earth from space, I will be the first to become concerned. Just below the surface of naive globalism is a thought that perhaps no one should be thinking. I'm wondering if I shouldn't be more afraid of the good and able criticism than I am of the ardent eco-experts.

To call the mentality that leads to the indiscriminate display of the earth seen from space "naive globalism" or "naive environmentalism" is not to say that it comes to us from naive, marginalized people. This, for example, is from the chairman's foreword to a report of the World Commission on Environment and Development. The report was titled *Our Common Future*:

> Perhaps our most urgent task today is to persuade nations of the need to return to multilateralism. . . . The challenge of finding sustainable development paths ought to provide the impetus—indeed the imperative—for a renewed search for multilateral solutions and a restructured international economic system of co-operation. These challenges cut across the divides of national sovereignty, of limited strategies for economic gain, and of separated disciplines of science.
>
> After a decade and a half of a standstill or even deterioration in global co-operation, I believe the time has come for higher expectations, for common goals pursued together, for an increased political will to address our common future.[1]

Five years after Gro Harlem Brundtland penned these words, it is hard to tell whether the principal effect of *Our Common Future* has been to bring about more global cooperation or to generate more global criticism of those who would urge us to think using terms like "our common future." And it is hard to tell whether the depersonalized, high abstractions of "multilateralism" and "cooperation" or the hyper-humanized counter-positions are more dangerous.

Frankly, I think it is neither the call for cooperation nor the explosion of criticism such a call always generates but the concatenation of the two that should concern us. Around the modern move to turn the environment into a fetish and the globe into an icon, the agonistic conversation being enacted between the environmental experts and the expert eco-critics has created a common "eco-cratic discourse." It is this discourse that makes it difficult for the rest of us to think for ourselves.

The eco-cratic discourse, as formulated by the experts and their critics, is cast in terms of systems thinking. The globe is a system that supports all its subsystems that support Hannah Arendt's "highest value," life itself. To understand what the eco-experts and the expert eco-critics have in common, one must understand systems thinking.

Ervin Laslo's introduction to systems theory is titled, instructively, *A Systems View of the World*. Systems thinking is offered as a corrective to the kind of vision that apprehends the complexity of a thing by seeing it, as Descartes taught the West to do, in terms of the simple parts that compose it and in terms of the simple relations that drive it. To see the world from a systems perspective, one must see connectedness instead of boundaries and irreducible organization instead of well-articulated, interacting parts. Systems thinking gathers everything together without discrimination or prejudice. It allows for the appearance of experts in everything, men like García Márquez's Frenchman, a man who had "an insatiable need to demonstrate . . . his universal knowledge regarding the enigmas of this life and the next."[2] And it allows for the excessiveness against which the Frenchman warned. It is not systems thinking alone that should be of principal concern; it is the sophistications of thought to which it can lead that threaten, as he put it, to "dehumanize history."

Some Signs of (Subtle and Sophisticated) Systems Thinking

I came to appreciate the dehumanizing effects of subtle and sophisticated systems thinking by studying the system that produced the first atomic bombs.[3] Even though saving the earth seems to be on the opposite end of the moral spectrum from building those bombs, it may be useful to become aware of the effects of a mentality—systems thinking—common to both. We can see the signs of sophisticated systems thinking emerging out of the eco-cratic discourse. What are these signs?

➤ Standards Become Merely Topics for Cynical Commentary
Don Worster, a historian of ecology at the University of Kansas, says that he asked a group of ecologists a "critical question": "What is a healthy ecosystem?" Their inability even to define an ecosystem was proof, Worster says, of the intellectual poverty of all the "systems talk." But it is possible that Worster's experts were stumped by his adjective, "healthy."

Sophisticated systems thinkers know that while systems might be described, they cannot be judged by simple standards such as "healthy." They are just too complex to admit simple assessments.

Indeed, in the institutional arena devoted to concerns about health, doctors gave up trying to organize their work around a concept like health decades ago. Medicine now tries to "help patients realize their unique potentials," to "optimize life experiences along life-course trajectories." This kind of rhetoric, which dominates contemporary medical discourse, enables action even without the old-time, commonsense standards like medicine had in that word "healthy" by which to judge those actions.[4] Indeed, having standards would limit the scope of possible action by placing some actions out of bounds. If one can affect a little cynicism with respect to any standard, there are no limits to what one can do. And cynicism is just what one gets from the potent combination of, on the one hand, experts knowing that simple standards are untenable and, on the other, critics laughing at the experts who can't answer simple, so-called "critical questions" like, "What is a healthy ecosystem?"

Systems thinking is encompassing and leaves no outside from which to develop standards according to which something can be judged. So it is not surprising to hear the eco-critics saying that a term like "sustainable," so central to Chairman Brundtland's work, has no real meaning. "Sustainable," the expert critics tell us, must be kept around only because of its effectiveness in mobilizing populations to political action (because we live, they tell us, in democracies in which people must be mobilized to meet the threats that they don't understand might threaten them) even though the experts can agree only on the fact that they cannot agree on the meaning of this term. By claiming that a word like "sustainable" can have viable utility only as a rallying cry, other words like "democracy" are also eviscerated. What remains when words like these are no longer available for use in civic discussion is only the cynicism with which they are dismissed. And cynicism is hardly a firm foundation for political discourse and action.

➤ Diversity Becomes a Scarce Resource
The Ecologist, in an effort to critically counter *Our Common Future*, proposed to publish a report called "Whose Common Future?" for the Rio eco-summit. The report will look to the "local people," not to multilateral cooperation, for redemption. The report to be written, we are told, "will portray clearly the vitality, innovativeness, and dynamism of local people in meeting the challenge of the environmental crisis" and will "document how they are actively seeking solutions themselves and what their solutions are."[5]

I do not personally know of any local people anywhere who think of themselves as "meeting the challenge of the environmental crisis." Most local people are, at least, more modest than that. But I do know that this new approach, exemplified by *The Ecologist*'s interest in the local people, is right in line with so many other developments of our day that come under the heading of *making diversity into a scarce resource*. People, cultures, thought, and actions become important not because *they are* but for what they might represent. Everyone and everything are no longer worthwhile but are, instead, valuable for their possible contribution to diversity. Diversity becomes the basis for a new, sophisticated colonization of the mind, of people, of nations, of regions. Diversity is a scarce resource.

The Ecologist's proposal says, "[Part 2] will argue that there is no need to 'invent' alternatives: they already exist." One principle of systems thinking is that there is rarely a need anymore to invent new knowledge; all the knowledge that one would ever need exists already in any system with sufficient diversity. The job of the system manager, of which breed I count Oppenheimer among the first, is to mobilize existing knowledge. And one does this by respecting and nurturing diversity, eccentricity, individuality, local knowledge, and so forth. Hence it is not surprising, if one understands systems thinking, to see now the eco-critics' turn toward celebrating the diversity of the local people and their successes vis-à-vis the environmental crisis. We preserve diversity (of seed stock, of semen and ova) in the cryogenic labs of private corporations because it—diversity—is valuable. *The Ecologist* will preserve the diversity of wisdom of local people everywhere in their report because their diversity is valuable too.

➤ People Become Resources; Everyone Becomes "Dead but Real"
The Ecologist's proposed report anticipates one of the risks of taking an interest in the diverse resources of the local people everywhere and of bringing their knowledge together so comprehensively in a report. Part 2— the part that will portray the vitality, etc., of the local people—we are told, "is not to produce a dry, technical compendium of alternatives." The risk in becoming part of a system, which *The Ecologist* seems to anticipate intuitively, is to enter a new category: "dead but real."

The term "dead but real" comes from a marketing manager at Weyerhauser who was describing some new plants that the company was marketing for use in modern offices filled with artificial air and light. The plants, he said, look real and smell real because they are made from real plants, but they metabolize nothing. When asked to describe them, Stephen Barger said, "They are not live, not artificial, but in between. It is a new category. Dead but real."[6]

The local people who lend their experiences to this comprehensive report stand at risk of having their stories become part of a "dry, technical compendium of alternatives." Unless the stories of the locals find their ways into the hands of a good writer well cautioned far in advance, their vitality, dynamism, and innovativeness might not be well portrayed. And it is only if people can be seen as contributing stories of redemption to the scarce resource of diversity that they will be valued at all in these times.[7] And if they go unvalued, someone may notice that all of one's efforts are being devoted to making everything *seem* vital, dynamic, and innovative. At that point, the very best the local people can hope for is to be put to sleep or stored in a deep freeze so that they might possibly contribute to diversity sometime in the future when their stories are deemed less dry and technical, or more "alternative."

Hans Achterhuis talks about the history of the concept of "nature as enemy," our collective Western history since the time of our conceptual "separation from nature."[8] I would suggest that somewhere in that two-hundred-year history there was a point where human beings came to see themselves as part of this "enemy" that "nature" has become. We are today in the peculiar situation of being at war with ourselves. (And this applies more broadly than just to the farmers in Holland who, Achterhuis tells us, are at war with themselves over the new EEC regulations that will require a reduction of their numbers by 40%.) We are in the very peculiar position of not just being torn away from nature, but of being torn away from ourselves, of being in a position not to see or otherwise sense our roles in cause-and-effect relations in the places we live[9]—dead but real.

➤ Professional Philosophy Becomes Essential
When all standards come under the sway of cynicism and when people become "dead but real" resources in a battle to preserve diversity (instead of being, say, consolations for being alive), new and very sophisticated philosophical justifications for action become essential. They are already appearing in the literature of the expert eco-critics.

Gary Snyder, an old poet and a new ecology guru, says he organizes his thinking about ecology around "a balance between cosmopolitan pluralism and deep local consciousness."[10] Wolfgang Sachs argues for "cosmopolitan localism."[11] Once expert systems thinking creates the "world" as a manageable or doctorable entity and once the expert critics create the "local people" as an aspect of the scarce resource of "diversity," sophisticated philosophy is necessary to join these elements in a relationship of complementarity. It requires a form of thinking well beyond common sense to join globalistic concerns with a valorization of the local. As Robert Oppenheimer tried to tell us some 40 years ago, science has voided common sense and that we require professional philosophy to show us how to think to justify all our modern undertakings.[12]

In these times and under the rise of systems thinking, ethics will be a growth industry. In a situation where there are no standards of judgment that cannot be cynically dismissed and in which systems can only be managed but not controlled, ethics will offer up intellectual and moral rationales for action. Ethics becomes a cheap political activity, a way of justifying the drawing of the lines and the making of the choices that the critics, as well as the experts, tell us will have to be drawn and made. We would do well to think about Ch. von Weizsäcker's prediction that ethics will become as much an object of idolization as technical ability in these times. And we should think about what happens to the "local people" whom we rush to value if they find themselves unable to participate in sophisticated, professionalized thought.

Be Careful about What You Think

I once taught with a woman from one of the tribes of the Iroquois Confederation. She tells me that members of her tribe try to be collectively careful about what they choose to think about. She says that they think about only those things that they want to bring about and, if they decide to think about something, that means they have decided to deal with the object of their thought completely, no matter how many generations it might take.

Her words are a caution to those who might be inclined to think things better left unthought.

This caution to be careful about what you think receives a dark echo in the first public report of Robert Oppenheimer following the end of the war with Japan. He said, "If there was any great surprise in [the] first explosion it lay not in any great new discovery. It lay rather in the fact that what happened was so like what we thought would happen."[13] Just thinking things together by writing an equation on the board or making a model in a computer can have effects. I think we should exercise a little caution in even thinking about joining everything together—including all the ideas and experiences of all the local people everywhere—in any way, in any respect, under any rubric, no matter how humane it may sound, no matter how philosophically sophisticated the rationale.

I recall a rancher in northern California. His name is Bo. One afternoon, he told my son an old story about some boys who stole some beans from a garden some 15 miles from his place and how, when the rancher there appeared with a gun, the boys ran the whole 15 miles back. Then he told John that when he recently walked that same path he had been able to see how the land had been changed by fencing and grazing. Then he told my son about the last 100 years of water use on his ranch, including how the gold rush affected "his" water, and about how he was sitting now with the local water board to think about water use in the area for the next 100 years.

As I listened, I immediately associated Bo's stories with two "dimensions of living" I had read about in the literature that appeals to those inclined to be thoughtful eco-critics: (1) a circle with a radius of 22 kilometers (about 14 miles) that Ivan Illich calls a "Kohr" to honor Leopold Kohr and that is, many seem to agree, the geographical area that one person can actually come to know and care about over time; and (2) Elise Boulding's planning unit of the 200-year present, a unit of time extending 100 years into the past and 100 years into the future. I said to myself, and to other ecologists, academics, and scientists who would listen, how ecologically sensitive Bo seemed and how smart Bo was to live within these academically respected ecological dimensions without ever having been schooled to know about, much less live within, them. He was only one mile off from a Kohr and he was right on the dimensionality of Boulding's present. Yes, how smart Bo was, we all agreed. A fine example of a small-is-beautiful or appropriate-is-just-right critic, we noted.

But then it occurred to me that the only "smart" person party to this encounter between Bo, my son, and me was me.

Bo—a person who finally agreed that he was an old timer because, as he put it, "All the others *I* knew as old-timers are dead"—was only doing what he always did: He was contending with the situation as it presented itself to him. He was well aware (and he told other stories to make this point) that if you make a mistake with the water or the soil or the plants on the ranch, the ranch makes you pay for your mistake, but most of the time the price, even over the long term, is not very high. You just continue on: contend and pay.

It only falls to the well-schooled few, I finally realized, to think together the many ways many different people contend and pay into such things as "dimensions for living" or some such pretentious phrase as I used in order to represent Bo's stories. Bo strikes me now as a person who is trying only to live well until the time when other people are the old-timers of the area. He is not contributing to diversity or thinking in terms of Kohrs or 200-year presents or anything else. He was, on this day, simply filling part of the afternoon by telling stories to a young boy who was, for a few days, in this old man's company and without television. Bo's mistake, if I may speak this way, was to tell his stories within the hearing of a well-schooled person—yours truly—who would be so "smart" as to think him to be a representative of the natural wisdom of local people everywhere, and not just Bo.

I don't think there is much chance to escape the expansion of systems thinking, at least the sophisticated variety that wants to nurture diversity and mobilize it under comprehensive approaches that will help initiate and strengthen local movements for change. Modern systems are too good to leave much room for escape. It is very difficult today, in the face of so many good and smart people so concerned about the welfare of everyone and the protection of everything, to remember who we are and to resist becoming a dead but real example of a solution to a global crisis, or some such thing, but it may be possible.

Gary Snyder opens his *The Practice of the Wild* by recounting a visit he made, along with a friend ("a student of native California literature and language"), to an old Indian in the hills of the Sierra Nevada, coincidentally very near Bo's ranch. After some small talk, Snyder's friend proudly announced the reason for the visit. "Louie," he said, "I have found another person who speaks Nisenan," a native language spoken at that time by two or, maybe, three people. In the name of preserving diversity and respecting a dying culture, this well-meaning young man had sought out another speaker so that the two old people could speak, probably into a tape recorder, perhaps on video, so that a soon-to-be-dead language might be preserved in the audio and video collections of a local university. "'Who?' Louie asked. He told her name . . . [and he—Snyder's friend, the expert—said], 'She lives back of Oroville. I can bring her here, and you two can speak.' 'I know her from way back,' Louie said. 'She wouldn't want to come over here. I don't think I should see her. Besides, her family and mine never did get along.'"

Snyder comments,

> Here was a man who would not let the mere threat of cultural extinction stand in the way of his (and her) values. . . . Louie and his fellow Nisenan had more important business with each other than conversations. I think that he saw it as a matter of keeping their dignity, their pride, and their own ways—regardless of what straits they had fallen upon—until the end.[14]

I would put it this way: Louie seems indifferent to the progress of systems thinking and the "help" that it brings to a world in need. But he also seems positively uninterested in making a contribution to the enhancement of the scarce resource of cultural diversity. In his polite way, he seems insistent on not becoming a datum for this no-doubt-smart student of literature and language. In his own way, he seems a man who will probably remember who he is. He seems a man unlikely ever to enter that new category of "dead but real." Saying no to being helped to contribute to diversity and saying no to global cooperation, especially when so much is at stake, is, I suspect, very difficult. But it is possible.

I know it is possible to refuse to participate in the eco-cratic discourse because both Louie and Bo did just that. But both Louie and Bo have an advantage over our children: Neither of them went to the schools that are just now learning how to talk about and value the environment.

CHAPTER 29

No Futures, Please, These Are Our Children

I don't know which memories and which thoughts nightly swell in our dreams. I dare not ask for information, since I, too, had rather be an optimist. But sometimes I imagine that at least nightly we think of our dead or we remember the poems we once loved.

Hannah Arendt, "We Refugees"

If schools would forget the future, they would have a chance of educating our children. As it is, schools will probably keep teaching our children to forget how to remember who they are, where they came from, and where they stand now.

The new superintendent of the local schools accepted our invitation to talk to the first class of students in the Master in Teaching Program. One of the first things a new superintendent does, he told the students, is to rethink the mission of the schools. A superintendent has to have a vision, and in the four months since he had been appointed, he had done his duty and had come up with one. The vision statement he'd like to think about, he said, was "Helping kids invent their lives."

As he uttered his vision, the superintendent looked at the floor and sort of kicked at the carpet—an "aw shucks" kind of gesture. I liked it. Here's a guy, I thought to myself, who will satisfy parents' and school board members' need for hucksterism and hype, but at least he has the good sense to be embarrassed. He'll be able to make the chamber of commerce-Rotary-Elks-League of Women Voters lunch circuit, leave a little dollop of a speech about "Helping kids invent their lives" and still be able to look carefully at what goes on in the public schools. Here is a man, I thought, who knows that true visions are not for the faint of heart or bureaucrats; he probably knows that people who presume upon the future are often locked up until they forgo their mad ravings. He was treading cautiously and I liked him.

Two years later there came in the mail a glossy, folded brochure hardly distinguishable from the piles of vote-for-me political pleas that arrived during this fall's election season. On the cover and bannered across the side was: "Olympia School District Strategic Plan." In the middle of the cover and across the back was: *"Helping kids invent their lives."* The superintendent had taken himself seriously!

In the body of the brochure I learned how this man who had seemed so promising had been spending a lot of his time: He had been forming committees, converting his vision into "Visionary Goals" (six of them), communicating throughout the community, soliciting support and input, receiving feedback, touching base, formulating "Target Objectives and Action Plans," and, finally, getting his communications director to design this brochure and send it to me, Residential Postal Customer.

I read the brochure closely. It contains not one fact, not one idea, not one acknowledgment of one aspect of our current situation. The whole thing is written in the future tense.* Even the "parameters," a term that most planners use to mean something like "constraints" and where one expects to find at least a bow toward the reality of one's situation, are framed with an orientation absolutely toward the future.** The plan's passive voice construction ensures that no one will think that anyone is responsible for the future, except maybe the plan itself. And while the superintendent is pleased, he writes, to introduce the plan, the plan does not even have an author; instead, it emerged from a process:

> The Strategic Planning Committee was comprised of 38 members who wrote the Belief Statements, Mission Statement, Parameters and Visionary Goals. From there, 65 individuals worked in six Visionary Goal Subcommittees to formulate the Target Objectives and Action Plans. Prior to presenting the plan to the Board of Directors, a nine-member writing committee reviewed and refined the plan. In an effort to receive additional input on the plan, two community forums were held by the Board of Directors and a parental survey based on the Strategic Plan was developed and distributed. In all, over 1,300 community members provided feedback to the Strategic Plan.[1]

The only way to have so many people so successfully involved in something is to make sure that they don't deal with anything real. Let them, instead, come to a consensus about the constraints they are willing to permit the bureaucrats to place on the future. Don't ask them to think about how; encourage them think ahead.

Chip Conquest, a certified teacher who works his farm in Vermont and teaches sometimes in the local schools, has reflected on the utility—the utility *to the schools*—of being concerned only about the future. He writes,

---

* And the bureaucratic banality of the future proposed in this brochure is certainly stunning, if hardly surprising. See "Visionary Goals" at the end of this essay.

** See "Parameters" at the end of this essay.

> Schools . . . are in the business of *general preparation*. School's job, as
> many educators see it, is to prepare students for their futures. . . . Schools try
> to prepare students by providing a well rounded curriculum that will keep
> open all the possibilities of the future. This means, of course, that they don't
> have the time or the inclination to pursue the questions, the complexity, the
> details of a specific thing—of a real thing.[2]

By being allowed, by public complacency, to be concerned only about the
future, schools are able to teach nothing that is important at the same time
that they take as their challenge anything that pops up over the cultural
horizon and announces itself as the latest social problem. So schools jump
headlong into the war on drugs; they invite the police into their classrooms;
they fret over policy issues like whether to put dopers out on the street or to
set up a special cell in the school for those who need special help living
their chemically challenged lives (where not even a D.A.R.E. cop, much
less an everyday teacher, would dare to try to teach). The schools teach
children "drug resistance skills," but they steadfastly refuse to teach them
about the particularities and the specifics of drugs, the kinds you buy on the
street or the other kinds, like Valium or Halcyon, that find their way through
legal routes into most American homes. Or schools get terribly concerned
about the state of the American family and prospects for the American
future implied by the tired, the huddled, and the haggard that they see
coming through the schools' doors every morning. But teachers and schools
will spend more time lobbying for immunity from prosecution for reporting
cases of abuse than they will spend demanding living wages for everyone or
studying contemporary economic reports that show, among other things,
that the gap between the rich and the poor is worse now than at any other
time since 1929. Schools release themselves from the hard work of pursuing
"the questions, the complexity, the details of a specific thing," from the hard
work of making critical assessments of the reality of our contemporary
situation, by taking as their task the making of a better future.

Chip Conquest contrasts the general preparation pursued by the schools
to the particularity of preparation that apprentices received under their
masters. He writes,

> The apprentice knew he would have hard work to do, that he would have
> real and increasing responsibilities, and that when the term of the
> apprenticeship was up he would know how to do his work. There was no
> pretense by either the apprentice or the master that the former was being
> prepared for all the possibilities of the future. . . . The apprentice simply
> learned his work by doing it, more and more of it, with less and less
> instruction and supervision. The master's teaching was an extension of his
> own work, which he would be doing anyway, with or without a "student." He
> could teach about something real because he was teaching something
> particular.[3]

If the apprentices had any future at all, it was simply as masters of their craft. Apprentices who were dreamers might look forward to the regard of their community, but I suspect that apprentices who looked forward at all saw only the reality of their situation: another day of hard work—"more and more of it, with less and less instruction and supervision"—as their bodies and minds slowly became suited to the real work they would do.

Anyone who has been an apprentice, or who seriously reflects on the possibility, will immediately appreciate the absurdity of entering an institution that proposes to make people ready for anything, that has as a visionary goal "prepar[ing] each student to be a lifelong learner and to function successfully in a diverse and changing society." There are no masters of that task, except perhaps someone like Tom Wolfe's protagonist who fancies himself a master of the universe.[4]

Once I saw a swallow teaching her young to pluck insects from the air. She would swoop low to the golf-course ground, catch a small goose feather in her beak, take the feather about twenty feet into the air, and release it. Then she would swing away from the floating feather, make a circle and dart back under it, folding her wings and releasing the intensity of her arc just as she snapped the feather in her beak. Then she'd release the feather again, circle around the watching golfers and wait for her offspring to try. They were not good at the task. One would swing up under the feather and, having misjudged its rate of fall, beat his wings wildly to still himself in the air as he repeatedly thrust his beak toward his "prey." Mom would fly by, grab the feather and repeat the lesson.

Some might think this was future-oriented "child rearing," the teaching of the young to face the problems of survival that would confront them tomorrow. And, if one thought that way, one could certainly learn important lessons from this little display: the importance of repetition, the place of patience on the part of the teacher, the need to look forward to improvement day by day.

I don't think I would be offending the bird or her kind if I suggested that this mother bird probably didn't think like that. This lesson was to be, I imagine, simply *today's* lesson.*** The young bird might be better at

*** But maybe this was not a lesson at all, and the mother was not teaching. A friend whose virtuosity in critical reading always surprises me wrote to ask,

> Is it true that the mother bird is teaching her young to pluck insects out of the air? Are you sure? This is one of those situations where you can't actually go up to her and ask, "Excuse me, madam, are you by any chance using that feather trick to teach those young ones to . . .?" So I guess we are tied to hunches here. My counter-hunch is that she may be showing off. She wants them to see how elegant her feather-plucking skills are. They'll try it too and maybe even worry about misjudging the feather's rate of fall. Maybe the wild wing-flapping is thrilling enough to satisfy them for the moment.

catching the feather tomorrow. And days later he might catch his first insect. But that was not the point of this lesson now. This lesson now was just what had to be done—now. Both lesson and learner proceeded under one rule: Do this or die. But, I imagine, this imperative gains its force for those swirling little birds and compels them to act now as they *must* act now simply because the rule has the status of a fact of life, not because they awaken some nights in a bird's equivalent of a cold sweat, suffering under the nightmare vision of a world from which death has absented them. It is only, I like to think, members of the advanced species that can be moved to act by bleak and egocentric visions of the future. It's only people, I suspect, who are moved to try to condition the future because of a fear of death. And what else could it be besides something huge—like the fear of death—that would motivate the construction of such huge institutions as schools? It is as if we think that no one will know how to live unless we build institutions to teach them. So we teach them—everything—even, as Arendt put it, "the art of living."[5]

Of course, the schoolteachers and the politicians among us would never admit that it is the fear of death that makes us act as if we could guarantee a better future. They would say that it is their belief in the goodness of the future that moves them to act. They are our optimists.

One can be an optimist or a pessimist only if one is concerned about the future. Unalterably opposed to both the optimist and the pessimist is the realist. The realist insists on paying attention to what has happened and to what is happening now. The realist can even illuminate the present effects of a culturally pervasive optimism. Hannah Arendt, author of "We Refugees," was one of many during her time who were forced to leave their homes, their occupations, their languages, and their friends and who found themselves in America. There, she says, "We were told to forget; and we forgot quicker than anybody ever could imagine." The Europeans transplanted in America were assured and reassured that everything would be okay, that their futures would be bright in this land of refuge and plenty. Some of them, she says, forgot their immediate collective and personal pasts so completely that they began to affect the optimism that was all around them. But, she wrote,

> There is something wrong with our optimism. There are those odd optimists among us who, having made a lot of optimistic speeches, go home

---

Later, when the mother bird gets the insect, they'll get an urge to try that move too.

Alright. I *don't* know if the mother bird was teaching her young anything. And I do know how much "teaching" is really just "showing off." But let the anthrocentrism serve for now. Even my friend allowed, finally, "A bird story has a greater chance of being a counterweight to the nutty school brochure than almost anything else I can think of."

and turn on the gas or make use of a skyscraper in quite an unexpected way. They seem to prove that our proclaimed cheerfulness is based on a dangerous readiness for death.[6]

Those who forget how to remember their past run the risk that it will sneak up on them and suddenly remind them who they are. Those who, in a rush to embrace the future optimistically, forget to think nightly of their dead or remember the poems they once loved as children can only be surprised by their past; they can never come to terms with it. Those who prepare themselves generally for the future, without regard for who they are, may become flexible and cheerfully ready for anything that a "changing and diverse society" may throw their way. But the realist will insist on looking at the statistics on how many optimists forgo their futures in favor of death. The realist will insist on asking the optimists how much violence they are willing to inflict in the name of making the future better.

It would be good if the schools would renounce all interest in the future. That would eliminate any possibility of acting around and on children out of an egocentric fear of death or out of a smiley-faced optimism that masks "a dangerous readiness for death," motives that are two sides of the same coin. It would force the schools and everyone in them to be properly embarrassed anytime someone thought in phrases like "Helping kids invent their lives," and it would permit teachers and students alike to experience the humility of thinking of their dead and the delight of remembering the poems they once loved. Renouncing the future would give everyone a chance to remember who and where they are.

Those who cling to visions of a better future have to be always on the go; they can never settle down. The superintendent's introduction to the "Strategic Plan" relies on traveling metaphors:

> The vision for the OSD is to create an environment in which each day, each student experiences success. The vision is a statement of the ideal, a mental journey, if you will, of what can be . . . .
>
> [I]t may be useful to think of the Strategic Plan as a road map. Not only does it show a destination point, but it also indicates the various roads one can take to get there.[7]

We should remember that maps are only good if you know, already, where you are. And people who rely on them are usually those anxious to get to a destination rather than those interested in paying attention to the details of their journey, details that are not on the maps. Being on the go is different from undertaking an important journey.

Some people who argue that schooling should concern itself with the future remind us that "education" comes from the Latin *educare*, meaning "to lead out," and that "teach," if it is rooted in Latin at all, comes from the same root as "digit" and involves "pointing," as in "pointing the way." Conquest, reflecting on these words and their derivations, wrote to his colleagues, all teachers in training,

> It is tempting to see ourselves as Virgils, lamp in hand, leading students out of the wilderness. The problem is that as teachers we often forget, as Virgil did not, that the education is in the journey. We, for some reason, want to get students out of the woods as quickly as possible, so at every junction, at every uncertainty we point clearly to the most direct path and then shepherd our flock along.

He said that some would even think that Dante's "journey and his resulting education were undertaken to achieve a specific goal—his salvation." But Conquest knows the story better. He knows that the journey begins when Dante says, "Midway in the journey of our life I found myself in a dark wood, for the straight way was lost" (Canto I, 1-3). Conquest writes, "Dante's education . . . begins at the moment he notices he is lost. . . . He begins, on his own, to search again for the 'true Way,' but finds his efforts so impeded that, 'more than once [he] turned round to go back'" (Canto I, 36). This is where Virgil enters and, Conquest says, "it's only at this point—when Dante finds his own sense of his place and his circumstances inadequate—that a 'teacher' becomes of any use to him in furthering his education."[8] But this teacher does not lead Dante out of his fix or point to the "true Way." Virgil is not interested in getting Dante "on the go."

We can only try to imagine what schools would be like if teachers pointed out things along the way that they thought children might find useful, or if teachers encouraged students to take note of where they are— and did so under the stark realization that they cannot save even one child. We can only imagine what schools might be like if teachers were there as guides—but as guides who appeared only after a child had realized he was lost and had struggled, without success, to find his own way. Maps like our local school district's "Strategic Plan" are not for those who are lost. They are for those who submerge any idea about where they might be under a consuming passion for getting somewhere else, and for those smart enough not to enlist a guide who might slow down the getting there.

Illich distinguishes the political and the cultural revolutionary in this way: "The political revolutionary wants to improve existing institutions— their productivity and the quality and distribution of their products. . . . The cultural revolutionary risks the future on the educability of man."[9] The children of the sixties have become the "political revolutionaries" of the nineties. They have ascended to school superintendencies and other positions of influence from whence they issue optimistic assurances that the future can be better if only we muster the collective capacity to improve the institutions that supposedly serve us. They are willing to risk nothing, most especially the future. That is why the people in their schools stand so little chance of ever being educated.

* * *

"Visionary Goals" of the Olympia School District

1. The Olympia School District [hereafter OSD] will develop a plan that will increase the involvement of the community, business, parents, and students in the educational process and include the involvement of students in community service.
2. The OSD will explore and implement educational reforms and management models which promote collaboration, flexibility, and accountability.
3. The OSD will implement a variety of student assessment procedures designed to correspond with the instructional program and to evaluate individual student achievement.
4. The OSD will provide integrated, challenging curricula which will prepare each student to be a lifelong learner and to function successfully in a diverse and changing society.
5. The OSD will provide a stimulating/dynamic learning environment through staff recruitment and development practices which will facilitate an integrated, educational program using all available resources.
6. The OSD will plan and provide facilities and resources to support the educational system.[10]

"Parameters" of the Olympia School District's Strategic Plan

> The paramount duty of the school is to maintain the integrity of the instructional program.
> The addition and continuation of programs will be evaluated based upon consistency with the district's mission, value for students, and adequate funding, training, and planning.
> Prejudicial discrimination and sexual harassment will not be tolerated; mutual respect and dignity for all will be expected.
> Physical facilities and instructional materials within the school district shall not prevent student achievement."[11]

CHAPTER 30

School Choice, or What Is Important

"Dear Mr. Arney, . . ." It is my first note home from a public school teacher; it's only two weeks into John's time in the second grade, and already there's a note. Jeff, John's previous teacher at the school down on the college's beach, would call or just speak to me when I dropped by the school. John is now in the school of four hundred around the corner, a school where no one drops in without signing the log at the front desk and pinning a badge on his or her pocket before walking the halls to a classroom.

> Dear Mr. Arney,
>   John is confused about the difference between his capital letters and his lowercase letters. Please work with him on this.

Already it's started, I think. They have taken such an interest in John that they have issued their first diagnosis: "John is confused." The problem I now face is how to get their attention off John and back on themselves, how to give John at least the chance of settling anonymously into this school that cares so much about him so early in his career there, how to give John a chance at an education?

"DEAR L——," I print at the bottom of the note, ALL IN CAPITAL LETTERS because that is how I print:

> DEAR L——,
>   JOHN IS NOT CONFUSED. NO ONE HAS EVER TOLD HIM THAT THE DIFFERENCE BETWEEN SMALL LETTERS AND CAPITAL LETTERS IS IMPORTANT. IF THE DIFFERENCE IS IMPORTANT TO YOU, TELL HIM. HE LIKES YOU.

A radio program: the pendulum is swinging and the interview this time is with *opponents* of home schooling. "I've seen kids coming to school in the sixth grade who don't know their multiplication tables. Kids have come from home schooling into junior high school and they can't write in cursive. Now, I admit, they learn these things quickly, but you've got to wonder."

Stop right there! Yes, you've got to wonder, but not about the kids who have been taught by their parents. You've got to wonder about these people who care so much about having kids so perfectly aligned with the curriculum that they can easily dismiss the fact that "they learn these things quickly." You've got to wonder about people so attuned to deficiencies that they are blind to students' capabilities. One of the things one learns outside of schools (and this is as true for children as it is for adults) is that it's very useful to be able to figure out what you have to know to get along in the settings in which you find yourself and then to be able to learn those things quickly. Learning multiplication tables when you have a reason to (even as meager a reason as getting along in school) is not hard. It's hard to learn multiplication tables in school because schools never show children that multiplication is important. Learning cursive writing is not hard. Anyone can learn these things quickly, if the person senses they are important to learn.

"School Choice" vs. Educational Possibility

Over thirty years ago Kenneth Boulding, hardly a Milton Friedman clone, proposed a school voucher system. Give parents vouchers for the schooling of their children and allow them to cash those vouchers in the schools of their choice. Boulding's simple proposal has been overwhelmed for thirty years by the much louder calls for nationwide "school reform." Recently, however, Boulding's idea resurfaced from the middle of the stream and we are debating "school choice." We arrived at this by a circuitous route. First, schools abdicated the responsibility for establishing the curriculum. In some cases, teachers traded a say in curriculum design for collective bargaining rights.[1] In other cases, school districts took to buying the latest fad from curricula publishers instead of thinking about what is important and teaching that. In other cases, people in schools decided that they had to take over the functions of dysfunctional families; consequently, substantive matters would have to take a back seat to "social skills."[*] For whatever reason, teachers and administrators lost control over curriculum to such an extent that in 1991 a national educational summit led to the formation of a national commission that would set national educational standards and formulate national curricular designs. Teachers and administrators lost control of the curriculum to such an extent that many people would come to think, again, that the best way to design a school is to "let the market decide."

Boulding had some liberals with him all along. At the heart of his proposal was an outline many liberals could love: Make schools competitive with one another, and make them accountable to students and parents. If schools didn't measure up, parents would take their children to other

---

[*] At a continuing education program for public school teachers held at my college, one teacher announced to the group that she had had to spend a significant part of her class time teaching her students which fork to use at dinner. The prom was coming up, and they didn't know these things, she said, so they had to be taught them. Everyone seemed to understand.

schools and withdraw their voucher-based financial support. The voucher system appealed to many because it expressed a faith in people to be able to make the best choices for their children. School choice, the liberals thought, would also provide a chance for poor people to take advantage of the better schools across town. Students would not be caught in the horrible disparities that result from schools being funded principally from local taxation.[2] The voucher system had immediate appeal in left-of-center politics because it offered yet another way to complain about politics as usual.

The recent reincarnation of the voucher system under the rubric of school choice has given even the liberals pause. Beginning with the Bush administration, school choice became an undisguised effort to use governmental money to fund religious schools, many of which were founded to avoid earlier efforts to integrate schools. Also, in the heat of the presidential election of 1992, the Carnegie Foundation for the Advancement of Teaching issued a report that concluded that it is primarily well-educated, financially better-off parents who take advantage of school-choice programs and that school choice can sometimes widen the gap between rich and poor districts. In one peculiar case in Massachusetts, 135 students took advantage of a school-choice program and transferred from schools in Brockton, a city in financial trouble, to schools in the relative wealthy suburb of Avon. Those 135 students took with them $1 million in state aid to Brockton *and* Brockton had to pay Avon the difference between its own low per-pupil expenditure and Avon's high per-pupil expenditure. The overall result was that Brockton had to fire teachers and increase class size to 40 students per room.[3] The difference between the theory of school choice and the way choice is being put into practice will probably lead to another round of calls for school reform. If we must say that it is a vicious circle, then we should do so with a knowing smile. After all, these debates have been going on in one form or another for over two decades.

Around the same time Boulding was arguing that the market should be allowed to decide school programming, Ivan Illich was making a radically different proposal. "It is difficult now to challenge the school as a system because we are so used to it,"[4] he wrote in 1968, but challenge it he did with a proposal that every citizen be granted an equal share of a country's educational budget. He did not mean that all people ought to be given a credit card that could be used at the school or university of their choice; he meant that people ought to be given credit cards that could be used to acquire an education in any way each saw fit. A friend of mine recently wrote that he is "convinced that school people will never admit that learning is a natural and naturally lifelong characteristic of human beings."[5] But

Illich's proposal was based on an insistence that derives from his faith that people can and do learn by living, that learning is "naturally lifelong."[*]

As if his proposal to grant everyone an equal share of a country's educational budget was not radical enough, Illich coupled it to the proposal that educational budgets be drastically cut back.

> We should consider a radical reduction of the length of the formal, obligatory school sessions to only two months each year—but spread this type of formal schooling over the first twenty or thirty years of a man's life. . . . Two months a year of formal schooling should be considered ample time for what the Greeks meant by *schole*—leisure for the pursuit of insight.[6]

Instead of proposing school choice, Illich was proposing that people—all people—be granted educational possibility. By radically curtailing formal schooling, such a proposal gives everyone the chance to discover that many of the things now taught in schools only because they are part of the curriculum are actually important in life. By arguing that schooling be spread out over many years, such a proposal admits that the importance of knowledge can be rediscovered many times in a person's life. By locating the right to decide how to allocate one's educational resources in the person, such a proposal replaces the possibility (for many, the likelihood) of being termed a "failure" with the right to make mistakes. That is, people would get to make their own mistakes in the allocation of resources; they would not have to suffer the mistakes made by teachers and school administrators, mistakes that, by the nature of the organizations in which they occur, are much larger than the mistakes that could ever be made by even a sizable group of people.

A Case for Indifference

Boulding's voucher system resurfaced as "school choice" because it could be made to fit the needs of regressive politics. It is highly unlikely that Illich's proposal will receive any kind of a hearing in these times, even if anyone notices that the proposal contains the idea that expenditures on

---

[*] Anyone who enters into these debates must begin with the recognition that most colleges and universities have tacitly (very quietly and discreetly) agreed with Illich's position. Most public colleges now have programs called something like "Credit for Life Experience." If students are willing to convert their life experience into creditable, documentary evidence that they have, by living, learned something that schools recognize as learning, the schools are happy to certify the educational value of that learning/living with credit. The programs strive for a schoolish rigor by imposing enormous bureaucratic hurdles on students or by requiring that the lifelong learning be rendered in the idiom of the schooled. In that way such programs can *avoid appearing* to acknowledge that people learn outside the walls of a classroom while awarding them credit for doing just that.

schooling should be radically reduced. Schools consume ever-larger proportions of governmental budgets, and even in times of economic contraction, schools are among the last budgetary items to be cut. Schooling is still a sacred cow.[7]

There may be some hope in the severity of recurrent budget crises and contracting public support for more taxes, more levies, and so forth. It may be that schools will finally lose some of their funding. If the state of California is still leading the nation into everything good and bad, we can expect more widespread and more vicious budget battles that will result in, among other things, larger school classes. If the teachers do not decide to burn out even faster than the five years it now takes the average California teacher to do, there is the possibility that teachers could rediscover the value of *indifference*. Teachers have shown that they can sustain an interest in 25 children per classroom, 30 children per classroom, even 35 children per classroom. The heroes carry on bravely with 40. Perhaps when 45 and 50 students enter every public school classroom, teachers will finally remember that no one can care for that many people, not even if they are small people. In classrooms of 45 and 50, the good teachers will be able to recall how they were able to teach their students before the schools insisted that teachers care for the children.

Annie Dillard recalls the evening when she finally saw "the famous amoeba" in a "scummy drop of Frick Park puddle water" under the lens of the microscope her parents had given her. She ran to tell her parents that they, too, could see this beast, if only they would hurry "before his water dried." It was after dinner and,

> Father had stretched out his long legs and was tilting back in his chair. Mother sat with her knees crossed, in blue slacks, smoking a Chesterfield. The dessert dishes were still on the table. My sisters were nowhere in evidence. It was a warm evening; the big dining-room windows gave onto blooming rhododendrons.

> Mother regarded me warmly. She gave me to understand that she was glad I had found what I was looking for, but that she and Father were happy to sit with their coffee, and would not be coming down.

> She did not say, but I understood at once, that they had their pursuits (coffee?) and I had mine. She did not say, but I began to understand then, that you do what you do out of your private passion for the thing itself.

> I had essentially been handed my own life.[8]

The indifference of Dillard's parents had allowed little Annie the chance to find out what was important to her.

If we insist on continuing to debate school choice, we will only be able to debate choices among different schools' ideas about what is important for children to learn. And we will debate only different ways of designating as "failures" those who can't, don't, or won't learn what their chosen schools say is important. If we continue to fund schools at current levels, through vouchers or through reformed versions of old mechanisms, teachers will be able to continue to care whether students learn what schools say is important for them to learn. (And, of course, they will continue to issue their diagnoses of those who are "confused" or worse.) If, willingly or unwillingly, we cut back on schoolish caring for every child, we open up the possibility of handing to each child his or her "own life." And in that act we open up another possibility: the possibility of rediscovering noninstitutional ways of caring about, and even caring *for*, one another.

CHAPTER 31

Ivan: "In Book after Book . . ." (as promised)

On the outskirts of Havana, they call friends mi tiera, *my country, or* mi sangre, *my blood.*

In Caracas, a friend is mi pana, *my bread, or* mi llave, *my key:* pana *from* panadería, *bakery, the source of wholesome bread to sate the hunger of the soul;* llave *from . . .*

"Key, from key," Mario Benedetti tells me.

And he tells me how, when he lived in Buenos Aires in times of terror, he would carry five alternate keys on this key ring: the keys to five houses, to five friends: the keys that proved his salvation.

Eduardo Galeano, *The Book of Embraces*

There is a sense in which I have known the work of Ivan Illich for more than fifteen years. There is another sense in which I have known his work only since beginning to know him, something that happened only two years ago. I write about the work of Ivan Illich as I know it.

Bob Kugelmann says that the making of lists is a peculiarly modern phenomenon. You know the kind of list he has in mind: item 1, make a List; item 2, grocery shopping (see attached list); item 3, study (see reading list). Bob has written about these lists in his book on the history of stress.[1] Stress is a modern phenomenon, too, coming out of the "strain" of the 19th century and out of "grief" and "loss" before that. In times of stress, make a list. Prioritize and get started, the therapists tell us. Just make a list and check things off as you go. By your checkmarks of accomplishment will you be known.

There is another kind of list. A friend in New Hampshire has a daughter who, as she was learning to talk, would wake up each morning and recite the list of all the words she knew: Mama, no, dog, eat, it, me . . . The list grew longer as she grew older. Every morning, she would recite all the words from memory. Eventually, I imagine, she developed a sense of security about the fact that this list of words by which she was known and by which she made herself known in the world would not be lost to her because of a night's sleep. She eventually stopped rehearsing her list every morning. But I dare say she keeps that list, which grows longer still, with her, even now.

Illich concludes his lecture "The Educational Enterprise in the Light of the Gospel," his call for paying attention to dropouts, with a plea for the construction of lists.

> None of [the educational research money in the U.S.] is focused on the transformation of the status of the dropout from that of an escapee who must be caught and brought back into the fold into that of a world wise, reasonable person. I do not plead for some new form of institutionalized haven. Rather I think of niches, free spaces, squatters arrangements, spiritual tents which some of us might be able to offer, not for "the dropout in general" but each of us for a small "list" of others, who through the experience of mutual obedience have become able to renounce integration into the "system."[2]

This small list of others is not the to-do list of the stressed-out people suffering their losses under a regime of what Kugelmann calls "engineered grief" and trying desperately, with a little organization and a little perseverance, just to keep less far behind than yesterday. This is not the list of the roll call with its implied or explicit list of "individual needs" to which the teacher can respond through the mobilization of resources. Illich's small list of others is more like Jennifer's morning recital of her words. It is a list of other people through which, via the intimacy of "mutual obedience," one is known and makes oneself known in the world.

The creation of this kind of list has one possible (but certainly not necessary) outcome: enabling oneself and others "to renounce integration into the 'system.'" For many years Illich and a list of associates have undertaken what they call "an archeology of modern certainties." This involves a particular kind of historical inquiry into those terms that we all take for granted, terms and practices that we think give orientation if not meaning to life and living. For example, Barbara Duden has inquired into the appearance of that modern thing—the "fetus"—in the place previously occupied by the *nondum*, the "not yet" in a "woman's innards."[3] Illich has been interested in the appearance of the notion of "life." He, like Foucault, has studied the appearance of "sex" on the recent historical scene. Other associates have undertaken studies of "progress," "helping," "development," and so on.[4] Illich has either discovered or invented (the distinction is not, I think, of great importance here) something called "gender" and "gendered society" to demonstrate that this modern given, sex (a variable characteristic of a similarly recent thing, the "human being"), is historically and culturally contingent. The list of the modern certainties with which Illich has concerned himself is much longer. What I am concerned with today is not the items on that list but rather Illich's attitude toward them. We must, he says, say, firmly and resolutely, "No, thank you," to these modern certainties in order to avoid integration into the system.

At first glance there seems a parallel between Illich and Foucault on this matter of saying no. Foucault, in his "Preface to Transgression," says something like, "Use the positive voice to say no."[5] Boundaries must be breached and limits transgressed to affirm something like the limitlessness of life together. Illich's no is not the same sort of no. It is a complementary form of "no." The comparison is worth attention.

Foucault's histories are of the social, one might even say artificial, placement of boundaries in social life. His first studies were of the boundaries between the mad and the sane and the diseased and the well. Later he became interested in the normal and in the processes of normalization in which boundaries are seemingly fluid and have the capacity to capture everything under a regime of "discipline." But still there was the implied boundary of the system, the boundary of the prison wall, the boundary of the social within which everyone was a delinquent, "at risk," and all those other terms that the normal inflicts on us. These are the boundaries that must, he says, be transgressed (in the name of nothing).

Illich is interested in the ways in which things—social institutions in particular, tools in general—grow in utility beyond their own limits. In medicine he would be interested in the way that limited knowledge of the uses of a few plants or a few techniques has grown into the modern world's principal industry and has claimed, in the name of health and wellness, authority for the management of living. In education, he has been interested in the way an experience he calls "bookishness" has grown into the business of compulsory, age-graded, universal stuff that we call "schooling." For Illich, the threat to good living comes not from teaching and learning per se or from efforts to help people in times of illness per se; the threat comes from the expansiveness of the institutionalized forms of these activities, from the way that there is seemingly no way to live unless one submits to the system or becomes a good and faithful critic of the system.

So Illich says no. No, I do not want to accept the generous offers of systematized help. And equally forcefully, no, I do not want to debate how to make systematized help better, regardless of what criterion happens to be the reigning measure of "better" at the time. By saying no in this doubled form one does not transcend limits; instead, one is able "to renounce integration into the 'system,'" the system that is based on the grounding concept of "needs."

Most of Illich's analyses proceed from a concern with the assertion and imputation of "human needs." Institutions come into being, according to Illich, through their ability to assert that people have needs: the need for health, the need for certified knowledge, etc. It just so happens that the institutions that name your needs are the institutions that say they are able to meet those needs. But, historically and empirically, institutions have a "specific (or paradoxical) counterproductivity" that leads them to effect the opposite of what they claim they will do. Medicine causes not ease from illness but dis-ease. (Illich said medicine is "iatrogenic.") Schooling causes a peculiar kind of illiteracy. This sets up the sort of social dynamic that Foucault outlined with prisons, viz., institutions bring with them their own impulse for (and, indeed, their own rhetoric of) reform. What Illich and Foucault both recognize is that the proponents and the reformer-opponents of social institutions both accept the underlying premise that there is a human need that must be met. The only question—the thing that separates proponent and opponent—is how to meet those needs. So Illich's no is directed more against the foundational notion of need than it is against the institutions that presume to meet those needs.

Of course, in these times, this can be a silly kind of posture to adopt. A gentle critic might ask, "Are you saying, Professor Illich, that the human body does not have a need for a certain number of calories to keep going?" or, "Don't you think that children need some knowledge?" Instead of saying what his understandings might lead him to say (e.g., "I would prefer not to think thoughtlessly about a person *having* a 'human body' that can be conceived as an energetic device" or "I don't think it's good that we have turned a certain portion of our number into 'children.'"), Illich just says no to such invitational questions. He renounces the questions themselves and thereby renounces integration into the system.

Marianne Gronemeyer has written a book called *The Power of Needs*.[6] In it she writes about the power that institutions come to have in our lives if we accept the premise that humans are needful beings. She finds an opposition to this power not in power of another sort: the power of reason, the power of historical contradictions, the power of well-assembled critical groups, etc.—pick one depending on your theory of social change. She finds opposition to this form of power in *Ohnmacht*, a German word that has two meanings: powerlessness and fainting. To oppose the power of needs one must accept one's total powerlessness. One must faint away[*] in the face of

---

[*] Lenny Bruce: "I'm doing a new bit that you'll just flip out with. It's social commentary. I do it with a colored guitarist, Eric Miller. The bit is on integration.

"So anyway, we do the bit together. Halfway through the bit—there is this party of four to my right, and they're really bugging me, you know, saying, 'I don't unnerstan it.'

"So I give this woman a quick stab: 'You *schlub*, you wouldn't understand anything'—you know.

"The other guy says, 'What'd he say to her?'

"The other guy says, 'He said something dirty in Jewish.'

"So I said, 'There is nothing dirty in Jewish.'

"So dig, she takes this old-fashioned glass, and starts winging it, man *vvvooom!* Right past me, man. I'm shocked. It crashes behind me.

"So I say, 'You've got a bad sense of humor, and bad aim.'

"So she gets bugged again, throws a second glass.

the reasonable demands that one enter into the dominant discourse, either as an advocate or as a member of the loyal opposition.

Illich's no is, for me, not a protest against or even a critical attack on modern institutions in the usual sense. His no is more a protest against the presumed adequacy of human knowledge. His attack is on the *presumptuousness* of knowledge and understanding, and on the seeming limitlessness of our presumptuousness. He is opposed to the presumed elimination, through the operations of reason, of mystery from life—not, I am quick to add, the sort of "mystery" of which Joseph Campbell speaks, which is an excuse for not pursuing knowledge of anything, but the mystery that one encounters at the end of a life of loving struggle to know something. This is part of the reason, I think, that Illich has started writing not as a theologian, as he cautiously insists, but in a more theologically informed language. In his call for a new "askesis in higher education," Illich opposes not the search for knowledge and the love of wisdom but the posturing that results from the assumption that the proper way to know and be known in the world is to involve oneself in the plays of power that develop around knowledge. I hear in this a call to accept the posturelessness of one who has fainted away in an embrace of one's powerlessness.

Illich's inquiry into our modern condition, an inquiry marked by his insistent no, is entirely negative. Erich Fromm called his approach "radical doubt." Illich's criticisms are pointed and harsh but they are not intended to be productive. They do not point toward a better future. In *Gender*, what he calls his first "book," Illich shows why it is important for him *not* to be interested in even the causes of our current situation. He writes,

> In this essay I have not tried to explain why society places the man on top and the handicap on the woman. *I have controlled my curiosity* in order to be free to listen more attentively to the report of the losers, to learn not about them but about the battlefield that is the economy.[7]

You must say no even to the general mode of inquiry that seeks causes for each obvious effect so that you do not develop a prurient interest in the situation of others whom you cannot know. You have to say no to the all-too-easy business of turning the subjects of history into objects of inquiry. Why? So that you stand a slight chance of developing an understanding of things as they have come to be.

"I said, 'Well, assuming I'm the most vulgar, irreverent comedian you've ever seen, you've capped it with violence. You realize what a terrible thing—you threw a glass at me!'

"So dig what the husband says: 'What else would a lady have done?'

"I said, 'Faint!'"

(John Cohen, ed., *The Essential Lenny Bruce* [New York, N.Y.: Random House, 1967], pp. 116-117).

After that, after renouncing an interest in the dominant mode of inquiry, you also have to renounce the kind of interest in the future that is a commonplace of what passes for politics today but which is a kind of an interest in the future that is allowed to only a privileged few. *Gender* begins to end with this: "I have no strategy to offer. I refuse to speculate on the probabilities of any cure. I shall not allow the shadow of the future to fall on the concepts with which I try to grasp what is and what has been."[8] Illich's work is a thorough-going critique of the modern condition. And somewhat like Foucault, he refuses to go further than the present. He refuses to suggest some presumed grand plan which might attract disciples and foundation grants and which might lead to the formation of utopian communities composed of nothing but the blind.

Indeed, the only interest I can find in Illich's work is an interest in having eyes open. He writes in the introduction to the lecture on education, "I will argue that—in this instance—the Gospel sharpens our eyes for the perception of the obvious, which our schooled minds cannot admit."[9] His work is a kind of invitation to look and see, a "celebration of awareness."[10] His readers are invited to see not through his eyes and certainly not through the theory-bound eyes of the well-schooled but through their own eyes, using whatever devices help sharpen their own visions of things as they are. We are back to a Lenny Bruce–like notion that people ought to be taught what is, not what should be. And to show what a thing *is* in these well-schooled times, when everyone knows what everything is truly *and* has an opinion about it, you have to proceed negatively. Sometimes, when the nature of a thing is so obvious and yet there are so many competing well-schooled visions of what a thing could be if it were better fitted for life, you have to proceed by showing people what a thing is not. So, schooling is *not* about transmission of knowledge. Medicine is *not* about healing the sick. Because he is interested not in reform but in making a way for people to seize a good life lived well together, Illich tries to dismantle the visions that support social institutions that erode and undermine the possibility of living well.

Illich proceeds down his negative way with only one thing that some might consider positive. He has hope. *Gender* ends, "I strongly suspect that a contemporary art of living *can* be recovered. . . . The hope for such a life rests upon the rejection of sentimentality and on openness to surprise."[11] Josef Pieper says that hope, in the tradition from which Illich writes,

> is the condition of man's existence as a knowing subject, a condition that by its very nature cannot be fixed: it is neither comprehension and possession nor simply non-possession, but "not-yet-possession." [This construction recalls Duden's *nondum,* her "not-yet."] The knowing subject is visualized as a traveller, a *viator,* as someone "on the way." This means, from one point of

view, that the steps he takes have significance, that they are not altogether in vain, and that they bring him nearer his goal. Yet this thought has to be complemented by another: as long as man as "existing being" is "on the way," just so long is the "way" of his knowing uncompleted.[12]

Through his constant critiques, Illich offers no vision, no ideas for renewal, no scheme for reform. He offers only the hope of the not-yet.

With what are we left in this condition of the not-yet, in this condition of hope? We are left with our lists. One might be a person left with the list of the sort that Kugelmann writes about. In the face of the not-yet, there are things to do. Just list them and get them done. The not-yet may remain, still, the not-yet, but at least you will have a sense of accomplishment. One might, alternatively, be a person with the sort of list that Illich writes about, a small list of others with whom you live in relationships of mutual obedience. It is worth reminding ourselves what Illich means by "obedience":

> unobstructed listening, unconditional readiness to hear, untrammeled disposition to be surprised by the Other's word. . . . When I listen unconditionally, respectfully, courageously with the readiness to take in the other as a radical surprise . . . I bow, bend over towards the total otherness of someone. But I renounce the searching for bridges between the other and me, recognizing that a gulf separates us. Leaning into this chasm makes me aware of the depth of my loneliness and able to bear it in light of the substantial likeness between the other and myself. All that reaches me is the other in his word, which I accept on faith.[13]

Illich's notion of a list has a material manifestation in his life. He has a list of several hundred names he carries with him all the time. When he writes something, he sends it to some of the people on this list. They listen. When someone on the list calls on him or writes, he listens in order to give a conscientious response. It is through this list of people he knows—and not through, for example, his list of books—that Illich knows himself and is known.

Now I will make what may seem a rather sudden turn. I want to turn away from the nature of the lists by which one is known and ask, finally, what it is that is obvious once one's vision is sharpened and one's eyes are opened and able to see? To do this, I must turn toward one interpretation of the work and life of Thomas Aquinas, acknowledging that Illich works in this tradition of a Christian appropriation of Aristotelian thinking. A colleague says that, out of the boredom of her schooling, she was moved to read all of Aquinas's *Summa Theologica*. This is something that no one can do, of course, because his *Summa* is incomplete. Several months before he died, Thomas Aquinas suddenly stopped writing his great work. He told his assistant, "Reginald, I can write no more. All that I have written before seems to me nothing but straw." Aquinas spent the last months of his life almost totally in silence. He broke his silence once, to speak to an order on Song of Songs, that book of the Bible that recounts the sensuousness of embodied love. It was a fitting last talk for a man who knew it was impossible to separate the love of truth from the love of other human beings.[14] When I look into Illich's writings to find the "obvious" for which the perception of our eyes is to be sharpened, it seems, at first, obvious that we no longer live with Aquinas's conviction. It seems obvious, today, that a lover of truth need not make any declarations about his or her relationship to any other human being. It seems obvious that the love of one's fellows is something conducted on a different plane from the love of truth. But then it appears equally obvious that right there, in Ivan's work, in book after book, there is an invitation to make the connection again and again, all the time, everywhere. The loving search for the truth is inseparable from the search for loving friends. Illich writes his critiques of our modern condition, yes, but he also has his list, his list that embodies and enfleshes his hope. The two are obviously connected. But Illich never makes the connection. He never writes about it; he never speaks about it. But if something is obvious, one, finally, doesn't have to say anything. We know that at least one of the great philosophers fell silent when everything became obvious to him.

CHAPTER 32

Second Thoughts: Valedictory

I am not a critic; to me criticism is so often nothing more than the eye garrulously denouncing the shape of the peephole that gives access to hidden treasure.

Djuna Barnes, *Silence and Power*

The opening line of Illich's notes on the concept of "askesis" reads, "I want to cultivate the capacity for second thoughts, by which I mean the stance and the competence that makes it feasible to inquire into the obvious. This is what I call learning."[1]

I have been having some second thoughts recently. We, your teachers in this program, have been quite critical of schools. You have taken us seriously, so seriously that I have listened to, heard about, and read *your* critiques of schools and *your* critiques of teaching. Hearing criticism of teaching and schooling coming from would-be-but-not-yet teachers has given me pause.

I have the sense that we have, to a certain extent, delivered you a message about the schools. Many of you have taken this message to be an indictment of the schools. Philip Rieff writes in his wonderful 1973 bombast of a book called *Fellow Teachers*, "Messages and positions are the death of teaching. As scholars and teachers, we have a duty to fight against our own positions."[2] To the extent that we have delivered the message that the schools are indictable, to the extent that we have professed a position that is critical of the schools, to that extent I want, today, to fight against that message and that position.

In the last months in this program criticism of the schools has become too easy. It has become so easy that, for some of you, your criticisms of the schools are at the root of your wanting, even your aching, to become teachers in the schools. Many of you have taken a stand that you think will serve you well in teaching—a stand in favor of children, a stand in opposition to discipline, a stand in favor of humane treatment of children, a stand in opposition to modern management techniques. When criticism comes so easily and when stands in regard to teaching are taken so firmly, so publicly, and so obviously by people who are not yet teachers, it is time to have some second thoughts.

I will cut to my point. I ask that you take careful notes because I am going to be, this once, highly directive. I am going to give you advice that I ask you to accept as guidance, even as an injunction on your behavior. My wish is that for the first three years of your employment in the public schools, *you will not have a single critical thought*—not one. To emphasize: I did not say that I wish you not to *express* a critical thought; my deepest hope is that you will not *have* one. I encourage you to take no stands and make no indictments. I encourage you, instead, to do your work well.

Are these second thoughts defensible after all that has gone before? Barely, but let me offer a defense anyway, thin though it is. The first line of defense is to suggest that becoming a critic and taking a stand is an activity that runs the risk of being merely fashionable. Again, here is Rieff:

> I cannot begin to recount the metamorphoses of that ur-text of modern intellectuals: Luther's famous, "Here I stand." I hope he never said it; if he had to say such a thing, knowing full well how he was shifting about, even as he said it, then I hope that Dr. Luther thanked every member of the Committee on Stands, in the first footnote qualifying his stand. How many deceits of resistance have followed since Luther's, to that same self-serving effect? Faith in criticism continues to shake the world without end. What makes Kierkegaard the last and greatest of the Protestant virtuosi, a genius never to be surpassed in his manner, is the way in which he protected himself against saying anything like "Here I stand." That kind of public utterance is far too ambiguous for Kierkegaard's spiritual and intellectual supremacy; he was too smart to set some fashion.[3]

Two things generally happen to critics who take a stand. They are either ignored (and under that response I include the official means of ignoring someone: being shot or being disappeared) or they catch on and become the next neatest thing around. (The child abuse bureaucracy started as a critical movement; they now flow in the mainstream.) Sometimes both things happen to critics: One year, they are adored; the next year, they are ignored. Call it fickle, call it bureaucracy, but recognize it as true. If I wanted to be a good teacher in the public schools today, I would try to avoid being ignored and I would make sure my work never became the basis for the next pedagogical reform. To do this means to avoid becoming fashionable; to avoid being a good and faithful critic; to do your work well.

A third thing can happen to critics. They are played with: critics are especially useful in schools that call themselves progressive because critics provide entertainment value and show that the institution is really more liberal than it ever could be. Critics are encouraged to point out the places where the institution can do better what it does already. And if they can come up with another name and another funding source so that the old thing can be done under a different label and with more money, all the better for everyone. So, by encouraging you not to have a critical thought for three years I am encouraging you not to let yourself become fashionable or useful.

A second reason I ask for a three-year moratorium on critical thoughts is that you are not yet enough *of your discipline* to become a critic of teaching or of the schools. You must become truly a teacher before you can ever presume to be a critic. Again Rieff writes,

> True teaching can acquire its strictly limited, easily challenged authority of resistance only after it develops institutionally in teaching orders. . . . Our academic institutions lack a presiding presence. Our expert devotions, endlessly critical, can never be commanding. We are stuck with our faith in criticism, only marginally different from popular versions of the endless expressional quest or liberated understandings. A true critic, I think, would be one who teaches in an institutional order opposed to the established ease of questioning.[4]

Three years is a very short time to begin to develop an understanding of what you are involved in as a teacher. The easy questioning of schools and of the communities in which the schools operate (expressed in terms of how "society" demands "too much" of schools), the questioning that I read about and that I hear about in teachers' lunchrooms, permits you the luxury of not facing what is going on in the schools. It creates a situation in which what Rieff calls the "authority of resistance" that lies at the thin-walled heart of "true teaching" will never have the chance to take root, a situation in which teachers will never establish the commanding, presiding presence that true teachers always have. You must permit yourself to become totally involved in the discipline you have chosen if you ever wish to have the opportunity to truly act out of that discipline. And, yes, I mean "act out" in both senses: "acting out," as in using the discipline as the firm ground of all your actions, and "acting out of," as in transcending the discipline.

Rieff says that a true critic works only in an "institutional order opposed to the established ease of questioning"—first, an "institutional order" where order is clearly linked to the monastic orders that function with each under its own rule; second, an order "opposed to the established ease of questioning." I encourage those of you who have chosen to be teachers, first, to become teachers. To do that, you must enter the school for what it is; you must avoid the easy questioning of that place; you must order yourself in opposition to the easy questioning that is established practice in lunchrooms and boardrooms. I suggest you do this for three years.

I can give you one exercise that you might find useful as you try to apply yourself to this difficult but short (three years only) discipline of holding all criticism in abeyance. If it were not for the confusion that it would cause, I would call this exercise a "critical exercise," but here it is:

Write down on a regular basis just exactly what you are doing in your school. (I stole this exercise from the diet plans. If you want to lose three pounds just write down everything you eat for one week—everything, in writing.) Set aside a regular time and make that time inviolate. Use that time to record your behavior. Don't write about "them" or about "the students." Write about what *you* are doing. Do this for three years. If you do this conscientiously and rigorously (which means, in part, using this exercise as a means of expunging from your thoughts any criticism of the schools), you will, at the end of three years, have a very good appreciation of what it means to teach in the public schools. This exercise and the appreciation it leads to will make you forever disinclined to indict the schools; it will instead permit you to recognize them. And it is only to *recognition*, not to indictment, criticism, and questioning, it is only to what Rieff calls "close, personal, positionless understanding," that true teachers devote themselves. It is only by recognizing the obvious that you will ever be able to cultivate the capacity for second thoughts and thereby learn anything. It would be very rapid, indeed, but I strongly suspect that in three years some of you will be able to recognize the schools that employ you. Good luck.

CHAPTER 33

Testing: Letters to Which No One Wrote Back

Our state, too, requires all districts to subject all students to standardized tests three times: once in elementary school, once in middle school, once in high school. Some districts test all students every year. On one Thursday late in the year, I got a note from school saying that testing of all students would take place the following week. I spent Friday trying to find out why.

First, I talked to teachers. They did not seem to know why all students were being tested. All the teachers knew was that it was a great imposition on them, at least on those who had to proctor parts of the test. One teacher ventured, "Sometimes you see something interesting in one child's scores. But the scores are so complicated to read. And there are so many parts to the test. I'm just not sure it's all that valuable." In fact, a couple of teachers in the "alternative" program across town had written to parents saying they did not see much use in the tests.

Second, I talked to principals. They had rationales. "Well, frankly we don't make any decisions based solely on test scores, but they do give us a picture, don't they?" said the principal at my son's elementary school. "Certainly not the complete picture, but something like a snapshot. It can tell us, sometimes, if a child is having some sort of systematic difficulty. We also get to see how the district is doing against national standards, and that is very important for all the children in the district."

Third, I called the district superintendent's office and was referred to a curriculum specialist. She told me that the tests were very helpful in getting a diagnosis of their efforts at the "building level" and at the "district level." "We can compare buildings to one another, and often we can tell if a building is deficient in one curricular aspect or another. The tests permit us to compare buildings to nationally published curricular standards—those that come with the textbooks. Sometimes, but more rarely, we can spot elementary teachers whose classes are having some difficulty relative to the average, but that should be a building concern."

"What about the children?" I asked.

"Well, these tests may be an element in the overall picture, but often tests are not very helpful at the level of the child. How a particular child scores depends on how he or she feels that day, what he or she had for breakfast, how he or she tests. You know."

"So you test all the kids mostly for the district's benefit?"

"More or less, yes."

Fourth, I called the chief tester at the state superintendent's office. "They [the tests] don't have anything to do with the kids at all. They can't. There aren't enough questions on any given form to do an adequate test of any area of knowledge. If a kid's score is way out of line—I mean *way out of line*—with the rest of his performance at school, then someone might look at why. But these are helpful for the administrators, only for them, for those who can read them anyway."[*]

"But the state requires these tests only three times in a child's passage through the system. Why do you think my district does it to every child every year?"

"Oh, that's easy. There's a lot of grant money that rides on your ability to demonstrate that you have gifted children and children of special needs. A lot of districts use these tests to demonstrate their qualification for grant money."

Back to the district: I talked to Stillman Wood, the assistant superintendent, the boss of the curricular specialist. "Oh, of course, the district has to demonstrate need, and these tests are the best way we can do that. They're very helpful in other ways, too, but, yes, we have to show the distribution of ability in the district so we can qualify for the grant programs. They're very important to our operational base."

Back to the principal: "I've just learned quite a lot about these tests. I would like to write a letter to parents explaining what I've found, and, even though the testing starts Monday, I'd like to try to get this letter to them tomorrow. May I have a mailing list?"

"That wouldn't be in the best interest of the school."

"But . . ."

"I can give you phone numbers."

"I think this is complicated and a letter is the best way to do justice to that."

"Do you want to pick up the phone list or should I mail it to you?"

I wrote to Stillman Wood. I suggested to him that by testing all students, he and the district were engaging in a research project that was not simply incidental to the established curriculum. I told him that I thought he ought to obtain informed consent from each and every parent. He eventually wrote back to thank me for my letter and to tell me that they were thinking

---

[*] This man showed me a study from California that demonstrated that 70% of public school teachers could not interpret scores from standardized testing. My son's principal could not understand why a student could answer all questions on a test section correctly and not end up in the 99th percentile. She did not realize that the test items varied from form to form and that some test forms contain items that are statistically discriminating, i.e., difficult, while others contain items that are not so difficult. It is only when a child gets a form with at least some difficult questions that that child has even the opportunity to score, comparatively, at the highest levels.

about ways to improve testing and assessment and they would be very happy to have me on a committee that would take a lot of work but that if I cared to do that, they would appreciate my efforts on their behalf and on behalf of the children in the district. Sincerely yours.

* * *

That weekend I spoke to my son about the tests. He decided he didn't want to take them. On Monday, I told the principal of John's decision and asked that she make an arrangement for him so that he would have some non-stigmatizing activity to do while the other kids were taking the test. She arranged for him to sit in the library.

In the library, something happened, something that pushed John to demand that he be allowed to take the tests. But then, as with any snowball set in motion, this one got bigger and some problems that had been hidden were revealed.

I wrote some lettters. Those letters addressed some of those problems. The first letter was to the principal at John's school.

April 19

Dear [Principal],

This may be a moot point since John tells me he finished the test today, but: I don't want John to be led to think that he is required to take the rest of the MAT6 test. I talked with [the district's curriculum specialist to whom I had spoken earlier] and learned that there are no rules requiring students who take only part of the test to make up the rest of it. Your practices have stigmatized him once. Don't do it again.

This has been a real horror show from my perspective (but not John's; kids are more resilient than their parents, usually), and I wonder why you persist. . . .

I had hoped you might find some non-stigmatizing way of accommodating John's and my desire that he be excluded from testing. I should have known that such a thing was not possible in a school. On the second day of John's exile in the library, something happened. As best I can tell, John tipped over a chair in a corner of the library and then hid. The librarian said something to him that, together with being singled out because of his and my decision, scared him. He spent 15 minutes that night sobbing about that event. Not the sobbing of sadness or remorse, but the sobbing of a person who is scared and mad and who has suffered some kind of assault. He talked about how he doesn't fit in at school, how he would like to go back to OCS [his school on the beach], and about how he would like, now, to take the test. He ordered me to go in the next day and find out if he could.

Me: "Why do you want me to ask? Can't you just ask them if you can take the rest of the test with your class?" Him: "If kids ask things like that, they ask questions and I might not know the answers."

So I came in. [His teacher] tells me she doesn't know if he can start taking the test in the middle. You tell me he can take the test if he makes up the rest of it. So I go to John and, despite the fact that I feel like a shit[*] doing this, I explain to him that he will have to make up the rest of the test and, given the tight schedule of schools, it might mean sometimes doing this during recess. "Okay." Very subdued. Very sad. Very heartbreaking for me.

So he took your test for two days.

Last night I came in and asked him how the test went. "I have thirty-eight pages to go." "What?" "It's fifty-one pages long and I have thirty-eight to go." Very subdued. An attitude of resignation you rarely see in children.

We talked over dinner. I told John that if he wanted not to waste time on this test, he could just use his #2 pencil to fill in the "bubbles" however he wishes. "Just make a pattern. Anything. Just get out of there as fast as you can." "But, dad, they have to read me some of the questions. It would take just as long anyway. And it's so easy. They say 'three' and I have to pick out the 3. Duh." So I told him to take the test seriously or not (schools are in favor of "choices" for kids, right?), and that I would write to his principal to say that he might be a subversive or he might not be a subversive but that he is smart enough not to tell either one of us if he is or not. And I would ask that this letter be put in his file if anyone in the future cares to try to interpret his second-grade test scores.

This is a much longer version of this than I was planning to write. But there you have it. Just don't subject this child to more of your testing, testing that almost everyone I've talked to agrees has almost nothing to do with my child.

Sincerely,
W. R. Arney

The principal did not write back.

The following letter went to Stllman Wood, the man who issued the invitation to sign up for the committee that was to work on alternative

---

[*] I understand that Rule Six of the School Handbook says to use appropriate language. I have thought about this word. In my considered opinion, I am not violating Rule Six.

And as for sending John home with his note about using "dam" (sic) and "God" on the playground and him not knowing why: I have an idea why. Its coincidence with all this other muck is really quite striking, don't you think?

means of assessment, a committee that would contribute to the strategic planning of the district.

May 8

Dear Dr. Wood,

I know that in these times it is darned difficult to speak plainly and look the truth in the face. But in these times, the only thing left to do is try. Here is my first response to yours dated April 30, which arrived only yesterday.

On the matter of my "thoughtful review": I did not give you a thoughtful review of anything. I sent you a rant. A thoughtful review would take much longer than the twenty minutes it took to bang out those letters to Al and Karen. I was angry—still am. Not about what you call "the educational disruption of the tests themselves," but about the way my child suffered in a place no one should suffer. I was angry about the fact that at every stage of my inquiry into my child's suffering, everyone admitted that the tests were educationally disruptive and not helpful to the children and so on and so on, and yet no one was willing to look this fact in the face and do something different. Out of my anger I tried a little bureaucratic ploy that has worked with less smooth bureaucrats: claim that they are doing a research project and ask them to obey the law about research subjects. But I'll get to that in a minute. For this point, let's leave it here: If you want me to give you a thoughtful review of anything, hire me as a consultant, pay me a lot, and expect a tepid report.

On the matter of your upcoming review of the district's assessment practices: I know that school administrators can ensure that a review of something everyone (including, as you put it, "increasing numbers of citizens, parents, and educators like [me]") knows is rotten will be "labor intensive and take considerable time for development." It's one of the best ways to make sure no one with ideas will have the chance to let their ideas have a definitive effect on anything. It's an especially effective technique when you, as the Director of Process for such a venture, are so presumptuous that you would assume such a study would be contained within the district and would think the outcome of such a study would naturally go to the "board of directors."

Why is it impossible for educational leaders to imagine bringing citizens together to create a public forum for the discussion of an important political issue and not prejudge the outcome? Is it because real citizens might say to educators something like, "Just obey the law (which in this case would have you test our children only three times in 12 years) and then educate our children well"? Is it because citizens might point out the obvious, viz., that "explor[ing] alternative approaches to student assessment" is one of the ways educationists have been able to keep themselves in business in the face of the fact that schools are not doing a good job, according to schools' present approaches to student assessment?

You are free to assume, as you said you would, that I will "lend [my] support and assistance" to any task that the district might wish to undertake. But you should do two other things: (1) ask if I will lend my support, and (2) know that my interest is in broad citizen involvement in serious discussion of crucial public issues that affect all of us. Any time any educational leader wishes to stand in front of the citizenry and initiate a public discussion (which, by the nature of such a beast, might go anywhere, not just into a report to some "board of directors") of the operations of these things called schools, I will, of course, lend my support and assistance to such a task. Wholeheartedly.

On the bureaucratic move of demanding that you gain informed consent for the participation of our children in your recent project: You said you do not agree with me. Dr. Wood, I did not ask you to agree with me. I did not wish you to repeat what [the curriculum specialist] told me, i.e., that the district separates "achievement testing" from "individual psychological testing" and that the district *thinks* (and acts as if it thinks) that only the latter requires informed consent. I was making an argument that your district's testing program is, in fact, a research project. I refer you no farther than to the first page of your letter. You say that the purposes of the test include the assessment of school and district achievement. That, in itself, makes this activity into a research project. In the context of this project our children provide the data for your activities. That makes them, in law, human subjects. Beyond that, [the curriculum specialist] admitted the obvious: some children could be harmed (and, as you know, in law and regulation "harm" has a broad interpretation which includes social and psychological harm) by their participation in this program. Human Subjects Review requires institutions to secure the informed consent of all human subjects put at risk by the research activities of organizations like the school district. Gaining informed consent does not mean that you would be unable to do your research. It's very likely that a good project administrator could make a case for conducting this research and convince a Human Subjects Review Panel to approve such a project. Gaining informed consent merely means that a researcher must think carefully about what he or she is doing, so carefully that he or she can explain the project to other researchers and, finally, to the subjects of that research. Please do not agree or disagree with me on whether you need to secure informed consent. Please tell me where my argument is flawed. Please tell me what facts of the matter I am missing. Please look the truth in the face. And please try to speak plainly.

Sincerely,
W. R. Arney, Ph.D.

Stillman Wood did write back, but only to say that it "appeared" he could "no longer be of assistance." He was, apparently, a man used to making what appears to him into reality for others.

I phoned. Apparently, he had read *Getting to Yes*. "What, exactly, do you want?" he finally asked. "I want you to get informed consent from every child you subject to your testing program." "I'll think more about it, and I will get back to you." "Why did it take you so long to get to this point?" "You know your problem? You called more than twice. Most parents never call more than twice. Are you sure you don't want to be on the committee to re-think alternatives?" "No, thank you."

He hasn't written back. Neither has he phoned.

CHAPTER 34

The Science Experiment: Two Letters

October 26

Dear [Teacher]:

Today John is to do his science experiment. He is bringing two glasses and a piece of foil to school. He tells me that he will put water in both the glasses, mark the levels of the water in each on the sides of the glasses and cover one glass with the foil. Then he is to wait two days.

When he first described this "experiment" last week I asked, "And what do you expect to learn from this?" "That the uncovered water evaporates. The water with the foil won't, because it's covered." "Sounds like you know what's going to happen." "Yeah, you are supposed to know." "I thought the idea of an experiment was to find out something you didn't know, to set up some circumstances that would allow you to learn something." "No, Dad, we were supposed to go to the library and look up experiments and do one for the whole class."

This conversation was going nowhere, so it became a good topic for cocktail party conversation with some scientists. "Yeah," said a physicist, "that's what a lot of science education is nowadays, demonstration of what's known, not experimentation around what's not known." "Yeah." This was also a conversation going nowhere.

This morning something curious happened. When John got out the materials for his experiment, including the foil, I told him I thought he had said he was going to cover the water with *oil*, not foil. Middle-aged ears, you know.

I told him it might be interesting to take a third glass and some oil. "Just cover the water with some oil and see what happens. That way you could think about what happens in the oceans when a tanker spills its oil on the water." "But, Dad, *I don't know what would happen.*" "That's the point. That's what I was saying experiments are about." "But, Dad, *I've got to know what happens.* That's what Mrs. ——— said. Just go with it, Dad." I avoided bringing up the fact that Washington's recent Nobel laureates got started by pursuing the results of a mistake—probably a more interesting mistake than mishearing "oil" for "foil," but mistakes come in lots of forms—because this was another conversation that was going nowhere. I told John, "Just do what you want."

But then it occurred to me that it is impossible for John to do what he wants because he is doing what he is supposed to do. He's in school. In school, the teacher does the wanting. The teacher wants him to demonstrate an "experiment"? John's a good student. He will comply.

I read in the Olympia School District's "Strategic Plan" that "The vision for the Olympia School District is to create an environment in which each day, each student experiences success." I have no doubt that John will experience a success today. That, of course, is guaranteed by the "environment" which you helped "create," which sent him to the library to find an experiment that he can successfully demonstrate. But where in this vision is the possibility for our children—my child—to face the fact that sometimes they don't know what is going to happen, to do so calmly, thoughtfully, with a spirit of inquiry, and with the possibility that they might not experience success for a very long time, maybe never? Where in this vision is a concern that our children not succumb to the desperation toward which John's "I've got to know what happens" points? Where, as you and everyone else in the district are "Helping kids invent their lives," is the opportunity for our children to learn? I have the feeling that, if you want to discuss these questions, this is a conversation that could lead somewhere.

Sincerely,
William Ray Arney

Both John's teacher and John's principal wrote back. They did not agree to have their letters published, but something of what they said can be inferred from my response, which follows, and from Don Finkel's commentary, "On Writing Back When It's Least Expected." So far, neither the teacher nor the Principal has replied to this second letter.

November 1

Dear ——— and ———:

I got both your letters. I apologize if my earlier letter made you think that I was providing feedback on the science lesson, or if I gave you the impression that I thought this was not a nifty thing to be doing. (If I can trust my cocktail party informant, lots of teachers, even college science teachers, think this is the way to teach science. Who am I to say otherwise?) I especially don't want you to think that my letter had anything to do with my "support for John and [your] efforts." Those are two other things altogether.

My letter was about an attitude toward living that happened to show itself in one particular manifestation at our breakfast table last Monday morning. I was concerned about the sort of desperation John expressed when I encouraged him to face a situation in which he did not know what was going to happen. That is an attitude toward living that I find deeply troubling when I see it in a fourth grader, in a college student, or in a national leader. I know the violence that attitude can lead to.

But my letter was more than that. I thought I could see, because I had read closely the Olympia School District's Strategic Plan, a direct connection between the ways in which the district has announced it intends to conduct itself over the next five years and this particular manifestation in my son of this peculiar but pervasive attitude. The questions at the end of my letter were real questions. I was asking if you did not also see this connection. I was asking if this connection might not get in the way of children learning something. I was really quite interested in your answers to those questions.

But my letter was more than that. It was an invitation to enter into a conversation about the education of youth. I am not interested in being reassured about the quality of the program to which my son is subjected at your school. I am quite interested in discussing important educational issues with you, with other parents, with children, and so on. Are you interested? Will you help arrange these discussions? I'll happily send copies of your letters to people who received copies of mine of the 26th and who are already having discussions about the questions I raised, but it seems like it would be much better if we, together, could create a public discussion of issues we face in common. I should think, [principal], that someone who would write, "Communication is a key in helping us work together," would jump at such an invitation.

By the way, [teacher], you wrote that you urged John to let his "experiment" sit around for several days. You said you did this because John "wanted to hurry his experiment." Here's a competing hypothesis: John wanted to end his experiment in two days because the method said to leave the glasses sitting for exactly two days. John may know that in science you establish your experimental conditions beforehand and then stick to them. How could one discriminate between these two competing hypotheses?

Sincerely,
William Ray Arney

CHAPTER 35

On Writing Back When It's Least Expected: Lecture
Donald L. Finkel

Ivan Illich emphasizes the importance of cultivating the capacity to be surprised. In the final sentences of *Gender,* he says, "I strongly suspect that a contemporary art of living *can* be recovered. . . . The hope for such a life rests upon the rejection of sentimentality and on openness to surprise."[1] "Surprise" is his final word in this book, and on it rests his hope. "School: The Sacred Cow," an essay from his earlier *Celebration of Awareness*, also ends by speaking of surprise. He says that public education, if it were guided by its original purpose, would presuppose "a place within society in which each of us is awakened by surprise; a place of encounter in which others surprise me with their liberty and make me aware of my own." And, he continues, "Our hope of salvation lies in our being surprised by the Other. Let us learn always to receive further surprises."[2]

This is jolting language. Indeed, this is surprising language. When have we heard anyone talk about education in terms of surprises? And why does Illich say we have to *learn* to receive surprises? Is it a capacity that has to be learned?

To begin to answer this question, I have to refer to a distinction that Illich makes between hope and expectation. In *Deschooling Society*, Illich says that *expectation* means "reliance on results which are planned and controlled by man. . . . Expectation looks forward to satisfaction from a predictable process which will produce what we have the right to claim." *Hope*, on the other hand, refers to a "trusting faith in the goodness of nature. . . . Hope centers desire on a person from whom we expect a gift." Illich says the history of modern man is the history of "the Promethean endeavor to forge new institutions" that will satisfy our expectations. (Of course, the institutions create our expectations at the very same time that they persuade us they can satisfy them.) This history "is the history of fading hope and rising expectations." "The Promethean ethos," he writes, "has now eclipsed hope. Survival of the human race depends on its rediscovery as a social force."[3]

This distinction makes it clear that one can never be surprised by the satisfaction of an expectation or, for that matter, by its frustration. When we enter modern institutions, we are forced to surrender the capacity for surprise because our entry is premised upon and shaped by the expectations that modern institutional life has cultivated in us. When you enroll in school, you *expect* to receive an education, to earn a degree, to learn skills, and so on. Can you be surprised by what you receive? It is more likely that you can only be satisfied, or dissatisfied, or fall somewhere on a continuum of partial satisfaction. What could surprise you? The laws of mathematics? The facts of history? The way your teacher says something peculiar to you? You *could be* surprised by any of these, I admit, but only if you have retained your capacity to be surprised. But the school—any school—will do all in its power to rob you of it. Illich's point is that the school, or modern life, generally, pervaded as it is by every variety of institution, has already, more than likely, robbed you of it before you enter its doors.

To be open to surprise, you must retain the capacity for hope, a trusting faith in the goodness of nature or, as Hannah Arendt might put it, in the goodness of the world, of the human condition. Even as hope awaits a gift, the hopeful person is still surprised when the gift comes. But to be capable of hope requires that one be able to recognize a gift when it is offered. Most people in institutions have lost this ability to recognize a gift when it is put right in front of their noses. I am reminded in speaking this way of the first paragraph of Illich's foreword to *Celebration of Awareness*: "It is always my hope that my statements, angry or passionate, artful or innocent, will always provoke a smile, and thus a new freedom—even though the freedom comes at a cost."[4] His words would provoke a smile if they were received as a gift. And I must say that is how I have always received his writings. I have been following his work since I was a graduate student and discovered some of his pieces in the *New York Review of Books*. Hard as he always was for me to grasp, I relished each of his new pieces because they always surprised me. Whether or not they provoked a new freedom, I cannot say. But if you read his words with the expectations we have been schooled to bring to social criticism, you will not only be disappointed; you will miss the gift. You must relearn your capacity to be surprised. And remember, we would never have to learn this capacity if it hadn't been taken from us. Hope is grounded in a well-nourished infancy, and surprise is as natural to infants as opening their eyes and looking around. It is only when we learn to expect satisfaction from predictable, institutionalized processes that we lose the capacity for surprise. And so we have to relearn it, or, better, we have to restore it.

Now a personal example: This past week, right in front of my reading eyes there has been a drama. Bill's son John came home with a science "experiment" to perform for his fourth-grade class. John had been to the library, had researched the experiment, knew the two experimental conditions he was to stage for the class, and he knew the results he *expected* to get. When Bill, through an accident actually, surprised John by suggesting a third experimental condition that might be interesting and informative, John reacted strongly. He said he couldn't enact the third condition because he didn't know how it would come out—he didn't know what to expect—and the whole point, John explained to his dumb dad, was that he had to know ahead of time how it was going to come out. Dad got the message and left his son to do his experiment properly. But he wrote a letter to John's teacher expressing his dismay over what was passing for science education. He invited the teacher to join him in a conversation over their differing views of the matter.

Here is my point. Bill's letter had to be a surprise to John's teacher. It is not the typical communication a teacher expects from a parent. The letter is, potentially, a gift to any teacher who has any capacity for hope left and who does not think of communicating with parents as a "management skill," a skill designed to keep parents out of teachers' hair while assuring the parents that they are "part of the process."

Is the Olympia school system a place that permits its teachers to retain or relearn a capacity for surprise? Is it "a place of encounter in which others surprise me with their liberty and make me aware of my own"? Not this time! I read the teacher's response to Bill and the response from the principal to whom Bill had sent a copy of his letter. Both letters said the same thing beneath superficial variations: "Thank you for your input. Don't call us; we'll call you. We always appreciate hearing from parents; now go away and let us get on with the important work we are doing as we teach your son science. And, by the way, if you had come to Parents' Night, you would understand why we do the experiment this way."

These letters were shocking to me even though I could have predicted their content perfectly. Writing them required the mangling of the content of Bill's original letter. But worse, the teacher and the principal demonstrated that they couldn't see the gift being handed to them. They couldn't see there was an Other—that is, a different but equal person—trying to talk to them. All they could see was a cranky, meddling parent. These educators could not be surprised because it is always only Otherness that surprises, and the schools will not permit the survival of Otherness. They can't even allow John to try out an experimental condition whose results no one knows. And they certainly could not engage in a conversation with Bill.

But the drama did not end there. Despite his initial impulse to be courteous and not be a troublemaker, Bill did not go away. He wrote back. His new letter pushed even harder than the first one. If you insist on not hearing me, it said, you're going to have to work harder than you did in those first letters. You are going to have to go another round with me. I am not a parent concerned with his son's education; I am not giving you feedback on your lesson; I am not part of the processes you learned to manage in your teacher training. I am not going to let you make me into any of those things: I AM TRYING TO TALK TO YOU. Would you please stand still and listen?

The answer, I am afraid, will be no. But regardless of what the educators do, what I appreciate more than anything is that, in this dismal instance, Bill retains *his* hope and his willingness to be surprised by his son's teacher and principal.

CHAPTER 36

Thinking One's Way Out of School

It had to happen, sooner or later, that John would be so upset by a class that I would have to go see the teacher. It was a surprise that he was upset enough to think about dropping out. The class was Science, several years after the "experiment."

"She's boring, Dad."

"You're bored by *science*?" I asked, trying to get the emphasis right.

My son, raised by the schools and our world at large on the see-through, thin gruel of "communications," said, again and for my benefit, what he had said the first time: "No, Dad. *She* is boring. Today, she wouldn't let me use the microscope because I didn't name all the pieces right. I said, 'Stage, lamp, objective lens, nose, fine focus adjustment, eyepiece . . .' And she says, 'I guess you'll have to try again tomorrow. It's nose*piece,* not just nose.' So, she's tested us on parts of the microscope for four days and still won't let us use them. *She* is boring and I don't think I want to be in Science anymore."

As it happened, that morning National Public Radio was running the first of a series on homeschooling. John listened and said, "I'd like to try homeschooling." I had my assignments: talk to the science teacher and find out how our district handled homeschooling.

Ambiguously Alive

Some comments about schools from the schooled and young have to be discounted for hyperbole, or at least checked out. So I just told the science teacher about the microscope quiz and waited for her corrections and qualifications.

Instead she offered, "That's right. The students have to be familiar with the instruments before they can use them."

"So you've been lecturing them about the parts of a microscope and quizzing them for four days and no one has looked through one yet?"

"Well, I've shown them slides of the kinds of things they will see when they use the instruments next week."

To avoid a Deweyan explosion about education and experience, I checked out another of John's reports: "John tells me you spent the first five days of class going over class rules and then testing them on the class rules."

"That's true, but we did discuss an important question in science." The Book of Lesson Plans was placed between us. "See, here in the first week, 'Alive or Dead?' That was our topic. We talked about what determines whether something is alive or dead."

This, in point of true fact, grabbed my full attention. It took me back thirteen years to a class of freshmen I was teaching with a biologist, Burt Guttman. Immediately after a lecture on cell biology, a naive new college student asked one of those silly, squishy, global questions that on the rare occasion cuts through 50 minutes of prepared talk and zooms like a dart to the heart of the lecturer's discipline. "Professor Guttman, what do you mean by 'life'?" Guttman wrenched up his face, thought for a moment, and said, "To a biologist, 'life' is not a very useful term." Then, this man, a specialist in bacteriophages, with a broad and firm grasp on his discipline, gave a long, memorable dissertation on the philosophy of biology, on what biologists *do,* on what it is possible to know, and on why 'life' is not something biologists worry too much about.

Some years later, I was reading Richard Preston's "Crisis in the Hot Zone," a scary report on the close call, near outbreak of a strain of Ebola virus in the Washington, D.C., area in 1992. Its discussion of viruses recalled some of Guttman's ideas:

> Some biologists classify viruses as "life forms"—ambiguously alive. . . . Viruses can seem alive when they multiply, but in another sense they are molecular machines—obviously nonliving, strictly mechanical, no more alive than a jackhammer.[1]

My fellow feeling for John's admittedly pedantic science teacher increased, and I thought we might divert ourselves from the Book of Lesson Plans to a potentially interesting discussion. I told the science teacher about my experience with Guttman and about the "Crisis in the Hot Zone" and about how "Alive or dead?" did, indeed, seem an important question in science; and I wondered, out loud, how she would think of a virus. Alive or dead?

"Are you asking me?"

"Yes, it's something that interests me, and I was wondering how you would think about that."

"This is just something we talked about with the students in that first week. And, yes, we did spend time on the class rules. I think it's important that the students understand the class rules, so I did test them. Just like I test them on the parts of the microscope."

It was clear where this conversation was going: It was going straight back to my son's unhyperbolic characterization of the science teacher. I recalled Preston's description of a virus—"compact, logical, hard, engineered by the forces of evolution, and totally selfish, the viral machinery is dedicated to making copies of itself"[2]—and momentarily this description of an object of science fit the science teacher, too. She seemed, dare I say, "ambiguously alive." I worried for my son.

But John had left me, and maybe himself, an out. He had said he'd like to try homeschooling.

The Pink Book

A friend had gone to the middle school principal with an extensive proposal for her son's education. Among other things, the proposal would have him spending half his days at the high school down the road. The principal's response was entirely accommodating. "Whatever you'd like to do, I'm sure it will be okay." My friend was disappointed by the absence of even a hint of resistance. Over the years, she had made various proposals and always there was some hesitation or reluctance or some anticipated difficulties. Not this time. "What's going on that the schools don't resist whatever resistance we might offer to them?" she wondered.

Sociologists might say schools are "coopting" resistance. Institutions that survive and grow have built-in schemes not just for responding to criticism but for incorporating it. Despite their relative clunkiness, schools are coming along on this score. More and more, schools are accommodating that which originated as harsh criticism of them.

Homeschooling was initially a multifaceted criticism of schools. Grown-up, liberal boomers and upright, not-so-liberal Christians had separate agendas, but both took their children out of the schools. Seemingly quickly, homeschooling took on all the trappings of a movement, with journals and opinion leaders and, only a little later, curricula, parental coop schemes, and so on.

Not quite as quickly but deliberately, the schools responded to those who thought they were voting with their feet against the schools. In our state, the legislature eventually required public schools to accommodate all parents who wanted to school their children, part-time or full-time, at home. Parents had to file a letter of intent with their district and had to make yearly reports, but the heavier burden was on the school. Principals had to schedule students into classes requested by parents; they had to make room in bands and glee clubs; they had to allow the students onto sports teams and into other extracurricular activities. All of this is spelled out in "The Pink Book," a publication of the State Superintendent of Education. It contains the law, the regulations, the forms, and everything a parent needs to take a child out of school.

While John was away at school, I read through "The Pink Book" and called his school. Band? Sure. Sports? Of course. Can he take a class with Lauri if he wants? I got my version of the "Whatever you'd like to do, I'm sure it will be okay." I was ecstatic. I began imagining the science we could do. I imagined John around truly alive scientists like Guttman. I imagined looking at the sky, the backyard, or under the couch like a scientist might. And my son, the guard, still had a place with his friends on the defensive line.

Thoughts Out of School

Schools are very powerful. In his earliest works, Illich spoke about schools becoming "oppressive idols" that protect those who succeed.[3] In schools, he said, "the pupil . . . is 'schooled' to confuse teaching with learning, grade advancement with education, a diploma with competence, and fluency with the ability to say something new."[4] It is not derogatory, but neither is it complimentary, to say that my son is very well schooled.

When John came home from school I told him, briefly, about the meeting with his teacher and, less briefly, about the possibilities of homeschooling.

"I don't think I want to do that."

"Really?"

"Really, Dad. It would be hard to leave the school."

And that's about all there is to say. It *is* very hard to leave school. The principal who says, "Whatever you'd like to do, I'm sure it will be okay," knows there is little risk of undermining anything crucial about schooling. The equivalence in the common mind between schooling and education, an equivalence that the schools worked a century to forge, is difficult to break. As Illich has said for more than a quarter of a century, schools are not just something useful; they have made themselves into something we think we *need.* Anything that can present itself as necessity is going to be very difficult to walk away from.

But the situation is far worse than Illich originally imagined. When homeschooling was still a potent protest movement, some children did leave the schools, some parents could think their way out of the schools, and there was some place to go to be a rebel. Now, when the superintendent provides the pink book and all the forms one needs to "leave," there is, in fact, nowhere to go. The school has literally incorporated its own alternative and there is no outside to which children and their parents might repair. My son knew leaving that school was "hard." It may be that even thinking one's way out of school, boring and brutal as school is sometimes, is impossible.

CHAPTER 37

Is It Hopeless?

We declare ourselves in favor of the jester's philosophy. . . . Thus we opt for a vision of the world that offers us the burden of reconciling in our social behavior those opposites that are the most difficult to combine: goodness without universal tolerance, courage without fanaticism, intelligence without discouragement, and hope without blindness.

Leszek Kolakowski, "The Priest and the Jester"

"So, do you think it's hopeless?"

The Seattle School District, like so many other districts, was "restructuring." In order to "decentralize" control, each school or program had to send a strategic plan to central headquarters. A friend and I were discussing one of those plans. Teachers and administrators had labored to produce twenty-five pages of "goal statements" like "In ——— years, ——— percent of all writing will be subjected to the writing process and multi-draft procedure." They had left the blanks to be filled in by "site-based coordinating committees," which meant that parents were going to have to labor, too. Eventually, the blanks would be filled, the goal statements would be approved and the whole thing would be shipped off to some office or other so that the local school could enjoy its "local control."

We laughed.

Then the tone turned serious: "Do you think it's hopeless?" "What?" "Improving the schools. Do you think there's no reason to hope for anything better?"

The questioner was a nurse. She has been in situations where she or another health official has had to say, "There's still reason to hope." This is a peculiar, modern perversion of that ancient idea. When an official utters this phrase, it usually means there are reasons to *expect* the preferred outcome, but the probability is small. Hope versus expectation: this is Illich's distinction again, an important distinction that helps answer the question, "Is it hopeless?"

Regarding the schools: It *is* hopeless. But by that I do not mean there is no reason to expect the schools not to improve. Improve they will. That is part of their business, and efforts to improve are sometimes more than just a tactic to keep the critics busy with work on site-based coordinating committees and their like. In saying, "It *is* hopeless," I mean that efforts to improve the schools will proceed in an arena from which all hope has been banished. The schools expect too much—of "the community" around them, of students, of parents, of teachers and administrators, of government agencies and officials, of themselves—ever to have the chance to have any hope. They spend too much time being reassuring. Every time a budget-pressed administrator or a teacher with too many students says, "There's still reason for hope," and means that maybe one more adjustment of the already-stressed mechanism or one more turn of the screw might just possibly work, they lead everyone willing to follow them through Dante's first portal. They are abandoning hope and trusting technique.

Illich traced the distinction between hope and expectation back to the myth of Pandora, whose box contained all ills plus one good, hope. The box opened, the ills escaped, and Pandora closed it before hope could get away. Modern history can be written, says Illich, in terms of "the Promethean endeavor to forge institutions to corral each of the rampant ills. It is the history of fading hope and rising expectations."[1] That is, we moderns have forgotten that along with all our ills came, in the same package, the one counter to them. We have struggled to engineer solutions to problems, and this work proceeds in expectation that the solutions will work. But our work proceeds without hope.

For example, the education of young people is not difficult. It happens everywhere, all the time, throughout time. Problems in the education of the young arise only when this common task is located in an uncommon place called school. It does not require a leap of genius to conclude that children forced to spend half their waking hours away from the common, everyday world of everyone else will have trouble learning what they must know to get along in life. But then, when young people fail to learn in the schools, we blame the schools and try to reform them. Or we "restructure" them. It seems obvious that if we continue to try to solve the problems of schooling in the schools through various technical means, the job of educating young people is, indeed, a hopeless one.

One route to readmitting hope is criticism. Saying what one sees using a language that forms a judgmental matrix but that strives always and only for precision of description is not an activity that will ever lead to rising expectations. It is not an activity that leads to a greater "reliance on results which are planned and controlled by man," as Illich defines "expectation."[2] It is an activity unlikely to lead directly to any solutions to any problems. Criticism is more likely to lead to a new set of conditions under which various alternative approaches to a task can be imagined. Criticism turns us away from the impulse to solve a problem until the nature of the problem can be discerned. If, for example, we could ever notice that in all the public discussions and debates about schooling, we are *only* talking about the education of the young, that might prove to be a surprisingly great and hopeful insight.

To be successful, criticism must be pointed and limited. When we live in expectation, our concerns become practical, global, and sloppy. Years ago, Wendell Berry noted, "The air is full of dire prophecies, warnings, and threats of what will happen if the Kingdom of Heaven is not precipitately landed at the nearest airport." This air is the exhaust of people who "have come to expect too much from outside [them]selves," he says. By living in expectation instead of in hope, we forsake the difficult discipline of criticism in favor of merely complaining. And a society of complainers is precisely what the modern state loves. Indiscriminate complaining allows the state an entrée into every aspect of life. It opens the way for the therapist, the pedagogue, and experts of all stripes to take away and take over what used to be the common tasks of living. And when their ways don't work, another restructured wave of reformed therapists, pedagogues, and experts of all stripes is waiting in the wings. As Berry puts it, "The public *demand* for perfection, as opposed to private striving for it, is almost always productive of violence, and is itself a form of violence. It is totalitarian in impulse, and often in result."[3] Criticism can counter this public demand for perfection and its accompanying expectations of a new and better future by focusing attention sharply on what is happening right now in front of wide-open eyes. The first task of criticism is to silence those who would cynically tell us, "There's still reason to hope." Once this is done, we might be able to realize there was never any reason not to live in hope.

Hope, says Illich, "means trusting faith in the goodness of nature. . . . Hope centers desire on a person from whom we await a gift."[4] Hope turns us toward what we have been given as a condition of our birth: nature and the other people who live with us. It turns us away from overreliance on our tools, including our social institutions, and everything else we have made. Hope inclines us to reflect on where we are, not to think about what might be in some perfected future. Berry says,

> We cannot look for happiness to any technological paradise or to any New Earth of outer space, but only to the world as it is, and as we have made it. The only life we may hope to live is here. It seems likely that if we are to reach the earthly paradise at all, we will reach it only when we have ceased to strive and hurry so to get there. There is no "there." We can only wait here, where we are, in the world, obedient to its processes, patient in its taking away, faithful to its returns.[5]

We might continue to try to solve the problems of schooling in the schools. We might continue to strive for an educational "there," somewhere in the indefinite future. If we can find a way to notice that this is, in a very deep sense, a hopeless enterprise, that simple act of recognition might allow us to remember how easy and enjoyable the education of young people can be— right here, right now. If we recognize the hopelessness of our reliance on schools, we might be able to hope for our children and ourselves again.

Notes

Introduction: Thoughts out of School
1. *Seattle Times,* December 11, 1998, p. A10.
2. Patricia L. Donahue, Kristin E. Voelkl, Jay R. Campbell, and John Mazzeo, *NAEP 1998 Reading Report Card for the Nation and the States,* March 1999; "Morning Edition," National Public Radio, March 5, 1999.
3. The Evergreen State College, graduating class of 1997.
4. See Donald L. Finkel and William Ray Arney, *Educating for Freedom: The Paradox of Pedagogy* (New Brunswick, N.J.: Rutgers University Press, 1995) for a description of The Evergreen State College.
5. James Hillman made a useful distinction between remembering what happens so that it can be rendered into a public story and what "actually happened." He said, "We're not conscious we're telling stories. I think Freud was getting at that when he said, 'It's how you remember, not what actually happened,'" James Hillman and Michael Ventura, "Is Therapy Turning Us into Children?" *New Age,* May/June 1992, p. 65, dialogue.

Chapter 1: It Matters
1. Cover letter from Michael McDonald, accompanying CTBS individual test scores, December 18, 1992.
2. Lynne K. Varner, "City Schools Downplay Poor Test Scores," *Seattle Post-Intelligencer,* December 25, 1992, p. B2.
3. Martin Buber, *The Way of Man According to the Teaching of Hasidism* (New York, N.Y.: Citadel Press 1966), p. 12.
4. Ibid.
5. Sherwood Anderson, "Certain Things Last: A Writer Warms to His Story," *New York Times Book Review,* December 20, 1992, p. 23.
6. May Sarton, *The House by the Sea: A Journal* (New York, N.Y.: W. W. Norton & Company, 1977), pp. 24–25.
7. C. Wright Mills, *The Sociological Imagination* (London, England: Oxford University Press, 1959), p. 226.
8. John Taylor Gatto, "What Really Matters? The Curriculum of Post-Graduate Life," a commencement address at The Evergreen State College, Olympia, Washington, June 7, 1992, pp. 2–3.

Chapter 2: What Should Be Taught in Teacher Education Programs?
1. Lawrence Kohlberg and Rochelle Mayer, "Development as the Aim of Education," in *Stage Theories of Cognitive and Moral Development: Criticisms and Applications,* Harvard Educational Review, reprint #13, 1978.
2. Donald L. Finkel, "Democracy in Education: Education in Democracy," The Evergreen State College, 1987.
3. Jones was a founding member of the faculty of The Evergreen State College. He wrote the first published account of the new college (Richard M. Jones, *Experiment at Evergreen* [Cambridge, Mass.: Schenkman Publishing Company, 1981]; Richard Matthew Jones, *Fantasy and Feeling in Education* (New York, N.Y.: New York University Press, 1968).

Chapter 6: Should We Value the Teaching of Values?

1. Peter Drucker, *The New Realities: In Government and Politics/in Economics and Business/in Society and World View* (New York, N.Y.: Harper and Row, 1989), p. 3.

2. Michael Oakeshott, "Learning and Teaching," in *The Voice of Liberal Learning: Michael Oakeshott on Education*, ed. Timothy Fuller (New Haven, Conn.: Yale University Press, 1989), p. 62.

3. Jean-Jacques Rousseau, *Emile, or On Education*, trans. Allan Bloom (New York, N.Y.: Basic Books, 1979), p. 321.

4. Shoshana Zuboff, *In the Age of the Smart Machine: The Future of Work and Power* (New York, N.Y.: Basic Books, 1988).

5. Harold W. Baillie, "Virtue in Its Place," in *Commonplaces: Essays on the Nature of Place*, ed. David W. Black, Donald Kunze, and John Pickles (Lanham, N.Y.: University Press of America, 1989), p. 27.

6. Robert Crawford, "A Cultural Account of 'Health': Control, Release, and the Social Body," in *Issues in the Political Economy of Health Care*, ed. John McKinlay (New York, N.Y.: Tavistock, 1984), pp. 61–103.

7. Zuboff, *Age of the Smart Machine*, p. 141.

8. Martin Ostwald, "Glossary of Technical Terms," *Nichomachean Ethics* by Aristotle (Indianapolis, Ind.: Bobbs-Merrill Company, 1962), pp. 303–304.

9. Baillie, "Virtue in Its Place."

10. Ivan Illich, Sigmar Groeneveld, Lee Hoinacki, and Friends, "Statement on Agriculture," Hebenshausen, December 5, 1990.

11. F. Forrester Church, *The Seven Deadly Virtues: A Guide to Purgatory for Atheists and True Believers* (San Francisco, Calif.: Harper and Row, 1988).

12. Martha Nussbaum, *The Fragility of Goodness: Luck and Ethics in Greek Tragedy and Philosophy* (Cambridge, England: Cambridge University Press, 1986).

13. Emilie Zum Brunn and Georgette Epiney-Burgard, *Women Mystics in Medieval Europe* (New York, N.Y.: Paragon House, 1989), p. 15.

14. Carl R. Rogers, *Client-Centered Therapy: Its Current Practice, Implications, and Theory* (Boston, Mass.: Houghton Mifflin Company, 1965), p. 523.

15. Benjamin DeMott, "Looking for Intelligence in Washington," *Commentary* 30 (October 1960), p. 294.

16. Ibid., p. 291.

Chapter 10: The Hard Work of Teaching vs. Teaching with Grace

1. Eugen Herrigel, *Zen in the Art of Archery* (New York, N.Y., Vintage Books, 1953), p. 51.

2. Maurice Friedman, introduction, *Between Man and Man* by Martin Buber (New York, N.Y.: Collier Books, 1965), p. xiv.

3. Ibid., p. xv.

4. Ivan Illich, "The Educational Enterprise in the Light of the Gospel," a lecture given in Chicago, Ill., November 13, 1988.

Chapter 11: Report Cards: An Exchange of "Letters"

1. C. Wright Mills, *The Sociological Imagination* (New York, N.Y.: Oxford University Press), 1959.

Chapter 12: The Evaluation Conference: Letter
1. Marilynne Robinson, *Housekeeping* (New York, N.Y.: Farrar, Straus, Giroux, 1980), pp. 76–77.

Chapter 13: Do I Need My Identity?
1. Michel Foucault, introduction to *Herculine Barbin: Being the Recently Discovered Memoirs of a Nineteenth-Century French Hermaphrodite*, ed. Michel Foucault (New York, N.Y.: Pantheon, 1980), pp. vii–xvii.
2. Homer, *The Odyssey*, trans. Robert Fitzgerald (New York, N.Y.: Anchor Books, 1961), pp. 60–61.
3. *The Oxford English Dictionary*, 2nd ed. (Oxford, England: Oxford University Press, 1989), vol. 7, p. 620.
4. All examples are taken from entries in *The Oxford English Dictionary*.
5. Roger Brown, *Social Psychology: The Second Edition* (New York, N.Y.: The Free Press, 1986), p. 551.
6. Benjamin B. Wolman, ed., *Dictionary of Behavioral Science*, 2nd ed. (San Diego, Calif.: Academic Press, 1989), p. 171.
7. Brown, *Social Psychology*, p. 551.
8. Raymond J. Corsini, ed., *Encyclopedia of Psychology*, vol. 2 (New York, N.Y.: John Wiley and Sons, 1984), p.180.
9. Uwe Pörksen, "Science and mathematical colonization of colloquial language," *Revista di Biologia—Biology Forum* 81, 3 (1988): 384–385.
10. Ibid., pp. 387–388.
11. Michel Foucault, *The Archeology of Knowledge* (New York: Pantheon, 1972), p. 17.
12. For example, see "Friendship as a Way of Life," an interview that first appeared in *Le Gai Pied*, April 1981, in *Foucault Live (Interviews, 1966–1984)*, by Michel Foucault (New York, N.Y.: Semiotext(e), 1989), pp. 203–209.
13. Stanley Hauerwas, "The Testament of Friends," *The Christian Century* 107, 7 (February 28, 1990): 212.

Chapter 17: What Do You Teach When the Students Know the Answer?
1. Richard P. Feynmann, *"What Do You Care What Other People Think?": Further Adventures of a Curious Character* (New York, N.Y.: W. W. Norton and Company, 1988), p. 14.

Chapter 19: Criticism of the Schools in the Schools
1. This quotation and others in this piece are taken from Ivan Illich, "The Educational Enterprise in Light of the Gospel," a manuscript for a lecture given in Chicago, November 13, 1988. I avoid giving page numbers because there are several versions of this lecture manuscript in circulation.
2. Ibid.
3. Ibid.
4. Ibid.
5 Raymond Williams, *Keywords: A Vocabulary of Culture and Society*, rev. ed. (New York, N.Y.: Oxford University Press, 1983), pp. 84–86.

Chapter 21: Who Will Manage the Self-Managers? Four Scenes from a Post-Quality School

1. William Glasser, *The Quality School: Managing Students without Coercion* (New York, N.Y.: Harper Perennial, 1990).
2. Ibid., p. 75.
3. Ibid., pp. 16, 22, 4.

Chapter 23: Reading

1. Comprehensive Test of Basic Skills, 4th ed. (Monterey, Calif: CTB, 1990), appendix A, "CTBS/4 Objective Statements," pp. 127–128.

Chapter 24: Gimme My Gun, I'm Working on My Self-Esteem

1. Olympia School District, "Strategic Plan," Olympia, Washington, 1992.
2. Christopher Lasch, "For Shame: Why Americans Should Be Wary of Self-Esteem," *The New Republic* (August 10, 1992): p. 29.
3. Gloria Steinem, *Revolution from Within: A Book of Self-Esteem* (Boston, Mass.: Little, Brown, 1992).
4. Charles Krauthammer, "Education: Doing Bad and Feeling Worse," *Time* (February 5, 1990): 29.
5. Ibid.
6. Joan DeClaire, "Kids and Guns," *View* 34 (September/October 1992): 32.

Chapter 25: Why I Won't Believe in Developmentalism

1. See, for example, Lawrence Kohlberg, "Education for Justice: A Modern Statement of the Platonic View," in *Moral Education: Five Lectures*, by James M. Gustafson, et al. (Cambridge, Mass.: Harvard University Press, 1970), pp. 57–83.
2. Carol Gilligan, *In a Different Voice: Psychological Theory and Women's Development* (Cambridge, Mass.: Harvard University Press, 1982); Mary Field Belenky, et al., *Women's Ways of Knowing: The Development of Self, Voice and Mind* (New York, N.Y.: Basic Books, 1986).
3. Uwe Pörksen, *Plastikwörter: Die Sprache einer internationalen Diktatur,* trans. Jutta Mason (Stuttgart, Germany: Klett-Cotta, 1989), pp. 33–34.
4. Hannah Arendt, *The Human Condition* (Chicago, Ill.: University of Chicago Press, 1958).
5. See William Ray Arney and Bernard Bergen, *Medicine and the Management of Living: Taming the Last Great Beast* (Chicago, Ill.: University of Chicago Press, 1984).
6. Hannah Arendt, "The Crisis in Education," in *Between Past and Future: Eight Exercises in Political Thought* (New York, N.Y.: Penguin Books, 1977), p. 189. The paragraph ends with an elaboration of the meaning of this "responsibility": "Vis-à-vis the child, it is as though he were a representative of all adult inhabitants, pointing out the details and saying to the child: This is our world."

Chapter 26: Halloween

1. Georges Bataille, *Erotism: Death and Sensuality* (San Francisco, Calif.: City Lights Books), 1986, p. 241.

Chapter 27: Saying vs. Knowing: A Sermon
1. E. L. Doctorow, *Billy Bathgate* (New York, N. Y.: Random House, 1989), p. 319.
2. Michael Oakeshott, "The Voice of Poetry in the Conversation of Mankind," in *Rationalism in Politics, and Other Essays* (New York, N.Y.: Basic Books, 1962), p. 198.
3. Martin Buber, *Between Man and Man* (New York, N.Y.: Collier Books, 1965), pp. 5–6.

Chapter 28: Experts and Critics and the "Eco-cratic Discourse"
1. World Commission on Environment and Development, *Our Common Future* (New York, N.Y.: Oxford University Press, 1987), p. x.
2. Gabriel García Márquez, *The General in His Labyrinth* (New York, N.Y.: Penguin, 1990), p. 120.
3. William Ray Arney, *Experts in the Age of Systems* (Albuquerque, N.M.: University of New Mexico Press, 1991).
4. See William Ray Arney and Bernard Bergen, *Medicine and the Management of Living* (Chicago, Ill.: University of Chicago Press, 1984).
5. Nicholas Hildyard, "Whose Common Future?: Proposed Structure," *The Ecologist*, January 1991, p. 6.
6. Les Gapay, "Preserved Trees Look Alive, Thanks to Weyerhauser," *Seattle Post-Intelligencer*, January 7, 1987, pp. B6, A1.
7. Leo Bersani and Ulysse Dutoit, *The Forms of Violence: Narrative in Assyrian Art and Modern Culture* (New York, N.Y.: Schocken Books, 1985); Leo Bersani, *The Freudian Body: Psychoanalysis and Art* (New York, N.Y.: Columbia University Press, 1986); and Leo Bersani, *The Culture of Redemption* (Cambridge, Mass.: Harvard University Press, 1990).
8. Hans Achterhuis, in his intervention at the conference "Conflicts in Global Ecology," June 27–30, 1991, Kulturwissenschaftsliches Institut, Essen, Germany.
9. As Ch. von Weizsäcker put it in her intervention at the conference "Conflicts in Global Ecology."
10. Gary Snyder, *The Practice of the Wild* (San Francisco, Calif.: North Point Press, 1990), p. 42.
11. Wolfgang Sachs, "One World," in *Development: A Polemical Dictionary* (London: Zed Books, 1991).
12. J. Robert Oppenheimer, *Science and the Common Understanding* (New York, N.Y.: Simon and Schuster, 1953).
13. J. Robert Oppenheimer, "The Atomic Age," New York Philharmonic Symphony Radio Program, December 23, 1945.
14. Snyder, *The Practice of the Wild*, pp. 3–4.

Chapter 29: No Futures, Please, These Are Our Children
1. Olympia School District, "Strategic Plan, 1992–1997," Olympia, Washington, 1992, p. 3.
2. Chip Conquest, "A Place Called School" (master's thesis, The Evergreen State College, 1992), pp. 30–31.
3. Ibid., pp. 31–32.
4. Tom Wolfe, *The Bonfire of the Vanities* (New York, N.Y.: Farrar, Straus and Giroux, 1987).

5. Arendt, "We Refugees," in *The Jew as Pariah: Jewish Identity and Politics in the Modern Age,* by Hannah Arendt and Ron H. Feldman (New York, N.Y.: Grove Press, 1978), p. 57.

6. Ibid.

7. Olympia School District, "Strategic Plan," p. 2.

8. Conquest, "A Place Called School," p. 32.

9. Ivan Illich, "A Constitution for Cultural Revolution," in *Celebration of Awareness: A Call for Institutional Revolution* (Berkeley, Calif.: Heyday Books, 1970), pp. 180–181.

10. Olympia School District, "Strategic Plan," p. 4.

11. Ibid.

Chapter 30: School Choice, or What Is Important

1. Dan Leahy, "Who's the Public in Public Education," Labor Center video, The Evergreen State College, 1989.

2. Jonathan Kozol, *Savage Inequalities: Children in America's Schools* (New York, N.Y.: Crown Publishers, 1991).

3. Susan Chira, "School 'Choice' Critiqued: Report Says Plan May Hurt Children from Poor Families," *Seattle Post-Intelligencer*, October 26, 1992, pp. A1, A8.

4. Ivan Illich, "The Futility of Schooling," in *Celebration of Awareness: A Call for Institutional Revolution* (Berkeley, Calif.: Heyday Books, 1969), p. 112.

5. Letter from Chip Conquest, November 1992.

6. Illich, "The Futility of Schooling," p. 118.

7. This is from the title of Ivan Illich's talk to the graduating class of the University of Puerto Rico in 1970. "School: The Sacred Cow," is reprinted in Illich's *Celebration of Awareness*, pp. 121–135.

8. Annie Dillard, *An American Childhood*, in *Three by Annie Dillard* (New York, N.Y.: HaperCollins, 1990), pp. 426–427.

Chapter 31: Ivan: "In Book after Book..." (as promised)

1. Robert Kugelmann, *Stress: The Nature and History of Engineered Grief* (New York, N.Y.: Praeger, 1992).

2. Ivan Illich, "The Educational Enterprise in Light of the Gospel," lecture notes, Chicago, Ill., November 13, 1988, pp. 30–31.

3. Barbara Duden, *Disembodying Women: Perspectives on Pregnancy and the Unborn* (Cambridge, Mass.: Harvard University Press, 1993).

4. Wolfgang Sachs, ed., *The Development Dictionary* (London, England: Zed Books, 1992).

5. Michel Foucault, "A Preface to Transgression," in *Language, Counter-Memory, Practice: Selected Essays and Interviews*, ed. Donald F. Bouchard (Ithaca, N.Y.: Cornell University Press, 1977), pp. 29–52.

6. Marianne Gronemeyer, *Die Macht der Berdürfnesse: Reflexion über ein Phantom rowohat* (Frankfurt: Verlag Reinbeck, 1988).

7. Ivan Illich, *Gender* (New York, N.Y.: Pantheon, 1982), p. 178, emphasis added.

8. Ibid., p. 179.

9. Illich, "The Educational Enterprise," p. 1.

10. Ivan Illich, *Celebration of Awareness* (Berkeley, Calif.: Heyday Books, 1969).

11. Illich, *Gender*, p. 179.

12. Josef Pieper, *The Silence of St. Thomas: Three Essays* (New York, N.Y.: Pantheon, 1957), pp. 69–70.

13. Illich, "The Educational Enterprise," pp. 18–19.

14. Pieper, *Silence of St. Thomas.*

Chapter 32: Second Thoughts: Valedictory

1. Ivan Illich, "Askesis: Introduction, Etymology, and Bibliography 1989, Introduction to Askesis for Discussion with David Ramage," notes dated June 13, 1989.

2. Philip Rieff, *Fellow Teachers* (New York, N.Y.: Dell, 1972), p. 6.

3. Ibid., pp. 31–32.

4. Ibid., p. 88.

Chapter 35: On Writing Back When It's Least Expected: Lecture

1. Ivan Illich, *Gender* (New York, N.Y.: Pantheon, 1982), p. 179.

2. Ivan Illich, "School: The Sacred Cow," in *Celebration of Awareness: A Call for Institutional Revolution* (Berkeley, Calif.: Heyday Books, 1970), pp. 134–135.

3. Ivan Illich, *Deschooling Society* (New York, N.Y.: Harper and Row, 1970), pp. 151–152.

4. Illich, *Celebration of Awareness*, p. 11.

Chapter 36: Thinking One's Way Out of School

1. Richard Preston, "Crisis in the Hot Zone," *New Yorker* 68 (October 26, 1992): 60–61.

2. Ibid.

3. Ivan Illich, "The Futility of Schooling," in *Celebration of Awareness* (New York, N.Y.: Anchor Books, 1970), p. 103.

4. Ivan Illich, *Deschooling Society* (New York, N.Y.: Harper and Row, 1970), p. 38.

Chapter 37: Is It Hopeless?

1. Ivan Illich, *Deschooling Society* (New York, N.Y.: Harper and Row, 1970), p. 151.

2. Ibid., p. 152.

3. Wendell Berry, "Discipline and Hope," in *Recollected Essays, 1965–1980* (San Francisco, Calif.: North Point Press, 1981), pp. 153, 220.

4. Illich, *Deschooling Society*, pp. 151–152.

5. Berry,"Discipline and Hope," p. 206.

Index

Studies in the Postmodern Theory of Education

General Editors
Joe L. Kincheloe & Shirley R. Steinberg

Counterpoints publishes the most compelling and imaginative books being written in education today. Grounded on the theoretical advances in criticalism, feminism, and postmodernism in the last two decades of the twentieth century, Counterpoints engages the meaning of these innovations in various forms of educational expression. Committed to the proposition that theoretical literature should be accessible to a variety of audiences, the series insists that its authors avoid esoteric and jargonistic languages that transform educational scholarship into an elite discourse for the initiated. Scholarly work matters only to the degree it affects consciousness and practice at multiple sites. Counterpoints' editorial policy is based on these principles and the ability of scholars to break new ground, to open new conversations, to go where educators have never gone before.

For additional information about this series or for the submission of manuscripts, please contact:

Joe L. Kincheloe & Shirley R. Steinberg
637 West Foster Avenue
State College, PA 16801

To order other books in this series, please contact our Customer Service Department:

(800) 770-LANG (within the U.S.)
(212) 647-7706 (outside the U.S.)
(212) 647-7707 FAX

Or browse online by series:

www.peterlang.com